# Groundwork:
# Writing Skills
# to Build On

# Groundwork: Writing Skills to Build On

Lucia Engkent
Garry Engkent

Toronto

**Canadian Cataloguing in Publication Data**

Engkent, Lucia Pietrusiak, 1955–
    Groundwork : writing skills to build on

Includes index.
ISBN 0-13-011480-4

1. English language — Rhetoric.  2. English language — Grammar.
I. Engkent, Garry, 1948–  .  II. Title.

PE1408.E484 2001          808'.042          C00-930145-3

ISBN 0-13-011480-4

Vice President, Editorial Director: Michael Young
Executive Editor: David Stover
Senior Marketing Manager: Sophia Fortier
Signing Representative: Natalie Witkin
Executive Developmental Editor: Marta Tomins
Production Editor: Joe Zingrone
Copy Editor: Kat Mototsune
Production Coordinator: Peggy Brown
Page Layout: Janette Thompson/Jansom
Art Director: Mary Opper
Interior Design: Carole Knox
Cover Design: Monica Kompter
Cover Image: Photodisc

1 2 3 4 5     05 04 03 02 01

Printed and bound in Canada.

# CONTENTS

## PART III: Readings

# Acknowledgements

This text was class tested at Seneca College, School of Computer Studies. We are grateful to the students and the staff — especially Rob Colter, Diane Hallquist, Veronica Abbass, Brian Flack, Betty Holmes, Maureen Lennon, Tom Orman, Kathy Pearl, Linda Siomra, Susan Stancer, and Kevin Topalian. They gave suggestions, critiques, and encouragement.

We also wish to thank the reviewers, Afra Kavanagh of University College of Cape Breton, David McCarthy of Centennial College, Beverly Allix of Humber College, Alexandra MacLennan of Seneca College, Barry Mathias of Camosun College, and Pat Rogin of Durham College.

We appreciate the talents and hard work of the Pearson Education Canada staff, especially those who had to deal directly with the "demanding authors" — David Stover, Marta Tomins, Kat Mototsune, and Joe Zingrone.

And finally, we acknowledge our children's contributions: David's computer program, Susan's *Star Wars* essay, and Emily's kadiddlehopper paragraph. They also listened to our discussions, offered suggestions, and occasionally let us use the computer. This book is dedicated to them.

# Introduction

*Groundwork: Writing Skills to Build On* is a practical, basic writing text. It is designed for remedial and developmental writing courses, including those for English as a Second Language (ESL) students. It is not intended to be a comprehensive grammar or rhetoric textbook. It bridges the gap between grammar books focusing on sentence structure and rhetoric texts focusing on essay writing.

The first part of this text establishes the structures the students will work with, focusing on the sentence, the paragraph, and the essay. Students are also introduced to summaries, oral presentations, and research papers. There are activities in this section, but few exercises that have right or wrong answers. Students are expected to practise what they are taught by writing paragraphs and essays. Some general topics are suggested; more specific ones are included with the readings.

The second part of the text deals with grammar and vocabulary. Instructors can dip into this section as they see fit. The grammar sections can be assigned as self-study for students who need them; the answers are in the back of the text. For instance, if an ESL student is making errors with non-countable nouns, the instructor can refer the student to the explanation and exercise in the text.

A selection of readings makes up the third part of the text. The selection includes fiction and non-fiction, newspaper essays and book excerpts. Almost all of them are from Canadian sources. Many are newspaper articles written in conversational English, and as such do not serve as models of academic writing. Instead, the sample paragraphs and essays in the first section fulfil that function. The reading selections help students improve reading and thinking skills. They also serve as a springboard to writing assignments. Following each reading are comprehension questions, vocabulary work, and writing topics.

The material has been arranged so that the chapters do not have to be taught sequentially. Instructors can pick and choose among the readings and do them in any order, having students write a paragraph or an essay about a particular topic based on a reading selection. The grammar troublespots and usage notes can be referred to when students are having difficulty with a particular point. We have based these sections on the errors that we see in our students' writing.

Students learn best by working with their own writing rather than with exercises dreamed up by textbook authors. The exercises in this text serve to illustrate particular points, rather than to provide drill and practice. Grammar lessons work best when taught in relation to the students' own writing.

We deal with students from a variety of academic backgrounds. Some cannot define a noun but rarely make a mistake using one. Some ESL students do brilliantly in grammar exercises but cannot apply their knowledge to their own writing. Some literature students can write about their feelings about a poem but cannot explain a process clearly. We tried to offer enough flexibility in this text to allow instructors to tailor it to their own classes.

## Native speakers and ESL students

*Groundwork* is designed to meet the needs of both native speakers and high-level ESL students. Native speakers are people who grew up using English and are therefore comfortable with its idiom. ESL students are those who are more comfortable speaking and writing in another language. Although ESL students make grammar mistakes that native speakers would not generally make, such as using the wrong article, both kinds of students need to learn about the writing process and the structures.

We expect that ESL students using this book would be at a fairly advanced level. In fact, some of our students are borderline—almost native speakers. They have spent many years in an English-speaking country and are comfortable with the idiom of the language, even though they have a slight accent and make some common ESL errors.

## Academic writing

*Groundwork* focuses on developed paragraphs and essays, but shows how academic writing relates to other kinds of writing the student will have to read or produce. We are trying to provide a bridge to the kind of writing students will be expected to do in the workplace; therefore, we have put less emphasis on personal essays and creative writing assignments. For instance, instead of asking students to write a description of a friend, we ask them to describe a Web site.

Because our focus is on academic writing, we encourage a more formal style of writing. Most of the sample paragraphs and essays in the text are in an impersonal, non-conversational style. For example, we ask our students not to use *I* or *you*. Many of our students, especially the native speakers of English, write in a conversational style and seem to have difficulty adopting another register. Thus, we teach them to write in a more formal register, so that they will learn to use a range of styles and be able to handle the style required in the work world.

## The five-paragraph essay

The five-paragraph essay provides a simple blueprint for students to emulate, practise, and then expand and develop as their skills and ability grow. We believe beginning and remedial writing students need structure as a foundation to build upon. Some teachers view the five-paragraph essay as being too limiting. After all, most real writing does not follow the neat structure of a one paragraph introduction (with thesis), three body paragraphs (with topic sentences), and a one paragraph conclusion. Of course, we do not want the five-paragraph essay to be the only way a student can write. However, once the students have mastered this structure they can expand and move on to other writing strategies.

# PART 1

# Structures

## CHAPTER 1

# The Writing Process

Writing is a form of communication. It tells your reader what you think. It is different from speech because it is more formal and precise. When you speak, some of your message is carried by your tone of voice, gestures, appearance, and physical surroundings. When you write, you do not have these additional ways to get your message across. Moreover, you do not have the luxury of facing your audience and making sure they understand you. Your meaning must be clear from your words alone. However, writing does have one advantage: As you write, you can reflect upon your words and revise them to make sure they communicate your message effectively.

Writing is a skill that you develop gradually. You never stop learning how to write better, but you have to work at it. Even professional writers are continually improving their skills. Most look back on their earlier work with dissatisfaction because they know they could now do better.

Writing is learned two ways—through practice and through reading. Grammar exercises may help you clarify points of grammar, but they do not teach writing skills. You can be taught the theory—how to structure an essay and how to use vocabulary, for instance—but you cannot really learn it until you do it yourself. When you practise writing, you develop the skill of expressing ideas. As you edit your work, you reconsider your words to make sure they are communicating your message. In addition, when you read, you acquire vocabulary, you are exposed to complex ideas, and you learn the forms and expressions of written communication.

One of the hardest things about learning to write is taking constructive criticism. The benefit of a second opinion is crucial because you may not be saying what you think you are saying. You strive to communicate with your reader; however, each reader is different and sometimes communication is not successful. Your words may be clear to you, but your reader may lack some of the information you have, or may not be able to follow the links between the ideas. Even professional writers rely on editors to give them a second opinion on their work.

# Why writing skills are important

Your need for good writing skills extends far beyond the classroom walls. Good writing skills are portable and practical. You carry them from job to job, or use them at home. When you use e-mail, send memos, put together brochures for your business, write a proposal, or compose a letter to complain about a faulty appliance, you need good writing skills.

Chances are that you will need to do some writing on the job. Even those who work in technical jobs must write, especially those at supervisory levels. The use of computers has increased our dependence on writing skills, as more people are responsible for the words that are published, mailed, or posted on the World Wide Web. For instance, in the past, managers could rely on secretaries to clean up their words, but now they compose their own business communication.

In addition, developing writing skills goes hand in hand with developing reading and thinking skills. Good writing demands careful thought and analysis. If you have a hard decision to make, for instance, putting it in writing is one good way of getting your thoughts clear.

---

### ACTIVITY  1.1

Find out about the writing tasks required for a job you are interested in. For example, ask an engineer how much of his day is taken up writing reports and correspondence, including memos and e-mail messages.

# How to get the most out of your writing course

How much you learn in a course depends on you—not the instructor, the textbook, or the mode of instruction. You get out what you put in. You have to make the effort to read the course material, do the assigned work, and, most importantly, learn from your mistakes.

When a piece of writing is returned to you, do not just look at the mark and put the work away. Instructors spend time making comments and corrections on a paper. You should make sure you understand what the teacher is telling you. If something is unclear, talk to your instructor. Go over the corrections. If a word has been marked as a spelling error, try to find the correct spelling. If you are making grammatical mistakes, make sure you understand the rules you are breaking. Seek extra help if you do not know why something has been marked wrong.

# Audience and purpose

When you write anything, the first things you consider are why you are writing and who will be reading your words. Writing is, after all, communication with your reader. Writers always tailor their work to their audience. For instance, we, as textbook writers, had to decide on a tone and style when we wrote these words. Our audience is you, the student, and the writing in this book has two purposes: instruction and demonstration. Thus, we have adopted a slightly less formal tone in the discussion parts of the text (where we explain what to do) than in the sample essays, which model academic writing. We made this decision because we wanted to approach the reader with a comfortable style, even though we are teaching students to write in a more formal tone.

In the work world, you have to consider the background of your audience. A report, for example, may be written for people with varying degrees of technical experience. For example, a product description written for the marketing department would be different than product specifications written for technicians. It would use less technical vocabulary. The term "layperson" describes a general audience who has no specialized knowledge of a subject. For example, doctors must be careful to use terminology that their patients— laypeople—understand.

If you have a problem at work, you may end up giving different versions describing the same situation. In a report to your supervisor, you might use technical language and give your opinion diplomatically ("the team members are trying to resolve a difference of opinion"). You may feel freer expressing your opinions if you write to a friend who is in the same business ("some people are using outdated methodology"). When you communicate with a family member, however, you may become more emotional but give fewer details and use less jargon ("it's a mess and every meeting is stressful").

## FIGURE 1.1    Sample of a Computer Program

```
'qBasic Program
'This program makes a record of the user's name and age.
'If the user's age is over 17, he is placed in the adult datafile.
'Otherwise, he goes in the student datafile.

'Variables
DIM name AS STRING
DIM age AS INTEGER
DIM choice AS INTEGER (1)

'datafiles
OPEN "adult.dat" FOR APPEND AS #1
OPEN "child.dat" FOR APPEND AS #2

LOOP
  'Input data
  INPUT "Type your name and press the Enter key or type [quit]
  to" _ & exit.";name

  'Check for exit loop conditions
  if name = "quit" then
    exit
  end if

  'input name and age
  INPUT "Hello", name, "How old are you? Type your age and press
  the Enter key"; age

  IF age >=18 then
    PRINT #1, name,", ", age
    PRINT "You have adult privileges on the network."
  ELSE
    PRINT #2, name,", ", age
    PRINT "You have student privileges on the network."
  END IF
END LOOP
'End Program
CLOSE #1
CLOSE #2
```

Note that punctuation marks on a computer are straighter than punctuation marks in print. In this program, the lines that start with a straight apostrophe (') are comment lines explaining how the program works. The lines in straight quotation marks ("") after INPUT and PRINT are written for users. The rest of the program is made up of instructions for the computer. These are specialized terms that the computer can interpret.

Computer programs offer a good example of audience and purpose (see Figure 1.1). Lines in a program that are targeted at other computer programmers contain jargon and technical language that non-programmers may not understand. Lines written for computer users are in simple, everyday English.

In addition to audience, writers must consider the purpose behind their work. Writing can be informative, reflective, persuasive, or creative. Instruction manuals are an example of informative writing; a journal is reflective; an essay is persuasive; and a short story or poem is creative.

In your writing course, you will probably not cover such a wide range of prose. This book focuses on academic writing, which forms a bridge to business and technical writing. You will write paragraphs, essays, and summaries, but not short stories or poetry.

Academic writing is, in a way, an artificial form of writing because it is not so much communication as demonstration. Generally, you are not giving your professor new information in your essay. Instead, you are showing your professor what you have learned and how you think. You may have to synthesize information, summarize and paraphrase other writing, analyze a problem, take a certain point of view, and support your ideas with facts.

The skills you develop in an academic writing course will serve you well even if you never write an essay again. For instance, you learn to organize ideas. You use the same skill when you write a job application cover letter, describing your academic training in one paragraph and your work experience in another.

## ACTIVITY 1.2

Consider the following writing tasks. In groups, consider who the readers would be and what kind of information and language would be required for the audience. For example, a letter to the editor of a newspaper would be read by regular readers of the newspaper. They would need a reference to the original story, but not a complete summary of the story.

- a brochure advertising a computer repair service

- a memo about job benefits

- a psychology essay on sibling rivalry

- a letter to a company complaining about a faulty product

- a report detailing new wiring standards to be used in construction

# What's the point?

Whether a piece of writing is an academic exercise or communication in the "real world," it must have a point—an argument, a main idea, a thesis. A paragraph, an essay, a letter, a book—each can usually be boiled down to one main point, something the writer is trying to get the readers to believe, such as the following:

- Smoking should be prohibited in all public places.
- The law of supply and demand should govern prices even in a crisis.
- The company will replace the broken appliance.
- Grieving people go through several stages when a family member or friend dies.
- The job applicant is qualified for the advertised position.
- Several expressions in English come from Aesop's fables.

Sometimes this point is clearly expressed, as in a thesis statement of an essay, and sometimes it is implied. As a reader, you should be able to determine the writer's main point. Consider why the author wrote the piece. What is the message that the writer is trying to get across to the reader?

# The three C's of good writing

No matter what kind of document you produce, the principles of good writing remain the same. You use different styles in a letter to a friend, a web page, and a business report, but the same factors determine how readable the document is and how well it communicates its message. Writing can be evaluated according to its content, clarity, and conciseness.

## Content

It does not matter how good your writing skills are if you have nothing to say. You do not need to be an expert on the subject, but you must have enough information and ideas to put forth a logical argument. Of course, you will have more to say if you are well-informed about issues and events in the news and in your field. Reading the daily newspaper is the best way to cover a lot of different topics and get up-to-date information. For instance, if a new law is proposed, a news story reports the facts, the editorial page gives the opinion of the newspaper staff, and the letters to the editor show different readers' reactions to the issue.

Some students complain that they have no idea what to write about. In English courses, students are generally offered a choice of topics. This kind of limited choice is good, because assignments are not so open-ended that students can write on absolutely anything. The problem here is not entirely a writing one, but one of having enough information and knowledge to think through the topic. Content problems can show up in argumentative essays on controversial topics. When students fall back on weak arguments, they reveal that they have not read enough, that they have not thought about the topic deeply, and that they are not developing a logical train of thought. For instance, a student writing an essay offering solutions to traffic problems may suggest only building more highways, but this idea is simplistic and does not consider problems of funding, space, and pollution.

Good content means that your main point is clear and well supported, and that you know what you are talking about. Your instructor will evaluate your ideas and how well they are supported.

## ACTIVITY   1.3

In groups, make a list of five current news stories and possible essay topics for each.

## Clarity

Because writing is all about communication, unclear writing has no value. Clarity is achieved through correct word choice, straightforward sentence structure, and signals for the reader, such as transition markers like "for example" and "in addition."

To communicate well, you must think an idea through first. Then you can write clearly and express yourself effectively. If your thinking is muddled, your writing will be too. Consider your audience and what your readers need to know. For example, in a business report, you might have to add a history of the project for a new manager. Whether or not you will use technical vocabulary in the report depends on the expertise of your audience.

Often you can achieve clarity in your writing by using plain English instead of ornate language. Keep sentences and paragraphs complete and brief. Some people think that good writing requires polysyllabic words and long, complicated sentences; they try to impress the reader with verbal complexity. Official writing ("bureaucratese") is often unnecessarily complicated, sometimes because the writer does not want to be perfectly clear. The military, for instance, might use the term "vertically deployed anti-personnel device" instead of the simple word "bomb." Many governments and businesses are trying to address this problem by fostering a "Plain English" approach.

It is important not to confuse clear and simple writing with simplistic writing. You do not want to write prose that sounds like it came out of a Grade 4 reader. Knowing your readers often determines word choice, level of expression, and complexity of ideas. In college or university, you are expected to write at a relatively sophisticated level.

Clarity also requires that you organize your ideas in a logical pattern and that you lead the reader from one point to another. Your sentences have to connect. Coherence in writing is further explored in Chapter 3 where we look at how paragraphs are organized.

---

### A C T I V I T Y 1.4

Discuss the following statements. Are they clear? If not, why not?

1. Sarah was not as unforgettable as she thought she was, but if she thought too long on the subject she was forgettable.

2. I hate gadgets. When that thingamigig rings in my pocket thing, I always press the wrong thing. And then I accidentally do something else.

3. The term cognitive dissonance in psychology illustrates a state of mind in which something or some idea a person sees or feels creates a sense of contradiction in his mind about what he understands and what he can accept as being true without violating his normalcy.

4. Just because he doesn't phone her every night doesn't mean that he doesn't have any affectations for her.

5. Drinking and driving is okay with me because on the highways sometimes I get thirsty and open a can of pop.

6. Watching too much television is a bad habit because you can learn about the world without ever reading a book.

7. Now, the Internet has become very common to normal people, so some advertisements which are part of computer web pages are very effective, better than television, radio and newspaper advertisements, because whenever someone uses the web page, he always sees it.

8. Eschew obfuscation by utilizing succinct phraseology, germane argumentation, and apt lexemes expressed in the vernacular.

9. The expression "Know news is good news" is confusing because it has too meanings.

## Conciseness

Concise writing is good writing. No reader wants to wade through irrelevant information or inflated phrases to get to the heart of a sentence, a paragraph, or an article. In the business world especially, where people are bombarded with so much information, a concise, clear piece of writing is as precious as gold.

Economy of words shows that you understand a reader's needs. Unfortunately, some students, desperate to fulfil a length requirement in an essay, pad their writing with unnecessary repetition and long-winded sentences. They only succeed in making their writing longer, not better.

Proper revising and editing are critical to achieving conciseness. Your words are not carved in stone: You can easily cut out what is superfluous. You may be reluctant to delete sentences you have laboured over, but professional writers know that careful pruning is essential.

Do not confuse brevity with lack of content, however. You may need to expand on an idea rather than leave it in an underdeveloped state. Make sure that you have covered the topic adequately for your readers.

This explanation of the principles of good writing can bewildering, to be sure. You are being told to put in enough content, but not too much; to keep it simple, but not simplistic; to keep it brief, but not too brief; and to make sure your writing is clear and organized—a formidable task, indeed. However, as you practise by writing paragraphs and essays, keep these principles in mind.

---

### A C T I V I T Y  1.5

Examine the following example of revising for conciseness. Determine which words have been deleted and discuss the methods used for eliminating wordiness.

Due to the fact that I have for a long time observed that students in college tend to like fast food over good, hearty, nutritious meals, I have come to realize that at certain periods of time these same people would go to fast food places such as McDonald's, Wendy's, or

Harvey's and pay a lot of money for a hamburger, fries, and beverage simply because at these places the service is fast, and the customer doesn't need to stand in line for a long time to get service. The food at any of these franchises is interchangeable and indistinguishable: the burgers and fries taste the same. Perhaps, at one place there are extra toppings and at another there is a special sauce melted into the meat patty and at the third place the meat is freshly grilled rather than defrosted and microwaved. Nonetheless and all in all, I have spent my $4.99, the average price for the "combo" in all three franchises, and have purposefully eaten all three kinds of burgers, chomped on all three kinds of fries, and sipped on all three medium-sized soft drinks. I cannot see the attraction of such food that draws university and college students day in and day out. After much consideration and personal analysis, I have come to the conclusion that students just go to these places to eat because everyone else does and because these franchises are within walking distance from the nearest classroom. [244 words]

**Revision for conciseness**

College students seem to prefer fast food over nutritious meals. Regularly, they go to McDonald's, Wendy's, or Harvey's for a burger combo simply because the service is quick. At any of these places, the food tastes the same despite minor differences in toppings and preparation. However, having eaten at all three places, I cannot understand the attraction of fast foods. I can only conclude that students go there because these places are conveniently located. [75 words]

# Choosing a topic

Writers are generally advised to write about something they know or can write about comfortably. Writing instructors give students different topics to choose from. Some teachers allow students to pick their own subject, but they usually reserve the right to approve it. Usually, this is not so much censorship as guiding you to a topic that can be dealt with easily within the confines of the assignment.

Generally, you may have a choice of topic for an assignment or an exam. It is important that you understand the question. Read it carefully.

Often you will be presented with a topic that you have to narrow down. An exploration of customs in Canada, for example, can be quite long; however, a focus on the meaning of some wedding superstitions is much more manageable.

Some essay topics require that you pick one side or the other of a controversial issue. You must take a stand. Even if you mention some opposing arguments, your composition must emphasize your side. Without focus, your paper will lack conviction.

Reading and talking to people will help you get ideas for your topic. Your instructor can help you with brainstorming techniques if you have writer's block.

Whatever the topic, you must think it through. Are you comfortable with the topic? How much effort is needed to cover this topic satisfactorily? Is it manageable as is, or can you choose an aspect of it? Do you have the resources demanded of the topic? Can you do an adequate job in the number of words required in the essay? Do you have enough time? As you gain experience as a writer, you will get a good sense of what you can handle.

## ACTIVITY  1.6

Rate the following topics from 1 to 10, with #1 as the topic you would most like to write about and #10 the topic you would least like to write about. You can choose to agree or disagree with the statement. Compare your evaluation of the topics with a classmate, and discuss the relative merits of each topic. Which topics are more interesting? Which are easier to write about?

_____ High schools should have designated smoking areas on the school grounds.

_____ Gambling should not be encouraged by government.

_____ An expensive luxury car is a worthwhile purchase.

_____ All students should learn to play a musical instrument in elementary school.

_____ Canadians should work shorter hours and have more vacation time.

_____ Learning a second language is an important part of education.

_____ Being single is not as good as being married.

_____ People should not give money to panhandlers.

_____ Violence in hockey must be reduced.

_____ Corporal punishment, such as spanking, should be allowed for disciplining children.

# Prewriting

Writers use different techniques to prepare to write. They do not sit down and write the document from beginning to end in one draft. The more you prepare your writing, the easier it is to do.

Brainstorming is the process by which writers think of many different ideas about their topic. Some writers jot down their ideas, some use diagrams to show the relationship between ideas, some use freewriting where they just write whatever comes to mind, and some ask themselves different questions about the topic. Mainly, they write down their ideas so that they can see the first steps of progress in the writing process. Then they choose which ideas to develop in their essay.

Word processors have affected the way writers work. Not only do computers make revising easier, they can also affect the prewriting process. For example, the outline may evolve into the actual piece of writing, instead of existing as a separate document. Writers can take a sketchy outline, add to it, and flesh it out until the composition evolves. If they get stuck on one part, they can skip ahead and then come back. They can move text around, easily using cut and paste functions.

Computers actually encourage movement back and forth between ideas or souces, instead of a linear progression. When you follow hyperlinks on web pages or in CD-ROMs you do not proceed in a linear way. Some writers find they must work in a straight progression; they write their draft from beginning to end. Others find that computers suit their way of thinking, and they move to another part of the work when they get stuck. For example, some writers find that it is easier to write the introduction once the whole essay is written. The organization of the final product (the essay), however, must be linear, so the introduction comes first no matter when it was written.

It does not matter how you brainstorm—what is important is that you generate a variety of ideas to start with. You will not use all the points in your essay, but it is better to start with more than you need. You have to look at your topic from all angles. If you are writing on a controversial topic, it is useful to think of the arguments against your point of view to help you think of points to argue. In your class, you might brainstorm in groups because it is useful to hear others' points of view, or your whole class might discuss the topic with your instructor.

Suppose, for example, your topic is this: "Discuss the advantages or disadvantages of working at home." Even if you already know which side of the issue you wish to argue, in the brainstorming phase, it is wise to consider both sides of the issue:

Advantages of working at home:

- reduces time, stress, and expense of travelling to work
- cuts down on the traffic jams and pollution caused by commuting
- flexible work hours
- can work around child care
- less distracted by co-workers and office politics
- makes residential neighbourhoods more used during the day, therefore safer
- develop a sense of community in neighbourhood
- can wear casual, less expensive clothing
- multi-tasking (put a load of laundry in while you are working)
- creates sense of independence
- less expenses for employers

Disadvantages of working at home:

- less contact with co-workers and supervisors
- employee bears office costs (space, office supplies, furniture, utilities)
- insurance problems, worker's compensation for injuries
- less solidarity with other workers, feeling of isolation
- workers can be taken advantage of by employers
- no separation of work and home, can lead to extended hours
- interruptions by family members
- others might intrude, not realizing it is work time
- might develop sloppy habits, in dress and workspace
- requires good self-organization and time management skills
- many are contract workers, receiving less pay and fewer benefits than "real" staff
- supervisor may have trouble monitoring work
- trying to keep track of home responsibilities while working can be distracting, neither job done well

These points form the raw material for an essay. Note that the ideas are expressed in point form. When brainstorming, you don't have to worry about essay structure and grammatical form. You should cast a wide net at this point: these ideas include advantages and disadvantages from different perspectives—the worker's, the employer's, and the society's. This is an illustration of the brainstorming process. From these ideas, you can choose to write an essay on the advantages or the disadvantages.

ACTIVITY   **1.7**

Choose one of the topics from Activity 1.6 and brainstorm. In ten minutes, write down as many points as you can for that topic. Don't write full sentences; just use point form. Afterwards, compare your brainstorming list with a classmate's.

# Writing

All writers suffer from writer's block occasionally. They look at the blank page or computer screen and cannot imagine how to fill it. The more you have prepared the topic, the easier it is to do the actual writing. In fact, the writing stage should actually take less time than the prewriting stage before it, and the revising and editing that follow it.

In your first draft, don't worry about getting the spelling and grammar perfect. Just get your ideas down. Don't worry about the length of the assignment; it's probably better to write more than you need at this stage and then to edit it down to the required length. You should also not worry too much about choosing the best possible words. You can always change your word choice in the editing stage.

You may find that the outline you have prepared does not match your essay. Revise the outline; it's not carved in stone and can easily be changed.

The problems that students have in the writing stage are often caused by anxiety. Thinking of the first draft as just one stage in the process can help alleviate the stress.

# Revising and editing

Revising your writing is one of the most overlooked steps in the writing process. Many students often produce a first draft and do little more than make a few corrections before they hand it in. Professional writers, on the other hand, keep revising, changing, and polishing their writing, and are often not fully satisfied even with the final draft. These writers move big chunks of prose around and sometimes delete a whole section of text. They stop writing to submit the piece for a deadline, but once it is published they still see ways that it could be improved.

When students think about revising their writing, they focus on mechanics—spelling, grammar, and punctuation. Although this is important, other aspects must be considered: paragraphing, sentence structure, sentence variety, and word choice. The word *revision*, after all, means "re-seeing." It is better to let your writing sit for a day or two before you edit. This will enable you to consider it with a fresh viewpoint.

Vocabulary choice can be improved during revision. You may find that you have used a particular word too often. As you edit, you can substitute synonyms. For example, you can use the word "employees" for "workers" in some of your sentences so that the writing does not sound repetitive.

Another useful thing to do in revision is to eliminate wordiness. Cutting out unnecessary words and rewriting sentences to focus on main ideas are actions better suited to the editing process than the initial writing.

The best way to learn editing is to do it with your own work. Get a second opinion of your draft. Your teacher, a tutor, or a fellow student can offer feedback. Ask if the main point is obvious, if it is sufficiently supported, and if your ideas are expressed clearly.

You may also be asked to edit a classmate's work. Peer editing can have varied results. Some students are better at seeing problems in other people's writing than they are in finding mistakes in their own work. Others, however, think that whatever their classmate wrote is perfect and make few suggestions. For classes with many ESL students, a peer editor should be someone with a different first language than the writer, so that the editor is less likely to make the same kinds of mistakes as the writer.

After you finish a first or second draft and are certain about the content, you should pay attention to cleaning up your paper. Proofreading carefully is important. If you are using a word-processing program, you may run the spell checking function to find typographical errors ("typos") and the grammar checking function to find clumsy sentence structures. However, these tools are very limited. Spell checkers catch errors such as "teh" for "the," but will not catch "there" instead of "their," or the misspelling of proper names or technical terms. Computers cannot understand language, and grammar checkers are very poor at figuring out the structure of a sentence. Often the suggestions are wrong. You can use these tools to guide you, but you cannot rely on them. You must carefully read over your entire paper yourself.

Here is an example of a paragraph as it is revised. The first draft is revised for unity, coherence, clarity and conciseness. The second draft is then edited to correct spelling and grammar mistakes.

### First draft

Their is not enough holidays in Canada. Other countrys have more holidays then Canada. Other countries, like Italy and Indonesia have longer holidays as well. I have cousins there who enjoy these extra holidays. In canada their is only Christmas Day, Canadia Day, New Year Day, Civil Holday, victorian day, Boxing Day, Labor Day and Thanksgiving. There's not any three day long holiday unless it falls on a Friday or Monday. Theres a long time from New Years Day untill victoria Day. That was a long time between holidays. Besides turkey, there is no festive meal to help celebrate each holiday. We need a special dish to symbolize that special day. I think people in Canada needs more time off so he or she can spent time with family and do thinks together. More holidays needed for Canada. No wonder people in Canada work so hard. They don't have free time and must depneds on Saturday and sundays, and sick leave to relax. The only long relaxing time is there vacation which is may be 2 or 3 weeks in the summer with the kids. They go to Disney land in Florida or elsewhere. Holidays are important for all Canadian peoples as a recent immigrant to Canada I am surpise to find so less legal days off work. Maybe this what is meaned by protesting work ethnics in canada.

### First Revision

Unlike other countries, Canada has less holidays. Their is only eight legal holidays; Christmas Day, Boxing Day, New Year Day, victorian day, Caanada Day, Civil Holday, Labor Day and Thanxgiving. There's not any three day long holiday, and theres a long time between holidays from New Years to Victoria Day. Because of this, canadians depend on weekends to relax and look forward to their three week vacation every year. As a recent immigrant, I am surpise to find so few days of rest.

### Second Revision

Unlike other countries, Canada has very few holidays. There are only eight legal holidays: Christmas, Boxing Day, New Year's, Victoria Day, Canada Day, Civic Holiday, Labour Day, and Thanksgiving. Canadians do not have three-day-long holidays, and have a long stretch from New Year's Day until Victoria Day for a rest. Because of this situation, Canadians depend on weekends to relax and look forward to the three-week vacation time. As a recent immigrant, I am surprised to find so few days of rest in Canada.

## ACTIVITY 1.8

Here is an example of a paragraph as it is revised. In groups, discuss the revisions. Find examples of improvement for unity, coherence, clarity, and conciseness. Look for changes in wording and explain why the new choices are better. Find the spelling and grammar mistakes that are corrected in the third version.

### First draft

They shouldnt have commercials in schools. There are lots of advertising that kids are exposed to. Schools should be a place to excape all this. Schools show commercials, they are telling kids they support the products being advertised in the comercials. Some schools make deals with Pepsi and Coke to sell only their stuff in the school, and the company gives the school some money. Schools today need more mony to run. And then there are big drink machines in the hall with big ads for the drink company. Schools teach good nutrition and than they go against this by making deals with soft drink companies. And pop is bad for their teath. Some schools had adds on computer screen savers. Kids in school don't have the option of turning stuff off like they do at home. They have to do what teachers tell them to do, even if that includes watching commercials. There are some really bad commercials, and some of them are boring, and yet they show them. Schools need to teech media awareness so that kids can see how companies are trying to seduce them with advertising. Making deals with companies isnt the weigh to make kids more media aware.

### Second draft

Commercials shouldn't be in schools. There are lots of advertising that kids are exposed to, but schools should be a place to excape all this. Students can't avoid this advertising as they do at home. They have to do what teachers tell them to do, even if that includes watching commercials. Some schools had adds on computer screen savers. If schools show commercials, they are telling kids they support the products being advertised in the comercials. Some schools make deals with Pepsi and Coke to sell only their drinks in the school, and the company gives the school some money. Schools today need more money to run. And then there are big drink machines in the hall with big ads for the drink company. Schools teach good nutrition in health class, but they go against this teaching by selling pop which is bad for their teath. Schools need to teech media awareness so that kids can see how companies are trying to seduce them with advertising. Making deals with companies isnt the weigh to make kids more media aware.

**Final version**

Advertising does not belong in schools. Even though students are exposed to numerous ads and commercials outside class, schools should provide an oasis to escape this over-commercialized world. However, some schools show advertising on computer screen savers and commercials on school television broadcasts. Students are a captive audience for this advertising; they have to do what teachers tell them, even if that includes watching commercials. Moreover, with in-school advertising, the education system sends the message that it supports the products. For example, some school boards make deals with soft drink companies to sell their drinks exclusively. Schools need the cash these deals generate, but they are making a deal with the devil, promoting products that go against the lessons in nutrition taught in health classes. Students need lessons in media literacy and advertising techniques, but commercializing the classroom is not good education.

# Using resources and getting help

Writers generally work alone, but they call on outside help and various resources to help them. This assistance can run the gamut from asking a friend to read what they have written to hiring a professional editor to clean up their work. Writers use resource materials ranging from dictionaries and grammar books to encyclopedias and the Internet. They acknowledge their sources of information.

Students must be careful not to cross the line between getting help and cheating. Sometimes this line is not clear. It may even vary across different educational systems or different cultures. In some contexts copying a writer's phrasing, for example, is the way students are encouraged to learn.

Instructors expect you to write your own essays with your own ideas and your own expressions. When you do take other people's words or ideas, you must acknowledge your research materials—you must not copy other writers' words and present them as your own. As a general rule, any source of information—from published to unpublished materials—may be included in your essay as long as you give credit to the original writer in both footnote and bibliography (and as long as the essay is not made up of more quotations than your own writing).

If you check the encyclopedia to find out the date of the French Revolution, for example, you do not have to cite the encyclopedia. This type of fact is considered general knowledge. However, if a historian has developed an unusual theory on what Marie Antoinette really meant when she said, "Let them eat cake," then you should cite that historian's work as reference.

If you state that white is the colour of mourning in Chinese society, you do not have to cite a reference; this is a general fact. However, if you refer to a specific study on the psychological effects of colour, you must include a citation.

If you give statistics, you must give a source for your figures.

How you cite your sources can vary. The format differs depending on the discipline. In the past, footnotes were used, but today writers generally put the author, year, and page number in parentheses after the reference or quote. Style guides have also needed to develop standardized ways of dealing with new sources of information—websites, newsgroup postings, and chat-room conversation. If you have to write a research paper, find out the citation style your instructor prefers. You can find out more about citation styles in Chapter 8, from style guides, and on Internet websites.

You must also be careful when deciding what does not need to be acknowledged. Like many students, you may be uncertain as to what "in your own words" really entails. Changing a word or phrase here and there in someone else's statement does not make it yours. Taking phrases and clauses from different writers and pasting them into a sentence does not make that statement yours. Any tinkering with someone else's statement does not make it yours. You have to write down the idea the way you normally would express it.

This does not mean that you have to avoid every vocabulary item the author uses. Obviously, you cannot write about a topic without using the same vocabulary other writers on the topic have used. Sometimes using one word the way an author uses it is copying because the author uses the word in an idiosyncratic way. Sometimes you can use an expression of several words that the author uses because it is a standard phrase in the language. For more about paraphrasing, see Chapter 7 on writing summaries.

Copying from other writers' works and failing to acknowledge sources of ideas is considered plagiarism. Academic penalties for plagiarism are severe because it is cheating—presenting something as your work when it isn't. Even copying a single sentence from another author can result in a grade of zero and official sanction. Check your school's calendar to find out more about the policy on plagiarism.

Another form of cheating to guard against is getting too much help with your writing assignments. Having someone read an essay to spot misspellings or to correct minor slips in expression is acceptable. If the person heavily edits or revises the writing, it is no longer your work. Remember that the instructor wants to see what you are capable of doing.

Many colleges and universities have writing centres where students can go to get help with their essays. The tutors at these centres are careful to avoid doing the student's work; they point out problem areas and make suggestions for general improvement.

Most writing courses include in-class writing assignments and tests. These allow the instructor to get a sense of the writing style of each student. Although instructors expect each student to submit better work when more time and resources (such as word processors and spell checking) are available, they also expect to be able to identify the out-of-class assignment as definitely the student's writing. Instructors can often tell when a student hands in an essay that is not his own work by the quality of the writing or by the differences in the writing style.

# Improving your skills

All good writers are readers. Reading is the most important step in becoming a better writer. It exposes you to ideas, vocabulary, and the flow of good writing. Moreover, the written language is different from the spoken language. The only way to learn the written language is from written texts. Good writers are also attentive readers: they pay attention to the language used, as well as to the meaning of the passages.

Practice is also important. It is easier to get your words down on paper (or on screen) if you do it a lot. One way is to practise writing is to keep a journal. Write in your journal for a few minutes at the end of each day. Do not keep a mundane record of what you did ("I got up at 9. I had a bagel for breakfast."). Instead, reflect on what you have experienced or seen during the day. You can write your opinions about the latest fashions, a new music group, or people you interact with. You may even find keeping a journal is good therapy—instead of telling off a classmate in real life, you can do it in the safety and privacy of your journal. Researchers have found that writing about problems can reduce stress levels.

You can also keep a journal for each subject you are studying. If you write a paragraph summary at the end of each section or chapter you study, you will not only improve your writing skills but you also find it easier to remember the material.

Letter writing is another way to improve your writing skills. Whether you send your messages by post or by e-mail, conducting a correspondence with someone is a valuable experience. Today, many people communicate by e-mail with "pen pals" all over the world. In addition to such one-to-one correspondence, the Internet allows you to participate in discussion groups, so you can practise your writing skills when you post messages. Indeed, the popularity of e-mail, chat rooms, and newsgroups has fuelled a comeback in writing skills, even though these forms of communication are less formal and structured than letters.

## How to improve your writing skills

1. Read.

2. Read a lot.

3. Read different kinds of materials.

4. Pay attention when you read, learning from other writers.

5. Practise writing.

6. Review your writing critically.

7. Correct your mistakes.

| SUMMARY |
|---|

## *The writing process*

- Choose a topic. The writing task may be assigned to you or you may decide on your own to write something.

- Think about your topic. Brainstorm. Look at it from different points of view.

- Limit your topic and decide on a thesis (the main point).

- Write an outline, organizing your ideas into sections or paragraphs.

- Write a first draft based on your outline.

- Make sure you have supporting points for your general statements.

- Read your draft, checking content, clarity, and conciseness.

- Rewrite your draft, eliminating unnecessary words and varying your wording.

- Check your draft for spelling and grammar errors, and correct them.

- Get a second opinion on your draft.

- When you are satisfied that you have said what you want to say in correct form and language, print your work.

## CHAPTER 2

# Writing Effective Sentences

Language is made of building blocks: Letters make words, which are combined in sentences, which make up paragraphs, which form written works ranging from essays or books. This chapter gives a quick review of sentence structure and establishes terminology. Students whose first language is English may be unfamiliar with traditional grammar terms, but they should be able to attach these labels to concepts they already know. Some ESL students, on the other hand, may be quite comfortable talking about grammar rules, so they may only need practice applying these rules to their writing. In either case, students need some familiarity with grammar concepts to be able to understand corrections to their writing. (Part II of this text revisits the world of grammar to look more closely at problem areas common in students' writing.)

## Parts of speech

In order to understand the structure of a sentence, you must be able to distinguish the different parts of speech and their functions. Nouns, pronouns, verbs, adjectives, adverbs, articles, and conjunctions are the building blocks of sentences.

Keep in mind that the part of speech of each word depends on how it is used in a sentence. The same word might be a noun, verb, or adjective.

**noun:**      I need a stronger <u>light</u> for my desk.

**verb:**      We often <u>light</u> a fire on cold winter evenings.

**adjective:**  It's not too cold, so I'll wear my <u>light</u> jacket.

Most words, however, have different forms for nouns, verbs, and adjectives. For example, *difference* is a noun, *differ* is a verb, and *different* is an adjective.

Although it is not necessary to know grammar terminology in order to be a good writer, you need to be able to understand these terms to discuss writing problems. In other words, if your instructor says that your sentence is incorrect because it lacks a verb, you should know exactly what a verb is. Pay attention to the part of speech tag (usually abbreviated to n., v., adj., adv.) when you look up a word in the dictionary to make sure you are looking at the right form. Students sometimes use the wrong parts of speech in their sentences, either because they do not know the correct form for the part of speech or because they do not understand the grammatical structure of the sentence.

## Nouns

Nouns are the names of persons, places, things, and concepts: *woman, James, home, Toronto, chair, beauty.* Proper nouns are capitalized: *Elizabeth, Canada, Ministry of Education, President Jones.*

Nouns may be singular or plural: *book, books.* Plurals are usually formed with the addition of *s.* Some plurals are irregular: *mouse, mice.* (If you are not sure of the plural form for a noun, check your dictionary.) Some nouns are uncountable nouns and are usually not found in a plural form: *information, water.*

You should be able to tell whether the noun is a subject or an object in the sentence. The subject is who or what is doing the action of the verb. Subjects are usually at the beginning of sentences in English. Objects generally follow verbs or prepositions. Objects are nouns that are affected by verbs or prepositions. For example, an object might receive the action of a verb.

Hiroshi made a wagon for his sister.

Hiroshi *is the subject,* wagon *is the object of the verb, and* **sister** *is the object of the preposition* for.

Nouns can also be used as adjectives to describe other nouns: *a car radio.* They also have a possessive form, shown by the addition of an apostrophe and *s,* which is used to describe another noun: *her sister's boyfriend.*

## Pronouns

Pronouns replace and refer to nouns.

When <u>Arthur</u> pulled the sword from the stone, <u>he</u> became king.

*The pronoun* he *refers to the noun* Arthur.

The pronoun must be the same in person and number as the noun which is the antecedent, which is the word to which the pronoun refers.

**As the subject of a sentence:**

|  | singular | plural |
|---|---|---|
| first person | I | we |
| second person | you | you |
| third person | he, she, it | they |

**As the object of a verb or a preposition:**

|  | singular | plural |
|---|---|---|
| first person | me | us |
| second person | you | you |
| third person | him, her, it | them |

**Possessive pronouns used before nouns:**

|  | singular | plural |
|---|---|---|
| first person | my | our |
| second person | your | your |
| third person | his, her, its | their |

**Possessive pronouns used without nouns:**

|  | singular | plural |
|---|---|---|
| first person | mine | ours |
| second person | yours | yours |
| third person | his, hers, its | theirs |

Notice that possessive pronouns have no apostrophes.

Pronouns also include words that some people do not think of as pronouns:

**Demonstrative pronouns:** this, that, those, these

**Indefinite pronouns:** each, some, many, one, few, anything, everyone, etc.

**Relative pronouns:** who, whom, what, which, whose, that

**Interrogative pronouns:** who, what, which, whose

Be careful to use the correct pronoun to refer to the noun. Also make sure you are not switching pronouns (from *we* to *they* to *you*) in your writing. Common errors in pronoun use are discussed in Chapter 14.

EXERCISE 2.1

Identify nouns and pronouns in the following paragraph. For each pronoun, say which noun it refers to.

The Trojan War started with the gift of an angry goddess. Eris, goddess of strife, was not invited to a wedding on Mount Olympus, so she tossed a golden apple, inscribed "To the fairest," into the middle of the party. Three goddesses vied for the apple: Hera, Zeus's wife, and two of Zeus's daughters, Aphrodite, the goddess of love, and Athena, goddess of wisdom. The gods and goddesses called on Zeus to make a judgement, but he did not want to decide among his wife and daughters. He called for an impartial judge. The judge chosen was Paris, the son of Priam, the king of Troy. Paris was living as a herdsman because he had been sent away from the city when a prophecy said that he would cause its destruction. The goddesses tried to bribe Paris. Athena offered him the gift of wisdom, Hera offered power, and Aphrodite offered the most beautiful woman in the world. Paris picked Aphrodite. The most beautiful woman was Helen, the wife of Menelaus of Sparta. When Paris stole Helen and took her to Troy, Menelaus went to his brother Agamemnon, a mighty Greek ruler, who assembled an army of Greek heroes. They sailed to Troy and surrounded the city in a siege that lasted ten years. Eventually, the Greeks won the war and took Helen back home.

## Verbs

A verb tells the action of something. It also describes the state or feeling of something.

Barbara <u>walked</u> around the park.

They <u>gave</u> him a promotion.

He <u>is</u> the new director of advertising.

Something <u>smells</u> bad.

They <u>completed</u> the report before the due date.

Verbs are often distinguished as transitive, those that require a direct object, and intransitive, those that do not. In the example sentences above, the verbs *give* and *complete* both take direct objects: *a promotion* and *the report*, respectively.

When you look up a verb in the dictionary, you see the base form. This form is the infinitive without *to* and it is used to make the simple present tense. Here are some base forms of verbs: *do, make, be, find, run, sleep, talk, seem, believe.*

To make the different forms of the verb you need to know three main parts:

| Base | Past Tense | Past Participle |
|------|-----------|-----------------|
| talk | talked | talked |
| whisper | whispered | whispered |
| sing | sang | sung |
| speak | spoke | spoken |

While regular verbs use the *-ed* ending for the past forms, irregular verbs vary. You can check your dictionary for the past tense and past participles of irregular verbs.

The verb in a sentence may be more than one word. The auxiliary or helping verbs *be* and *have* form part of the verb in the perfect and continuous tenses. Modal verbs can also be part of the verb: *could, should, may, would.*

The company <u>is installing</u> more security lights in the parking lot.

He <u>should have been working</u> harder.

Contrary to his expectations, he <u>did get</u> to the office on time.

Phrasal verbs are two-part verbs, completed by a preposition:

I <u>tore up</u> the bill.

I <u>looked up</u> the words in the dictionary.

Verbs have different forms depending on the tense:

Simple present: I study for my exams.

Simple past: I studied for my exams.

Future: I will study for my exams.

Present continuous: I am studying for my exams.

Past continuous: I was studying for my exams.

Future continuous: I will be studying for my exams.

Present perfect: I have studied for my exams.

Past perfect: I had studied for my exams.

Future perfect: I will have studied for my exams.

Present perfect continuous: I have been studying for my exams.

Past perfect continuous: I had been studying for my exams.

Future perfect continuous: I will have been studying for my exams.

(Note that some grammars use the term *progressive* instead of *continuous*.)

This list of verb tenses may look overwhelming, but you can concentrate on the forms that are used most often: the simple present, simple past, future, present and past continuous, and present perfect. Very few sentences require the future perfect continuous, but the simple present is often used in essays because it is the form used to express general facts. This paragraph, for example, uses the simple present tense in all the sentences.

Verbs can also be in active or passive voice. A passive sentence is formed when the object of the verb is made into the subject and the verb is used with the verb *to be* as an auxiliary.

Active: My boss gave me a promotion.
Passive: I was given a promotion.

Active: Somebody built that house in 1874.
Passive: That house was built in 1874.

Active: The new manager submitted the proposal.
Passive: The proposal was submitted by the new manager.

If you use a grammar checker with your word processor, you may see sentences flagged because they are in the passive voice. Your grammar checker is cautioning you because active sentences are preferable to passive sentences. Passive voice is harder for the reader to process and understand. Too many passive sentences make writing stilted and stop the flow. However, passive voice can be useful when you want to de-emphasize the doer of the action.

## Verbals

Verbals (gerunds, participles, infinitives) are forms of the verb that are not used as the main verb. Gerunds and present participles have an *-ing* ending: *going, skiing, playing.* The past participle has an *-ed* or *-en* ending, unless it is an irregular verb. The infinitive is the base form of the verb, usually preceded by the preposition *to: to go, to ski, to play.*

Gerunds act as nouns:

Skiing is my favourite sport.

Reviewing your lecture notes everyday is more effective than last-minute studying.

A famous author once said he enjoyed having written but not writing.

You can review the material by going over your lecture notes.

Participles are modifiers:

That man jogging beside the dog runs the city marathon every year.

Not understanding a word he said, they completed the task in their own way.

The infinitive can have different functions in the sentence:

I don't like to work on Sunday.

I need a screwdriver to open this.

To err is human.

---

**E X E R C I S E   2.2**

---

Identify which words are verbs or verbals (gerunds, participles, infinitives) in the following paragraph:

The verb "to coin," used to describe the action of introducing a new word into the language, has a double meaning when the names of coins enter the language. When the loon was chosen as the image on Canada's dollar coin, it made an indelible mark on the vocabulary of Canadian English. The new coin was dubbed the "loonie," and now the word is synonymous for the Canadian dollar as shown in newspaper headlines proclaiming "Loonie's value drops." It is fitting, perhaps, that the word "loon" refers not only to the waterfowl with the haunting cry but also to a crazy person, a "lunatic" or someone touched by the moon (from the Latin *luna*). With the loonie accepted into Canadian pockets and the language, a new bi-metallic two-dollar coin was introduced. The image on one side of the coin was a polar bear, another representative of Canadian wildlife. Several names were suggested. Some were built on the precedence of the loonie: "Doubloon" brought forth images of pirate gold, and "twonie" or "toonie" suggested a doubling of the loonie. Other names played on the image of the polar bear. "Bearback" and "bearbutt" were irreverent suggestions for a coin with the image of the Queen on the other side. However, simplicity won out in common usage, and the coin is now accepted as the "toonie." Coin designers must consider language as well as image when they choose symbols.

## Adjectives

Adjectives describe nouns: *bad, cautious, little, loud, marginal, plentiful, pretty, rich, sophisticated, tired, valuable, worthy.*

Adjectives have comparative and superlative forms. Comparatives are formed by using an *-er* ending on short adjectives or using the word more with longer adjectives: *cheaper, more expensive, friendlier, taller, more anxious.* Superlatives are formed by using an *-est* ending on short adjectives or by using the word *most* with longer adjectives: *fastest, longest, most troublesome.* Other qualifiers are also used with adjectives: *less, least, fewer, fewest, quite, rather, pretty* (in informal English), *very.* These qualifiers are adverbs.

## Adverbs

Adverbs are words that modify a verb, an adjective, or sometimes the whole sentence. They describe how, when, and where the action is performed. Adverbs can be positioned in different places in a sentence. Some adverbs are formed by adding *-ly* to an adjective: *quietly, quickly, happily.* Other adverbs include *already, now, then, yesterday, there, here.*

---

E X E R C I S E   **2.3**

---

Identify adverbs and adjectives in the following sentences:

1. Most students want a flexible, part-time job with a fair wage and a reasonable boss.

2. Teenagers generally do not have much work-related experience.

3. What employers really want from workers is willingness and enthusiasm.

4.  Unfortunately, some employees become bored with repetitious tasks, and demanding managers then accuse them of being unwilling to work hard.

5.  Because of the high rate of turn-over in "dead-end" jobs from the younger set, innovative employers now aggressively recruit senior citizens who want to keep active and have some extra cash to supplement their pension.

## Articles

The definite article is *the*, while *a* and *an* are indefinite articles. Articles are also called determiners. Article use can be tricky for ESL learners, especially when the usage is idiomatic. Essentially, the definite article is used when we are talking about something specific that has been identified, and the indefinite article is used in the sense of "one." See Chapter 14 for rules of use.

## Prepositions

Prepositions are connecting words that often show time or place relationships: *about, after, against, around, at, behind, beside, between, by, down, except, for, from, in, near, of, on, to, through, up, with*. They often introduce prepositional phrases: *down the road, in class*.

The basic meanings of prepositions are fairly straightforward, but students often have problems with the prepositions that are determined by verbs. For example, the verb *rely* takes the preposition *on* in a sentence such as "He relied on her to make the phone calls." We cannot say "rely with" or "rely to."

Prepositions are also part of phrasal verbs: *give up, step down, walk out*. In this case, they do not really function as prepositions because they are part of the verb. To show this distinction, some grammarians call these words particles or adverbs.

## Conjunctions

Conjunctions are joining words. The coordinate conjunctions are *and, but, or, so*, and *yet*. Subordinate conjunctions include *after, although, because, if, since, when, while*, and *whereas*. Coordinate conjunctions join two clauses of equal weight. When a subordinate conjunction is used, the more important idea is in the main clause. The subordinate conjunction introduces the subordinate, or dependent, clause, which has the less important idea.

Smokers choose to harm themselves, <u>but</u> they should not be allowed to poison the air for other people.

Although smokers choose to harm themselves, they should not be allowed to poison the air for other people.

I wanted a better grade, so I repeated the course.
I repeated the course because I wanted a better grade.

Whether you choose to use coordinate or subordinate conjunctions depends on how you want to emphasize your points.

It is important not to confuse conjunctions with adverbs such as *however, nevertheless,* and *therefore*. These words cannot join clauses. Therefore, sentences such as the following are ungrammatical. The asterisk shows that the sentence is incorrect.

*Smokers choose to harm themselves, however they should not be allowed to poison the air for other people.

*I wanted a better grade, therefore I repeated the course.

---

## E X E R C I S E  2.4

Identify the part of speech of each underlined word in the following sentences:

1. Every year in high school, the class studies a different play by Shakespeare.

2. My parents play Scrabble every evening, and then they go for a walk.

3. I walk quickly and my sister always has trouble keeping up with me.

4. After the reorganization, a calmer atmosphere prevailed.

5. When I go to the movies, I like to see a film with lots of special effects that take advantage of the big screen.

# What is a sentence?

A sentence is a group of words that starts with a capital letter and ends with a period (or a question or exclamation mark). It expresses a complete thought. It has a subject (something we are talking about) and a predicate (something we are saying about the subject). The predicate must have a verb.

Whether or not we have a grammatical sentence depends on what is between that capital letter and the final punctuation mark.

Sometimes the group of words is incomplete and we have a sentence fragment, a non-sentence.

Look at the following pairs of sentences. The first is an incomplete sentence; the second is a grammatical sentence. You should be able to feel that something is missing in the first example of each pair.

1. Ketchup.
2. I like to put ketchup on my French fries.

3. Because he was sick.
4. Because he was sick, he missed the test.

5. Being an ambitious person.
6. Being an ambitious person, he took the upgrading courses.

7. The stars shining brightly.
8. The stars are shining brightly.

9. After the disastrous party where he spilled wine down the front of his brand new white shirt that he had spend days shopping for and had finally found at a special half-price sale.
10. He vowed to drink more carefully after the disastrous party where he spilled wine down the front of his brand new white shirt that he had spend days shopping for and had finally found at a special half-price sale.

The odd-numbered sentences are incomplete: 1 lacks a verb; 3 is a subordinate clause with no main clause; 5 is a phrase with no main clause; 7 has an incomplete verb form "shining"; 9 is long, but there is no main clause.

# The anatomy of a sentence

The minimum requirement for a sentence is a subject and a verb. The kernel of the sentence is a subject plus a verb. Sentences also have modifiers such as adverbs, adjectives, prepositional phrases, appositives, and clauses.

Jim works.

Jim works slowly.

Jim in the head office works slowly.

Jim in the head office works so slowly that we are always behind.

Commands (sentences in the imperative mood) are considered to have "you" as the understood subject:

Stop!

Here are the basic patterns of simple sentences:

*subject + intransitive verb*
James shouted.

*subject + transitive verb + direct object*
Elaine hit the ball.

*subject + transitive verb + indirect object + direct object*
He gave her the promotion.

*subject + verb + adverbial*
They are here.

*subject + transitive verb + direct object + objective complement*
The group appointed him president.

I painted the room yellow.

*subject + linking verb + predicate noun or adjective*
Elizabeth is a neurosurgeon.

The pizza smells good.

Transitive verbs are ones that take a direct object. These basic sentence patterns are expanded with modifiers—adjectives, adverbs, phrases, and clauses. They can also be transformed into questions (also called interrogative sentences) with a change in word order the the addition of a question mark.

# Phrases

A phrase is a connected series of words that modifies or expands upon parts of the sentence. Depending on the construction of a sentence, the phrase is identified differently and used differently.

## Noun phrases

The <u>big yellow school</u> bus stops suddenly.

I saw the <u>big yellow school bus</u>.

The noun phrase "the big yellow school bus" is the subject of the sentence in the first example. In the second, it is the object of the verb "saw". While its relationship in the sentence changes, the noun phrase remains the same, a noun phrase.

## Verb phrases

I <u>have been wandering</u> all afternoon.

You <u>should have been</u> there.

A verb phrase includes the verb and helping verbs: *have been wandering* and *should have been*. In the first sentence, *wandering* is the main part of the verb phrase, and *have been* are the helping verbs. Similarly, in the second sentence, *been* is the main part of the verb phrase and *should have* are the helping verbs.

Verbals are often constructed in phrases. Verbals come in three forms: infinitive, gerund and participle, and each can have modifiers and complements within its phrase.

Infinitive phrase: <u>To meet the deadline</u> is an impossible task.

The infinitive phrase *to meet the deadline*, is acting as a noun and the subject of the sentence. Note that because of its verb qualities, *to meet* can take on the object of the verb *the deadline*.

Gerund phrase: <u>Snacking on sweets</u> is not healthy.

The gerund phrase is *snacking on sweets*, and it is acting as a noun and the subject of the sentence. Similar to the infinitive phrase, the gerund *snacking on* has verb qualities and thus can take on the object *sweets*.

Participial phrase: <u>Having recently seen the movie</u> I decided to stay home instead.

Participial phrase: The woman <u>holding the umbrella</u> is my aunt.

Participial phrases cannot act as nouns; they can only be used as adjectives and modifiers. So, *having recently seen the movie* and *holding the umbrella* are two participial phrases that modify respectively *I* and *woman*. In short, participles modify pronouns and nouns.

In addition, you can write participial phrases as present or past participles. Note that their function as adjective and modifier remains the same.

Present participle: <u>Running to catch the bus</u>, Hardeep stumbled and fell.

Past participle: <u>Abused by her spouse</u>, Jeannette sought help from the Women's Shelter.

## Prepositional Phrases

Prepositional phrases start with a preposition: *in, at, with, to, under, of, upon, beside, over*. They modify nouns and verbs. They generally give additional information pertaining to subject, time, or place.

Many antiques <u>of the last decade</u> are found in the house.

I put the book <u>on the desk</u> <u>in the corner</u>.

---

E X E R C I S E   **2.5**

---

Underline the phrases in the following sentences:

1. Once upon a time, there was a man, dressed in a red suit, who wanted to please children.

2. Living in the North Pole for most of the year, he was sheltered from the everyday hustle and bustle of crowds and other distractions.

3. For eleven months, he and his merry elves made toys of every sort and stored them for one special day.

4. During this time, some of his helpers kept a list of children who were naughty or nice.

5. With the help of eight tiny reindeer, he rode through the sky to every household.

6. Children, believing that this jolly old man would be wanting something good to eat after all this work, often placed cookies and milk near the fireplace, just for him.

# Clauses

In contrast to a phrase, a clause has a subject and predicate. It may be complete in itself (an independent clause), or it may be subordinate (dependent) to another part of a sentence. Subordinate clauses are a good way to put additional, but less important, information into a sentence.

Note the difference between clauses and phrases:

Phrase: The boys <u>wandering around the complex</u> were looking for trouble.

Clause: The boys <u>who were wandering around the complex</u> were looking for trouble.

A subordinate or dependent clause usually begins with a subordinate conjunction: *although, because, when, after, if, while.*

<u>When the rain stopped</u>, the baseball players resumed playing.

He refused the transfer <u>because he didn't want to move</u>.

Relative clauses begin with relative conjunctions: *that, which, where, why, who.*

John, <u>who really should have known better</u>, was disqualified.

The person <u>whom they selected</u> is well qualified.

Clauses are used to add extra information to a sentence. They allow a writer to maintain the focus on the main point.

The temperature increase in the Pacific Ocean called El Nino was blamed for many weather disasters. El Nino occurs every three to seven years. It caused flooding in parts of the U.S., drought in the West Pacific, leading to brush fires in Australia, and hurricanes in Tahiti and Hawaii.

### Revision using clauses

The temperature increase in the Pacific Ocean called El Nino, which occurs every three to seven years, was blamed for many weather disasters. It caused flooding in parts of the U.S., drought in the West Pacific, leading to brush fires in Australia, and hurricanes in Tahiti and Hawaii.

# Compound and complex sentences

A simple sentence has one clause. In a compound sentence, another clause is added with a coordinate conjunction: *and, or, but, so, yet.* In a complex sentence the addition is made with the use of a subordinate conjunction: *because, if, when, since.* Here are some simple sentences:

The computer lab is open twenty-four hours a day.

We can work on our assignment all night.

Our assignment is due tomorrow.

Here are some compound sentences:

The computer lab is open twenty-four hours a day, so we can work all night.

Our assignment is due tomorrow, and we can work all night.

The work is complicated, but we can work together.

Here are some complex sentences:

Because the computer lab is open twenty-four hours a day, we can work all night.

Although our assignment is due tomorrow, we can work all night.

We can work all night if the computer lab is open.

Here are some compound-complex sentences:

Although our assignment is due tomorrow, we can work all night and make the deadline.

We can work all night and make the deadline if the computer lab is open.

Although our assignment is due tomorrow, we can work all night and make the deadline if the computer lab is open.

In a complex sentence, the clause introduced by the conjunction is the subordinate or dependent clause, and the other clause is the main clause. The main idea is in the main clause. By using complex sentences, you can add more levels of meaning or depth to your sentence. For example, you can give less important information in subordinate clauses.

While he was cleaning out his desk, the phone rang.

Although I have never been a tele-marketer, I have related experience.

I will teach that class, if you help me prepare for it.

## EXERCISE 2.6

Identify the clauses in the following and decide whether the sentences are simple, compound, or complex sentences.

1.  Being a cautious man, James learned all he could about home-based businesses before he set up his office.

2. He started his consulting business while he still had a full-time job.

3. Once he was sure he could be successful, he quit his job.

4. He enjoyed meeting different people, not having to answer to a boss, and managing his own time.

5. After a while, however, James yearned for the good old days when he could talk shop by the water cooler and share a confidence or two.

6. He enjoyed the challenge of his new work, so he never regretted his decision.

7. Suddenly, without warning, disaster struck at the stroke of midnight.

8. Although he had prepared for the millennium bug, he could not imagine the magnitude of his troubles.

9. Some hacker broke into his files and stole all his data.

10. Luckily, having foreseen this disaster, James had made backups.

# Identifying the subject and verb

You should be able to identify the subject and the verb of each sentence you read and write. The subject + verb combination is the core of the sentence. To find the subject and verb, you must eliminate modifying phrases and clauses.

~~Before he put the papers in the box~~, the new <u>assistant</u> <u>entered</u> the file names ~~in the computer~~.

~~While waiting for the bus~~, the <u>students</u> ~~from the ESL class~~ <u>listened</u> ~~to the conversation around them~~.

Usually, the subject is the doer of an action. It is usually a noun or a pronoun. In special cases, it can be a gerund, infinitive, or a noun clause.

<u>John</u> works.

<u>I</u> read.

<u>Reading</u> is fun.

<u>To ski in the Rockies</u> takes skill.

<u>That he could still sing after the accident</u> is a miracle.

The verb shows the action. Sometimes the verb is more than one word; it may include helping verbs. A verb that ends in *-ing* is not a complete verb on its own.

The rain <u>stopped</u> suddenly.

I <u>could have asked</u> for more money.

The class <u>has been waiting</u> a long time.

They <u>were correcting</u> the papers.

The game <u>was developed</u> in 1998.

EXERCISE  **2.7**

Identify the subject by circling it. Identify the main verb by underlining it.

1. The attendant at the parking lot couldn't give us change.

2. While he was collecting the fees, his brother distributed the tickets.

3. On the bulletin board was the advertisement for student jobs.

4. Power-walking can be addictive.

5. The manager and her assistant were looking for discrepancies in the accounting.

6. At six o'clock I came home and found that my house had been broken into.

7. How can you say that?

8. The employees were in charge of identifying and tagging the defective goods.

9. That our government is undemocratic can be debated.

10. The store around the corner next the fire station is closing.

# Sentence variety

When you write, you should use long and short sentences, simple and complex. Long sentences explain; short sentences emphasize the idea. Long sentences generally slow down reading. Too many long sentences in a row may hinder understanding for the reader. However, too many short sentences in a row may create choppiness, or a staccato rhythm. Moreover, too many short sentences, especially if they contain simple vocabulary, make your writing sound juvenile. You should develop a mature style that includes both kinds of sentences. It is also important to have different sentence patterns in your writing. Try beginning sentences with phrases or clauses, for example.

The following three paragraphs say the same thing but use different sentence styles. Which is easiest to read?

Family studies is a course in Grade 8. It is popular. It is practical. In the past students took home economics. It was only for female students. Both boys and girls take family studies. Students learn to cook. They learn to sew. They cook meals. They work in teams. They serve these meals with pride. They do homework. They cook for their families. Students sew. They make tote bags and clothing. Students also study family life. They learn to be good parents. These life skills are important. They are not always taught at home. In many families boys do not cook. They do not sew. Working parents buy ready-made items. They buy prepared foods. The students accomplish something. This is good for their self-confidence. This is especially good for students who do not do well with academic work. Schools should do more than provide book learning. They should produce good citizens. Family studies is important.

A modern version of home economics, which was only open to female students, family studies is one of the most popular and practical courses in the Grade 8 curriculum for both boys and girls. Students get an opportunity to develop basic cooking and sewing skills, cooking meals in teams, serving these meals with pride, and then for homework, cooking for their families, and in sewing class, they make items like tote bags and clothing. Students also study family life, including aspects of psychology and sociology, such as child development, so they learn what it means to be a good parent. These important life skills are not always taught at home since in many families boys do not do much cooking or sewing, and working parents have to rely on ready-made items, including prepared foods. The students' accomplishments are also good for their self-confidence, especially for those who do not always have academic success, and this is a necessary part of education, since schools should do more than provide book learning in order to produce well-rounded citizens, and family studies is an important part of this goal.

Family studies is one of the most popular and practical courses in the Grade 8 curriculum. The precursor of this course, home economics, was open only to female students, but both boys and girls take family studies. Students get an opportunity to develop basic cooking and sewing skills. They cook meals in teams and serve these meals with pride. For homework, they cook for their families. In sewing class, they make items like tote bags and clothing. Students also study family life, learning what it means to be a good parent. These important life skills are not always taught at home. For instance, in many families boys do not do much cooking or sewing, and working parents have to rely on ready-made items, including prepared foods. The students' accomplishments are also good for their self-confidence, especially if they do not always have academic success. Schools should do more than provide book learning in order to produce well-rounded citizens, and family studies is an important part of this goal.

## E X E R C I S E   2.8

Make the following groups of sentences into one or two sentences. Use phrases and clauses to put ideas together. You can leave out unnecessary words and change the order of the ideas. Try for a variety of sentence patterns. Compare your versions with classmates' to see the different options.

1.  Queen Victoria chose Ottawa as the capital of Canada.
    She also considered Kingston, Montreal, and Toronto for the honour.
    Ottawa was farther from the American border.
    Ottawa was a small lumber town.

2.  Laura Secord was a heroine of the War of 1812.
    She overheard American officers planning an attack.
    The attack would be a surprise.
    She walked 30 km.
    She walked through swamps and forests.
    She warned the British troops.
    Today she has a chain of candy shops named after her.

3.  Louis Riel was a Metis leader in Manitoba.
    He wanted his people to have some choice in their place in Canada.
    He led the Red River Rebellion.
    He was hanged for treason.
    He died on November 16, 1885.

4.  D'Arcy McGee was shot on Sparks Street.
    Sparks Street is just two blocks south of Parliament Hill.

He is one of the few Canadian politicians to be assassinated.
He was killed in 1868.
It is believed his killer was a Fenian, an Irish revolutionary.

5. John A. Macdonald was the first prime minister of Canada.
   He wanted British Columbia to join the new Canadian
   confederation.
   He promised to link that Western province with the ones in the
   East.
   He proposed a national railway that runs across Canada.
   Based on this commitment, British Columbia joined in 1870.

## CHAPTER 3

# The Developed Paragraph

A paragraph is a group of sentences that form a unit of information: it has one main idea supported by examples, illustrations, explanations, facts, or opinions. Writers explore, explain, and expand upon that one idea so that their readers can understand it clearly.

Paragraphs can be distinguished by appearance. They are blocks of text with the first line indented, usually about five spaces or one tab space on a typewriter or computer. Sometimes, instead of an indent, paragraphs are shown with blank space between each paragraph; this block style is common in business writing. In books, the first paragraph after a title or subtitle is not indented. The reader must be able to clearly distinguish one paragraph from another, to know where each paragraph begins and ends.

In academic writing, paragraphs tend to be between four and eight sentences long, or 100 to 150 words. Some paragraphs may be longer, especially if they have to stand alone. Shorter paragraphs may be used for emphasis or transition. Developed paragraphs have a topic sentence, supporting ideas, and a concluding or transition sentence.

Other kinds of writing, however, favour shorter paragraphs because they are easier to digest. Newspaper and magazine articles often have one- or two-sentence paragraphs, since longer blocks of text are hard to read in narrow columns. In modern fiction, paragraphs are also generally quite short. Modern novels often include much dialogue, which necessitates a new paragraph each time the speaker changes. Novels written in the 19th century, in contrast, had long paragraphs that could sometimes fill a page or two.

The change to shorter paragraphs is a result of the influence of other media. For instance, television shows are broken up into small sections by commercials. Commercials themselves try to deliver a message in mere seconds. Hyperlinks encourage readers to flit from place to place in multimedia encyclopedias and Internet web pages.

Thus, it is not surprising that educators say students have shorter attention spans. Accordingly, most books published today have short paragraphs and many subtitles. Even though shorter paragraphs are much more common now than in the past, we still write some longer developed paragraphs for essays.

In this chapter and the next we will concentrate on independent developed paragraphs, ranging from 100 to 200 words. This chapter goes through the basic structure, while Chapter 4 gives more examples of paragraphs, classified by rhetorical type.

# The developed paragraph

For the most part, we will be dealing with developed paragraphs: those with a topic sentence to introduce the idea, and supporting details to explain and expand on the idea. Some paragraphs will need a concluding sentence or a transition sentence at the end. Introductory, transition, or concluding paragraphs may not follow this pattern, and thus we distinguish them from developed paragraphs. A one-sentence paragraph is not developed and is generally not acceptable in academic writing.

Sometimes you may be called upon to produce a piece of writing that is a single paragraph, an independent developed paragraph. For example, a summary or an abstract is often one paragraph. You may have to write an independent paragraph for an answer on a test. Paragraphs that stand on their own and are not part of a longer text are usually longer, perhaps eight to twelve sentences. They are fully developed with a topic sentence and concluding sentence.

Developed paragraphs are a foundation for essays and other longer pieces of writing. A body paragraph in an essay, for example, is a developed paragraph. Being able to fully develop an idea in a paragraph is a useful skill for all writers.

# Topic sentences

A topic sentence tells the reader what the paragraph is about. Topic sentences are usually the first sentence in the paragraph, although they can appear as the second sentence after a transitional sentence, as a middle sentence, or as the last sentence. Some paragraphs do not have a topic sentence at all; the topic is implied. However, for academic writing, your paragraph should start with a clear, specific topic sentence.

It is best to begin the paragraph with the topic sentence. The topic-sentence opening sets forth the main idea, and you can easily follow through by giving more details with examples, illustrations, analogies, and explanations. For students who are developing their writing skills, setting the topic sentence first makes it easier to write the paragraph. Moreover, when the first sentence is the topic sentence, it is easier for readers to follow the text. In fact, savvy readers use this common organizational pattern to their advantage: when they want to skim a text just to get the main ideas, they read the first sentence of each paragraph.

Picture the topic sentence like an umbrella. All of the other sentences in the paragraph should be covered by the topic sentence. If a sentence does not fit under the umbrella of the topic sentence, delete it, or rewrite the topic sentence.

The topic sentence is the least specific statement in the entire paragraph. The supporting sentences are more detailed and informative. The topic sentence introduces the main idea, but the supporting sentences explain it.

For an example, let us consider topic sentences for a paragraph about computer spell checkers:

> Computers are very useful machines.
> *(too broad, does not limit the topic enough)*

> All students should buy a computer.
> *(too broad, reader would expect a paragraph on the advantages of computers for students)*

> Computer spell checkers are programs which check the words you write against their electronic list to see which words are not in their dictionary.
> *(too specific, gives no room to explore ideas)*

> Word processors often come equipped with spell checkers.
> *(a fact with no room for development of ideas)*

> Computer spell checkers are useful, and word processors are fun to use.
> *(two ideas—a good topic sentence has just one)*

> I don't like computer spell checkers.
> *(personal, but simplistic sentence)*

> Spell-checkers are good.
> *(vague and simplistic)*

Computer spell checkers should be used carefully because they cannot really understand sentence structure.
*(too specific)*

Computer spell checkers have as many disadvantages as advantages.
*(somewhat broad, suitable for a paragraph on both sides of the issue)*

Computer spell checkers are not as helpful as people think they are.
*(good topic sentence, specifies topic and shows that the focus of the paragraph will be the problems or negative aspects of spell checkers)*

The topic sentence should be one idea, a supportable idea, neither too broad nor too narrow, and not too specific, but not too vague. These requirements are hard to understand in such relative terms, but you will get a better idea of a topic sentence by looking at good ones and bad ones and by trying to write your own. As you look at sample paragraphs and essays in this book, evaluate the topic sentences.

A C T I V I T Y   **3.1**

Which of the following sentences would make good topic sentences? Try to imagine what a paragraph based on this topic sentence could say. If you do not have a good idea, the topic sentence is probably poorly written. Decide if the topic sentences are too broad or vague, or too narrow and specific.

1.  People immigrate to another country for some reasons.

2.  Reading is good for you.

3.  If you stop and think about it, you will come to the same conclusion that I have reached.

4.  A paperback novel usually measures 18 cm by 11 cm.

5.  Businesses take advantage of part-time workers.

6.  I like watching commercials and so should you.

7.  Aluminum siding is the best way to cover up weatherbeaten, chipped exterior walls of a house.

8.  Use it or lose it.

9. There is no difference in having a natural gas range or an electrical one.

10. "When in Rome, do as the Romans do" is good advice.

# Focus

The topic sentence reflects the focus of the paragraph. A paragraph should not try to cover too much of a topic. It should have a single main idea. Often this means narrowing the topic.

For example, we could talk about different aspects of computer spell checkers:

- how spell checkers can help poor spellers
- the disadvantages of automatic word correction
- the difficulty of using spell checkers with technical writing
- how a spell checker works
- comparing spell checkers in different word processing programs

The purpose of the paragraph is also reflected in the focus. The paragraph describing how a spell checker works is giving information and explaining a process, while a paragraph telling the advantages of a feature is an argument.

# Supporting ideas

Supporting sentences are more detailed and more specific than the topic sentence. These supporting ideas can be examples, illustrations, analogies, explanations, quotations from a source, facts and statistics, and expert opinions. They must be related and relevant to the main idea. You may need two or three points to adequately support your main idea.

From the paragraph outlines below, see which supporting sentences fit the topic sentence "Computer spell checkers are not as helpful as people think they are":

Computer spell checkers are the greatest boon to writers.
*(positive aspect, but the focus of the paragraph is negative)*

Desktop publishing features also make word-processing packages useful.
*(not about computer spell checkers, so does not fit the paragraph.)*

Computer spell checkers are often included with word-processing software.
*(a fact about spell checkers, but does not further the main idea)*

The computer often does not recognize proper names and technical vocabulary.
*(gives a disadvantage of spell checkers, thus supporting the topic)*

Computer spell checkers are annoying.
*(too general for a supporting statement.)*

# General and specific

In a developed paragraph, general statements are supported with specific information. This information can be given in details, facts, statistics, examples, and illustrations. Here are some examples:

General: Children can learn skills that they will need when they no longer live with their parents.
Specific: They can learn how to prepare food, look after their clothing, and deal with home maintenance problems such as an overflowing toilet.

General: University students must learn to get information from lectures.
Specific: They must take notes while the professor is speaking.

General: Students must acquire the skills they need for the work world.
Specific: In group assignments, they can learn how to get along with others and finish a project as a team.

ACTIVITY  3.2

Write a specific supporting statement for each of these general statements:

1.  High school students may have trouble adjusting to the responsibilities of university studies.

2.  Writing with a word processor can be helpful for students.

3.  Sports can teach children many important life skills.

4. Hollywood blockbuster movies can bring in much more money than just the receipts from the box office.

5. It is not surprising that gardening is becoming a popular activity among middle-aged people.

6. Swimming has several advantages over other exercises.

7. Being the oldest child in the family can be difficult.

8. Fashion can be illogical and impractical.

9. It is important to have a good balance of different foods to stay healthy.

10. Women provide much unpaid labour in our society.

# Concluding statement

In an independent paragraph, the concluding statement wraps up the main idea and signals completion. A concluding statement often echoes or recaps the topic sentence.

For the paragraph on spell checkers, we could have a concluding sentence like one of these:

Spell checkers are good for catching typographical errors, but writers cannot rely on them to find all the mistakes.

While spell checkers can catch errors, they do not eliminate the need for careful proofreading.

Despite these disadvantages, spell checkers can be useful tools for writers.

Note that the concluding sentence echoes the idea of the topic sentence but does not repeat it exactly.

In an essay, a paragraph may end with a transition sentence instead of a concluding statement. The transitional statement links one paragraph to the next. You can see transitional sentences at work in Chapter 5.

# Putting it all together

Here is the complete paragraph about computer spell checkers:

Computer spell checkers are not as helpful as people think they are. First, they cannot distinguish homophones. For example, if someone types "brake" instead of "break," the spell checker does not catch the mistake because both words are stored in the computer's word list. Sometimes a spell-checker even makes spelling mistakes worse. If a writer types "a lot" as one word, the computer suggests "allot" as a correction. Other problems come from the words that are correctly spelled but not stored in the spell checker's dictionary. Canadian English uses a mixture of British and American spelling, but some software packages are not shipped with Canadian dictionaries. Moreover, the computer often does not recognize proper names and technical vocabulary. Spell checkers are good for catching typographical errors, but writers cannot rely on them to find all the mistakes.

Here is the outline of this paragraph, showing you the structure:

OUTLINE:

Topic sentence: Computer spell checkers are not as helpful as people think they are.

First supporting point: cannot distinguish homonyms

    Example to explain this point: brake/break

Second supporting point: makes spelling mistakes worse

    Example to explain this point: a lot/allot

Third supporting point: words that are stored or not stored in the spell checker's dictionary

    Example to explain this point: Canadian English

    Second example to explain this point: proper names and technical vocabulary

Concluding statement (echoes idea of topic sentence): Spell checkers are good for catching typographical errors, but writers cannot rely on them to find all the mistakes.

# Unity

A good paragraph has only one topic. This one main idea is set out in the topic sentence. All the sentences in the paragraph should relate to the topic sentence. If they do not, the paragraph is not unified. Putting too many diverse ideas into one paragraph loses the focus and confuses the reader.

Which sentences do not belong in the following paragraph?

Like a chess match, baseball is a game that involves strategy, move, and counter-move. First, the pitcher-hitter match-up takes some manoeuvring. Left-handed pitchers are usually more effective against left-handed batters, and managers often change pitchers or hitters to increase the odds. Home runs are really exciting to watch. As the catcher and pitcher chose which pitch to throw, they play head games with the batter. Should the pitch be a fastball, change-up, or curve ball? Should the ball go over the inside or the outside of the plate? The batter tries to predict which pitch is coming, and the pitcher tries to catch him off guard. When the pitcher is preparing to throw, the players in the field set their defensive alignment. For example, they may play farther back in the field if the hitter is a powerful slugger. Base runners have to be really fast. Baseball does not have the non-stop action of hockey or basketball, but its subtleties can be appreciated by knowledgeable fans.

This paragraph is about the strategy of baseball. Home runs are about power, but not really strategy. The same goes for the speed of the base runners. When you read the non-unified paragraph, the ill-fitting sentences should stick out. Read the paragraph again, taking out these two sentences: "Home runs are really exciting to watch." "Base runners have to be really fast."

However, the idea about base runners could have been worked into the paragraph by relating it to the topic: "The fielders' strategy might be changed if the base runner is exceptionally fast or exceptionally slow."

# Coherence

The verb *cohere* means sticking together as well as making logical sense. If your paragraph is coherent, the ideas in the paragraph are arranged logically. Readers should be able to follow your argument. The sentences in a paragraph can be arranged in chronological, spatial, logical, or climactic order. If you are telling a story, for example, you should tell what happened in chronological order. If you are describing a room, you might go from one side to the other. An argument should be constructed so that readers can see the logical relationship from one idea to the next. You might save your strongest argument for last and build towards it.

Coherence involves more than organizing the points you make in your writing. You can link your sentences by using transition markers such as "first" and "for example." Using pronouns, repeating words, and referring back to other points are other techniques used by writers. Here's an example:

The directors tried to improve cooperation among departments by changing the reporting structure. Their plan involved massive reorganization of the hierarchy.

"Their" refers to the directors. "Hierarchy" refers to "reporting structure"; the terms are synonymous (they mean the same).

E X E R C I S E   **3.1**

You can see how coherence works when you try to deconstruct it. The following sentences are scrambled parts of a paragraph. Put the sentences in the proper order to make a coherent paragraph. Use clues like pronouns and transition markers to help you. Look for logical order. Start with a general statement for the topic sentence.

_____ The solution to this problem was packet-switching—data would be broken up into packets and transferred over a network of computers.

_____ The Americans wanted a way to keep communication going in the event of an attack of Soviet nuclear missiles.

_____ Scientists soon found this network convenient for sharing research findings and discussing problems with other scientists.

_____ These providers became large companies as more people came online and the Internet became more commercial.

_____ If one system was down, the packet would be rerouted another way. Then the electronic packets were reassembled at the final destination.

_____ When they left the school community, they wanted to maintain their Internet access, so they turned to Internet service providers.

_____ It started as an American military project.

_____ Military computers were not the only ones on this early network; scientific institutions, including universities, were also connected.

_____ The development of the World Wide Web and web browsers made the Internet easy to use and led to its current popularity.

_____ Gradually, more of the university community came online.

_____ The Internet, a network of computers sharing information, has been growing steadily.

_____ Students became accustomed to the speed and ease of e-mail communication.

# Using transition markers

One way to ensure coherence is through the use of transition markers. These expressions help the reader see and follow the development of thought. They signal the relationship of ideas. Using transition markers is like using the signal lights in your car to tell the people in the car behind you where you are going next.

Transition markers can show contrast, continuity, addition, or relationship. Here is a list of commonly used signals:

Addition: also, finally, first, furthermore, in addition, moreover, next, secondly, thirdly

Cause and effect: accordingly, as a result, consequently, therefore, thus

Comparison: likewise, similarly

Contrast: however, in contrast, instead, nevertheless, on the other hand

Emphasis: in fact, indeed, of course

Special features or examples: for example, for instance, in other words, in particular, mainly, specifically

Summary: in brief, in closing, in conclusion, in short, on the whole, to conclude, to summarize

Time relations: afterwards, at that time, earlier, in the meantime, lately, later, meanwhile, then

Note that these expressions are adverbs, not conjunctions, so they cannot join two sentences. Compare the following sentences using the conjunctions *although, but,* and *because* with the ones using the adverbial transitions.

Although I don't have much time left, I should be able to make the deadline.
I don't have much time left, but I should be able to make the deadline.
I don't have much time left. However, I should be able to make the deadline.
Because they used the old procedure, we have to do it over again.

They used the old procedure, so we have to do it over again.
They used the old procedure. Therefore, we have to do it over again.

Using transition markers improves the coherence of the paragraph. They help the sentences stick together logically.

## E X E R C I S E   3.2

Add a transition marker to the following groups of sentences to show the relationship between the ideas.

1.  The parade route gets lined with people quickly.
    You should go early to find a good vantage point.

2.  Parents with small children may want to leave early.
    They cannot because their children want to see the last float in the parade.

3.  The clowns have several responsibilities.
    They distribute candy to the children in the crowd.
    They entertain spectators with tricks during pauses in the parade action.

4.  It is very difficult to march in step and play an instrument.
    Marching bands must practise more than other bands.

5.  The parade marshall leads the entire parade.
    She sets the pace for the marching bands and floats.

6.  Sometimes, unfortunate accidents happen.
    A horse bolted into the spectators last year, injuring two little boys.

7.  The celebrities don't do much except ride on the floats, smile, and wave at the crowds.
    They get paid well and have lots of perks.

8.  Normally the parade route remains the same.
    This year the organizers decide to shorten it by taking Elm Street instead of Maple Avenue.

9.  I have two reasons why I avoid going to parades.
    I don't like crowds.
    I get a better view from the television broadcast.

10. Parades are losing popularity in the 1990s.
    They cost too much to produce.

## *Check your paragraph*

- Does your paragraph look like a paragraph? Is the first line indented? Are all sentence boundaries clearly marked with capital letters and end punctuation?

- Does the topic sentence adequately introduce your topic?

- Do you support all the points you make? Are your statements clear and easy to understand?

- Is your paragraph unified? In other words, do all the sentences in the paragraph relate to the topic sentence?

- Is your paragraph concise? Have you eliminated unnecessary words and phrases?

- Is your paragraph coherent? Do your sentences follow logically? Do transition markers show the relationship between ideas?

- Are grammar, spelling, and word choice correct?

## CHAPTER 4

# Types of Paragraphs

In order to give you more examples, we have assembled a number of developed paragraphs in this chapter. We have classified them according to type, based on rhetorical mode, such as persuasion and narration. Your purpose determines the kind of paragraph you write. You may use a narrative paragraph to give background information, or a definition to clarify concepts and terminology. More on rhetorical mode can be found in the sample essays in Chapter 6.

As you read these paragraphs, check the structure. Does the topic sentence adequately define the topic? Check for unity and coherence—are all sentences related to the topic sentence and do they follow logically? Are supporting details used to explain the ideas? Is the paragraph clear and concise? We have included word counts for some, to give you an idea of common length.

## Narration

Narration is a story, usually told in chronological order. You write a narrative to describe a sequence of events in a report. When you have a car accident, for example, you write your version of the events for the police. In an essay you might include an anecdote to illustrate a point or to give background information.

Good story-telling requires that the audience follow what is happening. You have probably heard poor story tellers labouring through a tale, getting ideas mixed up, or giving too few or too many details. Writing a good narrative paragraph is telling a story. Make sure your points follow in a logical order that your readers can follow. As with all your writing, remember your audience. Give as much detail as you think your readers need.

You can see examples of narration in some of the readings, especially in the two short stories "Why My Mother Can't Speak English" and "Soap and Water," and in the essay "Another View of the True North."

> The ancient Greek myth of Echo and Narcissus has left a legacy on the English language. Echo was a talkative nymph who offended Hera, the queen of the gods. Hera took away Echo's speech, leaving her able only to repeat what others said. The sad nymph wandered the woods and one day happened across a handsome and vain young man named Narcissus. He thought that no woman was attractive enough for him. When he stopped by a pool, he saw a beautiful face in the water and did not realize he was seeing his own reflection. When he tried talking to the image, his words were repeated by Echo, so he thought that a lovely woman was trapped in the pool. Narcissus just sat there gazing at the pool, in love with his own reflection. Having fallen in love with him, Echo stayed nearby watching him. Finally, Hera turned him into a flower, which we still call a narcissus. We also use the word *narcissism* to describe excessive self-love. Echo, of course, gave her name to the sound we hear coming back to us in a canyon or an empty room. (191 words)

Melissa, Amin, Midori, and I worked together to produce this report on ESL websites. First, we met after class in the computer lab. Using two computers, we input "ESL" as a search term with several different search engines, such as Yahoo and Alta Vista. We got thousands of hits, so we eliminated sites that advertised ESL courses or textbooks. After bookmarking the most promising sites, each of us took a list of a half-dozen sites to examine more carefully. We sent the URLs to ourselves by e-mail to avoid having to write down the addresses. Individually, we each looked more closely at the sites. Then we met again to discuss preliminary findings and to put together a list of criteria to evaluate the sites. (See Appendix I.) For example, we considered how helpful the sites would be, how interesting they were, which level of proficiency they were aimed at, and whether there were errors in such things as spelling and grammar. We reduced our list to eight sites, with each student assigned two sites. We visited the web pages again and considered them according to our criteria. Each student wrote a description and evaluation of two sites. Then we met to read and comment on our individual sections. We assembled the final versions together in this report.

1. Tell the story of a myth or legend you know.

2. Tell the story of something that happened to you. It could be something funny, sad, frightening, embarrassing, or exciting.

# Description

A well-crafted description gives the reader a mental picture. You articulate how something looks, smells, tastes, or feels. Your words create a visual depiction of any person, place, or thing in the mind of your reader. Like all other methods of writing, a descriptive paragraph needs focus and a logical method of organization. For example, to describe a room, you may wish to order the elements from left to right, from near to far. You can incorporate descriptive paragraphs in all kinds of writing. In a business report, for example, you might have to describe the product.

> The book is a triumph of design that electronic technology has not improved upon. It is portable: You can put one in your pocket or handbag, read it at the beach or in the bath, and prop one on your chest or cradle it in your hands. A book offers pleasure for the senses: the feel of the paper, the smell of fresh ink, the beauty of illustrations, and the flow of the words on the page. Books decorate a home, whether you have a few coffee table books on display or shelves full of tomes in your personal library. The words have a physical presence, unlike those in ever-scrolling electronic pages, so you have a clear idea of how long the book is. The design is simple: pages are hinged at one side and contained within a soft or hard cover. You do not have to worry about a special reader to make the text accessible. Books that are hundreds of years old can still be read, while electronic formats go out of date quickly. You just have to remember eight-track tapes, Beta video, and 5 1/4" floppy disks, to appreciate the timelessness of bound paper. (199 words)

Note that the paragraph above is written in a more conversational style since it uses *you*. While it is a description, it offers elements of comparison and of persuasion.

> The kadiddlehopper is a revolutionary achievement in gizmo design. Its sleek, oblong plastic shell fits neatly in the palm of the hand. It looks as if it could slip out of your grasp like a wet

bar of soap, but with enhanced grooves along both sides, the kadiddlehopper can be held comfortably, even elegantly. The three function buttons across the top of its shell are easily accessible to forefinger or thumb. The buttons are colour-coded in red, white, and green, but they also have distinct raised symbols, so you can work the functions in total darkness, or in a coat pocket. Once activated, the kadiddlehopper responds quickly and quietly. The liquid diode screen emerges from its shell, displaying a personalized analyzer of blood viscosity, chicken intake level, the temperature at the centre of the Earth, and other essential information. This important contribution to your everyday life comes in a choice of puce stripe, lime green polkadots, or orange plaid patterns. (161 words)

Okay, okay, you caught us. The kadiddlehopper doesn't really exist. The point is that a description can help you "see" something even if you've never actually seen one.

---

| ASSIGNMENTS |
| :--- |

Describe your favourite restaurant, a web page, a room in your home, a car, or a person.

# Definition

A definition paragraph clarifies a term or idea at length when a single sentence does not cover the topic adequately. For instance, you might have to include historical information or classification in the definition. Examples can help make the definition clear.

Procrastination is the act of delaying something. The word comes from Latin: *pro* means "for" and *cras* means "tomorrow"; in other words, we procrastinate when we leave something for tomorrow. Some people procrastinate because they are lazy and prefer enjoyment. Others put off an unpleasant task by finding countless other tasks to do. By putting things off, they merely postpone the inevitable—a task that must be done. Unfortunately, the consequences can be troublesome. For example, when a car owner ignores the warning lights in his automobile and does not take the car to a mechanic, he may find himself paying more for repairs than if he had taken the car in earlier. Or, worse, he could be stuck on a busy highway when he needs to be at a business meeting. Procrastination is a bad habit that everyone would do well to avoid.

"B-movie" is a term used to describe a motion picture that does not attain the high standards of a regular feature film. In the early days of motion pictures, the feature would run about 90 minutes. The Hollywood studios thought that movie goers would feel cheated with such short entertainment, so they concocted the cheaply produced flick to accompany the main feature. The B-movie was the lesser film in a double-bill attraction. The second-string feature could be filmed in about a week, whereas the A-film usually took six to eight weeks to complete. Still, the B-movies provided solid entertainment even though they were full of theatrical cliches, stolen plotlines from famous movies, and formulaic endings. Hop-A-Long Cassidy westerns, Buck Rogers science-fiction yarns, and the Bowery Boys shenanigans fall into this category of motion pictures. The notorious Ed Wood, in *Plan 9 from Outer Space*, brought this art form to its lowest depth when he replaced the deceased Bela Lugosi with a personal therapist in mid-film. Yet, many of these B-movies are fondly remembered by an older generation who grew up on double-features and Saturday matinees. (198 words)

## ASSIGNMENTS

Write a definition paragraph of one of the following: software, happiness, home page, nerd, honour, justice, a good education.

# Compare/Contrast

Strictly speaking, comparison explains similarities, while contrast explains differences. If an assignment topic asks you to "compare" two things, you can discuss just similarities, just differences, or both.

Although e-mail is a written form of communication, it is more like oral conversation than like traditional letter writing. Time is the first important factor. E-mail messages travel so fast that their contents have more immediacy. Writers can talk about their current activities. They can ask questions and get direct answers, with parts of the previous message quoted in the response. Another obvious similarity is the informal, conversational style. Some e-mail writers do not follow standard written conventions like punctuation and capitalization. They even insert emoticons, or smileys, to imitate facial expressions and tone of voice. E-mail is almost like talking to someone directly.

Although e-mail is an informal type of communication, it is not exactly like conversation. E-mail is bound by the conventions of written discourse, even though some e-mail users think they can dispense with proper spelling and punctuation. Because people cannot see their correspondents, they have no visual cues like facial expressions to see how messages are delivered or received. They cannot hear a sarcastic tone of voice or see a twinkle in the eye. Smileys, or emoticons, are a weak attempt to inject this type of signal in e-mail messages. Using all capital letters in a message is considered the equivalent of shouting, but people may use all caps inadvertently or out of laziness. Another difference is that people rarely walk off in the middle of a conversation, yet many e-mail messages are left unanswered. People should never treat e-mail messages as casually as conversation; these messages are recorded and can come back to haunt their writers.

E-mail is a form of written communication that closely approximates, but does not duplicate, spoken language. Like conversation, e-mail often has informal language. Spelling and punctuation rules are less strictly adhered to. Because e-mail travels so quickly, it has more of a question-and-response style than traditional letter writing does. However, e-mail users find that misunderstandings are more common than in speech. They cannot duplicate clues like tone of voice that show someone is teasing. And while someone rarely walks away from an unfinished conversation, some e-mails go off into cyberspace and never get answered. Moreover, e-mail messages are recorded, so a thoughtless comment can come back to haunt a writer. E-mail users can enjoy the easy communication of e-mail, but they should not make the mistake of dismissing it as a casual conversation.

William Lyon Mackenzie King and Pierre Elliot Trudeau were two of the longest reigning prime ministers of Canada. King held office for almost 22 years and Trudeau, 16 years. However, their similarities do not end here. Both King and Trudeau belonged to the Liberal Party, led the Party to majority governments, and saw defeats and resurgence to power. Both men governed during times of crisis in Canada. For King, the overriding crisis was Canada's participation in the Second World War. He had to decide whether or not to proclaim conscription and thereby antagonize the French in Quebec. For Trudeau, his powderkeg was the Front de Liberation de Quebec (FLQ), a violent political group that desired Quebec independence. He invoked the War Measures Act to deal with it. King brought Canadians out of war victorious; Trudeau brought home the BNA Act and a Canadian constitution. Both political figures were controversial in their private lives as well. King talked to his deceased mother through his dog, and consulted astrological assistance in public decision making. Trudeau married a very young socialite and began a tempestuous relationship that spilled over to the public forum. Two men from different eras of Canadian history left giant footsteps for others to follow.

## ASSIGNMENTS

1. Compare two articles you have read on the same topic.

2. Write a contrast paragraph about two products you use, two homes you have had, or two people you have known.

3. Compare two products on the market or two methods of doing something.

# Cause/Effect

Sometimes when you consider a problem or situation, you need to discuss causes or effects. For example, racism is caused by prejudice and ignorance; the effects are discrimination and sometimes violence.

Creating a united Canada was not merely a dream of Sir John A. MacDonald and other nationalist politicians of the day; it was a necessity. First, there was the constant threat from the Americans. Having successfully established their republic, the Americans were venturing on an expansionist ideology that looked not only westward across the American mid-west but also northward into Canada. The wide expanse of the Canadian prairies, rich with fertile soil, was inviting territory. The developing economies of Upper and Lower Canada (Ontario and

Quebec) tempted American entrepreneurs and bankers. Second, the protectionist practices of Ontario, Quebec, New Brunswick, and Nova Scotia stagnated the growth of industries and trade, and threatened to weaken political stability. Like dominoes, each weak province fell into the inviting arms of the United States. Third, fledgling Canadians felt that they could retain ties to Britain and yet have a country to call their own. As a result of the political situation and nationalistic feelings, the Dominion of Canada was established in 1867.

Although business leaders maintain that a certain amount of unemployment is necessary to maintain a healthy labour market, unemployment creates a vicious circle of economic effects that rebound on business. Simply put, the unemployed cannot buy. Economic growth depends on people spending money. Those with no jobs will only buy the bare necessities of life. Henry Ford understood this basic economic principle when he tried to ensure that his factory workers were paid enough so that they could afford to buy one of the automobiles they were building. Moreover, in times of high unemployment, those who do have jobs become worried about the security of their positions. They do not spend freely because they want to save money for an uncertain future. When people avoid buying, retailers, manufacturers and service providers lose business. As a result, they cut back on staff, creating more unemployment and exacerbating the problem. (148 words)

## ASSIGNMENTS

Discuss the causes or effects of poverty, drunk driving, or poor academic performance.

# Persuasion

In a persuasive paragraph, you try to make the reader see your point of view. Your topic sentence introduces the argument. Your supporting details give reasons why your opinion is valid.

Although the government can pay for important services with the enormous profits generated by lotteries and casinos, these activities create more harm than good. Gambling is an addictive, destructive behaviour. Gamblers can ruin their family life when they use up their income and their savings to make bets. When they become desperate, they commit crimes to get more money for their gambling habit. As the government makes more gambling opportunities available, more people become addicted. Video lottery machines, for example, are known to be highly addictive. The government is supposed to safeguard the public good, but it is contributing to the ruin of people's lives. Society is harmed when people are impoverished by gambling, especially when they commit crimes. Therefore, encouraging gambling is an immoral activity and not the role of a responsible government.

Insisting on school uniforms is a misguided notion. People are confusing the contents of a book with its cover. If students lack respect or discipline, forcing them to dress the same will not change anything. Moreover, just because students wear a uniform, it does not mean they look good. Many teenage girls hike up their school kilts, exposing too much thigh. Students leave shirts untucked and wear pants that are baggy or too tight. In addition, school uniforms can be expensive and harder to clean than simple jeans and T-shirts. The cost is another burden for parents who already pay for books, school supplies, and field trips. Uniforms are also less comfortable to wear. Despite these disadvantages, some politicians and educators favour uniforms, seeking conformity and the appearance of control, without realizing that appearance is not reality.

School uniforms should be worn by all students. First, uniforms indicate a respect for authority. There is nothing so satisfying to a teacher as gazing out at a sea of smartly dressed students ready to learn. Second, students do not have to worry about being in style and can concentrate on school work instead. Designer names are meaningless in such an environment, and there will be no more muggings for expensive sneakers or jackets. Third, uniforms are less expensive than keeping up with fashion trends. Finally, uniforms teach conformity, a value highly prized in the workplace. Students who look the same feel the same. Uniforms are an important part of an effective school environment.

## ASSIGNMENTS

Write a persuasion paragraph giving your opinion on a current news issue.

# Process

Process paragraphs describe how something is done. However, they are not the same as instructions. Process tells how something is done or how it works while instruction tells the reader how to do something. For example, you can tell someone how to write an essay by giving instructions. You cannot tell someone how to make a star even though you can explain the steps by which a star comes into existence. Instructions include commands—"Fold along the dotted line."—but process paragraphs do not.

Pizza is a popular take-out food, but it is easy to prepare at home. Cooks can make the dough from scratch with flour, yeast, and water, or they can buy frozen prepared dough and roll it out to fit the pan. Already-baked breads are also available as a base for pizza. The pizza makers spread tomato sauce on the crust and then top the pizza with whatever ingredients they like. One popular combination is pepperoni, green peppers, and mushrooms. Meat-lovers can add ham, Italian sausage, cooked bacon, or browned ground beef. Vegetarians might load up their pizza with onions, olives, or sliced tomatoes. These are traditional toppings, but some people enjoy pizza with unusual ingredients such as eggplant, broccoli, or shrimp. After the meat and vegetable toppings are arranged, the pizza is topped with cheese. Mozzarella cheese is stringy when melted, so brick, cheddar, or parmesan can be used along with the mozzarella. The assembled pizza is baked until the crust is lightly browned and the toppings are bubbling hot.

When a volcano like Mount Vesuvius in Italy or Krakatoa near Java erupts and spews its hot lava, ashes, and noxious gases high into the atmosphere, it follows prescribed stages. First, a seemingly dormant or extinct volcano may have internal activity. Fissures in the core of the volcano spread, like the root system of a tree, down 90 kilometres into the depth of the earth's mantel, just under the crust, where molten magma sloshes and shoots like hot water through copper pipes to fill the empty space of the fissures. Often a volcanic cone caps the rushing hot liquid and burning rocks; however, when the seismic conditions are right, one of two things can occur. The volcanic crater might act like a pot of thick soup that has boiled over and dump molten lava down the crevasses. Its rivers of fire incinerate all living things instantly. Or, the volcano might explode its top like a geyser, and send its mixture of ashes and gases into the sky. The earth surrounding the mountain groans and shakes. The sky is blanketed with a darkness that even the sun's rays cannot penetrate. Depending on size and violence, a volcano can erupt continually for days, even weeks. When the magma stops flowing and cools, these solids extend land mass, if the volcano is situated near water. On the other hand, the gases and fine particles of volcanic dust are carried by wind over the stratosphere for hundreds, even thousands, of kilometres until rain and gravity take hold and carry them down to earth. Even this process can take years to complete, long after the volcano has returned to dormancy.

## ASSIGNMENTS

1.  Describe one of the following activities: changing a tire, planning a party, tying a shoelace, buying a computer, or training for a sport.

2.  Describe a simple biological process, such as a plant growing.

## CHAPTER 5

# Writing an Essay

The essay is a composition on a subject, usually presenting a personal view or opinion. According to Michel de Montaigne, the originator of the genre, an essay is an attempt at explaining an idea or subject to your reader. (The French word *essayer* means to try something.) An essay has an introduction, several developed paragraphs, and a conclusion. An essay can vary from 400 to 4000 words, although your school assignments may be generally under 1000 words. Teachers assign essays to find out if you can clearly explain your ideas. They may ask you to write on a personal experience or to give an opinion on a social issue.

Some students think the essay is an artificial structure that has little relation to real-world writing. After all, journalists and executives do not write five-paragraph essays. However, school activities do not have to be replicated in real life to be instructive. You may not ever use the essay structure outside school, but the communication and thinking skills you develop in essay writing are necessary for both writing and speaking tasks in the work world.

Practice in the essay gives you a grounding in expressing your ideas clearly, concisely, and coherently. It forces you to economize on words and expression. With only a limited number of words, you must think about the important details and ideas and forgo extraneous points. In short, essay writing gives you discipline in the writing process. It makes you organize your main points and develop them adequately.

When you have mastered the technique of essay writing, you can adapt the model to other kinds of writing. While the five-paragraph essay has a one-paragraph introduction, a longer piece could have an introduction of several paragraphs. You have to organize your ideas into different body paragraphs when you write business letters and reports, just as you would in an essay.

Some students argue that the five-paragraph essay structure is like a strait-jacket to their creativity, but we like to think of it as a warm sweater—something reassuring to hang onto. Students who are developing writing skills benefit from having a defined structure to follow.

# The developed paragraph and the essay

An essay and a developed paragraph are similar. Both have a statement that introduces the topic; both make points in support of the topic; both need supporting details; both have a conclusion. An essay is more than one paragraph, but it follows the same basic pattern as a developed paragraph. A developed paragraph is like a mini-essay, with less development of ideas. Body paragraphs in an essay are developed paragraphs.

**Paragraph:**

Although some people think that children's only responsibility should be school work, children's participation in household chores benefits both the family and the children themselves. When the housework is shared, there is less stress on the adults. The family can enjoy more leisure time when fewer of the parents' off-work hours are consumed by chores. In addition, children can learn skills they will need when they no longer live with their parents. They can learn how to prepare food, look after their clothing, and deal with home maintenance problems such as an overflowing toilet. Moreover, doing housework helps children develop their character. For instance, they learn responsibility when they have a regular duty, such as putting away the dishes every day. Work teaches children how to be industrious and cooperative. When children find out how much effort goes into keeping a house clean and running smoothly, they learn to be considerate and not leave messes behind them. Therefore, parents who do not ask children to participate in the daily household chores are doing their children a disservice. (178 words)

**Essay:**

Parents have different expectations of their children. Some feel that children should enjoy their childhood with few demands put on them. Some think that the only job children should have is doing well at school. In other families, children gradually learn to take on all the tasks they will have to do as adults, including helping with the housework. These parents recognize that <u>sharing household chores helps the family out, teaches children valuable skills, and lets children develop good character traits</u>.

All family members, including children, should share in the work required to keep a household going. Even young children can contribute by picking up their toys after they play. As they get older, they can learn to do more around the house. It is not fair to expect parents to do all the housework, especially today when both are likely to hold outside jobs. Moreover, if the parents are stressed from overwork, the whole family suffers. When all family members pitch in, they can get the work done in less time. Then the whole family will enjoy more leisure time.

The skills that children can learn doing housework are invaluable. When they move out an live in their own places, they will be able to deal with the cleaning and maintenance work a home requires. For example, they will be able to handle emergencies such as a toilet overflowing. Kitchen skills enable people to prepare more nutritious, better tasting, and less expensive food than restaurant or processed food. Another type of chore that children can learn is clothing maintenance— how to wash their clothes, iron shirts, and sew on missing buttons. Even though house-cleaning services can handle many tasks, most people, especially young adults starting out, cannot afford to pay someone else to do the work for them.

In addition to learning practical skills, children can develop character traits by doing chores. They learn responsibility when they have a regular duty, such as putting away the dishes every day. Work teaches children how to be industrious and get a job done efficiently. Children learn the benefits of cooperation when they have to work together. When children find out how much effort goes into keeping a house clean and running smoothly, they learn to be considerate and not leave messes behind them. They also learn to be careful when using household equipment.

Doing housework is an important learning experience for children. If parents do not ask children to participate in the daily household chores, they are doing their children a disservice. Children may grumble and complain about doing housework but, like many things that they have to do in life, these jobs benefit them in the long run. (449 words)

In the essay, the thesis statement comes at the end of the introductory paragraph and each of the three middle paragraphs is a developed paragraph starting with a topic sentence.

# The five-paragraph essay

The most common structure taught in school is the five-paragraph essay. It has a one-paragraph introduction, one paragraph as a conclusion, and three middle paragraphs (also called the body of the essay) that expand and explain the topic. The five-paragraph essay ranges from 400 to 800 words. This structure is sometimes likened to a hamburger because the body of the essay is the meat of the topic while the bun (the introduction and conclusion) holds it all together.

# Brainstorming

Before you begin writing, you must consider your topic. Brainstorming is the process of coming up with ideas for the topic. This is even more important for an essay than for a paragraph because an essay requires more ideas and more organization of the ideas. We discussed the process involved in choosing a topic and brainstorming in Chapter 1. Reread those sections if you need to review.

Your instructor will probably give you a choice of topics. Choose the subject you are most comfortable with. Often the topic will have to be made more specific so that it can be handled in a short essay. You may be asked to take one side in a controversial issue, and you will have to decide which side you want to argue.

For a topic such as "History is an important subject for all students. Agree or disagree," you should consider both arguments in your brainstorming session. Jot down points that show why history is important as well as points for why it is not very important. Looking at both sides means that you will come up with more ideas to work with. As you think of one argument, you might think of the counter-arguments. When you finish your brainstorming, it will be easier to see which side you should write your essay on. Here's an example of brainstorming:

Why do some immigrants adapt to a new country more easily than others?

- younger immigrants learn more easily
- education level determines rate of assimilation

- open-mindedness leads to acceptance of new culture
- environment (if they live in a ethnic community, they have less need to adapt)
- whether they speak the language of the new country
- family structure—children bring new language and culture from school to home, older relatives retain links to native culture
- work environment—how much they interact with people from new culture
- reasons why they immigrated, their motivation
- some are more outgoing
- their desire to integrate
- how different their native culture is from the new culture (the closer, the easier)
- their knowledge of other countries and cultures
- staying at home rather than working or studying

# Thesis statement

A thesis statement sets out your position, approach, and limits on the topic of your essay. It gives a condensed view of your essay to the reader. It is this statement that you will support in the rest of the paper.

Do not confuse a thesis statement with the topic or with the title. A thesis statement, just as its name suggests, is a full sentence. Your topic or title is what you are talking about, but in your thesis statement you say something about your topic. Your reader should know exactly what your position is from your thesis statement.

THESIS:

Topic: action movies

Title: Unrealistic Action Movies

Thesis statement: What irks me about action movies is the unrealistic dialogue, the illogical actions of the hero, and the clichéd chase sequences.

Some thesis statements, like the one above, introduce the topics of the individual body paragraphs. Some instructors demand thesis statements that give the main ideas of the three body paragraphs. However, this is difficult to do if you cannot reduce the topics to short phrases. You can write a more general thesis statement that tells your main idea, but does not specify what the body paragraphs are about. You can see examples of both kinds of thesis statements in this textbook.

If you want to include the three main ideas of the body paragraphs, you have to pay attention to several details. First, make sure that you can reduce those three main ideas to relatively short phrases. You don't want your thesis statement to be too long. Secondly, use parallel structure. "The Olympics changes the way a city looks, its economy, and people think about it differently" is ungrammatical; while "The Olympics affects a host city's appearance, economy, and reputation" is grammatical. (You can read more about parallel structure in Chapter 14, on page 183.) Thirdly, be sure to talk about the body paragraphs in the same order in the thesis statement as they appear in the essay. For the essay about the Olympics, for example, the first body paragraph should talk about appearance, the second about economy, and the third about reputation.

Here are examples of thesis statements:

> The rate of assimilation depends on an immigrant's background, individual qualities, and situation.

> Despite the bells and whistles of new gadgets, books stand up very well as sources of information.

> E-mail presents new and better ways to communicate with people.

> History is an essential subject for all students.

> The government should not encourage gambling by running lotteries and casinos.

The best position for the thesis statement is at the end of your introduction. This allows you to lead up to the thesis and provide background information or an attention-grabbing opening. If you start your introduction with your thesis, you will have trouble finding something else to say in the introduction. After you state your thesis, it is natural to start the support for the thesis.

> Hollywood action films have always stretched the credulity of the audience. After all, we go to the movies to be thrilled and entertained and to put reality out of mind for the next two hours. We expect fantasy, but only to a point. Unfortunately, Hollywood producers, directors and screenwriters think the moviegoers have no intelligence or appreciation of the genre. So they recycle the pap in almost every film. <u>What irks me about action movies is the unrealistic dialogue, the illogical actions of the hero, and the clichéd chase sequences.</u>

Learn to avoid the most common mistakes in thesis writing. A thesis statement should not be an announcement, such as "In this essay, I am going to show the differences between urban and rural life." Like a topic sentence, it should be neither too broad nor too narrow. It should not be a simple fact that leaves no room for discussion. It should set out a plan that is manageable in five paragraphs.

## ACTIVITY 5.1

Decide if each of the following sentences would make a good thesis. If not, are they too broad, too vague, too narrow, or an announcement? Discuss what kinds of sentences would make better thesis statements for the topic.

1. In this essay, I will prove that the government should not encourage gambling.

2. Some immigrants do not learn English because they are too old.

3. Using a car and taking public transit can be compared according to cost, convenience and health factors.

4. Families are important in society.

5. This essay is about the reasons teenagers smoke.

6. Colombia is a very interesting country.

7. Research, shopping, and making a deal are the three main steps to buying a car.

8. There are many reasons for electing a strong leader; that is what I think.

9. College students earn a diploma, while university students earn a degree.

10. Today I want to discuss homesickness.

## Organizing ideas

One of the most difficult tasks of essay writing seems to be organizing the ideas into body paragraphs. You may look at the points in your brainstorming exercise and see a possible essay organization clearly. Or, you may arrange and rearrange your ideas, struggling to fit them into the required three body paragraphs. Some points may obviously be related to other points, but some of your ideas could fit in more than one paragraph.

Let's consider the example we used to illustrate brainstorming:

Why do some immigrants adapt to a new country more easily than others?

- younger immigrants learn more easily
- education level determines rate of assimilation
- open-mindedness leads to acceptance of new culture
- environment (if they live in a ethnic community, they have less need to adapt)
- whether they speak the language of the new country
- family structure—children bring new language and culture from school to home, older relatives retain links to native culture
- work environment—how much they interact with people from new culture
- reasons why they immigrated, their motivation
- some are more outgoing
- their desire to integrate
- how different their native culture is from the new culture (the closer, the easier)
- their knowledge of other countries and cultures
- staying at home rather than working or studying

Some of these factors relate to character traits and personal motivation. Some factors are determined by the new environment—where immigrants live and work. Others are part of the immigrants' background. Therefore, you could divide the essay into paragraphs based on these three aspects.

Go through the list of brainstorming ideas above and label each factor as either character, environment, or background. Discuss other possible ways of organizing the points into three body paragraphs.

## Outline

An outline is the formal arrangement of thesis statement and paragraph ideas. Like the blueprint for a house, an outline is an organizing structure. It lets you put ideas and supporting details in order before you write. Outlines are generally written in point form; however, your instructor may ask for full sentences. Even if you choose to write full sentences in your outline, don't worry too much about the wording; you can revise it as you write the essay.

Here is the format of an essay outline. This generic form has three supporting points per body paragraph, but your paragraphs may have more or fewer points. You can also check out the outlines included with essays in this chapter and the next. (Note that you can number the paragraphs or the supporting points, or use dashes instead of numbers—just be consistent.)

THESIS:

Topic sentence for first body paragraph:

    1. supporting point:

    2. supporting point:

    3. supporting point:

Topic sentence for second body paragraph:

    1. supporting point:

    2. supporting point:

    3. supporting point:

Topic sentence for third body paragraph:

    1. supporting point:

    2. supporting point:

    3. supporting point:

Here is an example of an essay outline, using the essay about children and housework:

THESIS:

Children should do housework

Idea for topic sentence for first body paragraph: work should be shared

    1. supporting point: even young children can learn to clean up

    2. supporting point: not fair to parents, especially when they have outside jobs

        – extending the point: all family suffers

    3. supporting point: work done in less time, more leisure for all

Idea for topic sentence for second body paragraph: invaluable skills

    1. supporting point: care and maintenance of home

        – example: toilet overflowing

    2. supporting point: kitchen skills

    3. supporting point: clothing maintenance

        – examples: washing, ironing, sewing

Idea for topic sentence for third body paragraph: develop character traits

1. supporting point: learn responsibility
   - examples: putting away dishes
2. supporting point: how to be industrious and get a job done efficiently
3. supporting point: benefits of cooperation
4. supporting point: learn to be considerate
5. supporting point: learn to be careful

Another example:

THESIS:

The rate of assimilation depends on the immigrants' background, individual qualities, and situation.

1. immigrants' background prepares them for their life in new country
   - language
   - education
   - similarity between their own culture and new culture
   - how much they've travelled and seen the world
2. each individual has certain qualities that makes him adapt well or not
   - attitude towards new culture
   - open-mindedness
   - willingness to learn
     - some qualities may be affected by age
3. the situation the immigrants find themselves is also important
   - existence of ethnic neighbourhood
     - immigrants don't need to interact to survive
   - education
     - if they are taking language classes
   - work situation
     - how much they come in contact with people
     - women who stay at home don't adapt as quickly

# Introduction

The first paragraph of your essay is the introduction. It leads your reader to your thesis statement, which should be the last sentence in the introductory paragraph. An introduction is usually three to six sentences. It can give background information or narrow your topic down for your thesis. It should not include any of the points that will be made in your body paragraphs. The function of the introduction is to prepare your reader for your argument.

If you start your introduction with your thesis statement, you have no place to go after that. You will end up repeating yourself or launching into the ideas in the body paragraphs. Therefore, put your thesis statement at the end of your introductory paragraph and lead into it.

Your introduction could include the following:

- some background information on your topic

- a definition of a term, concept, or idea

- a brief narrative, such as an event in history or the recent past

- a personal anecdote

- an opinion contrary to popular belief or acceptance

- a startling statement

- an interesting fact or statistic

- a rhetorical question, one that you will answer yourself

- a glance at the opposition, if you are writing an argumentative paper

- an apt quotation

Introductions depend on the thesis statement. You cannot write an introduction if you do not have a clear idea of what your thesis will say. The introduction can be a stumbling block for students. If you are having trouble writing your introduction, write your body paragraphs first. Then think of how best to prepare your reader for your thesis.

If you are going to write an argument essay, you might want the introduction to explain why it is a contentious issue and what the opposing argument is. Here are three examples of different introductory paragraphs for the same topic:

THESIS: It is dangerous to rely on computers.

Computer technology dominates our lives. The machines store records, track financial transactions, and allow people to communicate more efficiently. It is hard to imagine any kind of modern business operating without computers. However, this reliance on computers comes with many dangers.

"I think there is a world market for about five computers." This statement was made in 1958 by the CEO of IBM, Thomas J. Watson. It is hard to fathom how Watson could have so wildly underestimated the use of computers. The machines have become ubiquitous. It is hard to imagine modern business and even home life without personal computers. Indeed, it can be said that our society relies on the technology too much. We need to recognize the problems inherent in our use of the computers.

Computers have developed from plodding, room-size behemoths to tiny, lightning-fast chips that can make millions of calculations in split seconds. As the machines have become smaller, less expensive, and more powerful, they have become more widespread. The machines are no longer related to large institutions like government, universities, and corporations. Many families own their own computers. While we cannot live without the technology, we must recognize the problems in using computers.

As you can see from these examples, there is more than one way to write a good introduction. You can see more examples in the sample essays in the next chapter. Remember your audience and purpose. Determining what background information your reader needs can help you write an introduction.

## Middle paragraphs

The middle paragraphs in the body of the essay follow the rules of a good developed paragraph detailed in Chapter 2. Each body paragraph should begin with a topic sentence and contain two or three points explained with supporting details or examples. Each paragraph should have unity (one main idea) and coherence (sentences following in logical order with transition markers).

Body paragraphs do not need a concluding sentence, but sometimes a linking sentence is used. It is a good practice to link your body paragraphs into a coherent, unified whole, so that one paragraph follows the next logically. For example, to join the previous paragraph to the next one, you can use a transitional clause or sentence: "Having noted the hackneyed, inane dialogue, we now turn to the illogical actions of the hero." Or, use a sequence marker: "Second, the actions of the hero contradict his personal philosophy concerning violence and revenge."

# Conclusion

Having a satisfactory, effective conclusion is important in essay writing. It gathers up all the ideas expressed in the introduction and the body paragraphs, and it gives you one last chance to impress upon your reader your main points.

A good way to start the concluding paragraph is to restate the thesis. Do not use the same wording, however. For instance, if your thesis statement is "A shorter work week would benefit the worker, the worker's family, and society as a whole," your concluding paragraph can begin with "The advantages of a shorter work week extend beyond the worker himself."

You may want to summarize in your conclusion, but you must do this judiciously. Summary conclusions are useful for longer essays, but in a short essay a summary sounds repetitious.

Another thing to avoid is a too short conclusion. Some students peter out at the end of an essay. Either they run out of steam or they cannot muster the strength to wrap up ideas. They may have a one-sentence conclusion or a vague ending.

Your conclusion depends on the type of essay you write. If you are explaining how a problem has come into being, for example, your conclusion might suggest a possible solution. In your last paragraph, you might want to offer the reader a "so what?" idea that shows how your topic relates to other, larger issues. Look at the sample essays to see various conclusions.

# Revising and editing

Once you have put your essay together, it is important to revise and edit it. First, you focus on your content, organization, and wording. Check to see that your general statements are supported with specific statements of explanation or example. Question the logic of your argument. Look for a sound argument, expressed clearly. Make sure your points are in the body paragraphs and not in the introduction or conclusion. You can ask someone to read your essay and give you feedback on how clear it is.

After you are satisfied with what you say, turn your attention to how you say it. If you find you have repeated the same word or phrase, look for places where you can use pronouns and synonyms instead. If you wrote your thesis statement when you were outlining your essay, you may have to reword it so that it flows smoothly out of the introduction. Eliminate unnecessary words and phrases to achieve conciseness.

The final step is proofreading and correcting. Your spelling and grammar mistakes don't matter much in your first draft, but they must be eliminated before you print your final copy.

You can make a checklist of the mistakes you are prone to make. Use assignments that have already been marked to pinpoint your weaknesses. For instance, if you have many sentence fragment errors marked on your writing, add "check for fragments" to your personal checklist. If spelling is your weakness, make sure you spend enough time checking your spelling before you hand in your work.

Use the spelling and grammar checkers that come with your word-processor, but be aware that they will not catch all of your mistakes, and they will question words that are correct—you cannot rely on these electronic aids. If the spell checker flags a word, look at the suggestions carefully. If you are unsure of what is correct, check your dictionary. Avoid making a mistake like the student who had the word *bicycle* appear throughout a paragraph when he really wanted the word *basically*.

The final proofreading is your responsibility. Read your essay over carefully; do not just skim it. Look for mistakes such as using *that* instead of *than*. Your spellchecker won't catch those mistakes and they are easy to miss.

## SUMMARY

# *Steps in the essay writing process*

- Consider the topic. Make sure you understand what is being asked. Limit the topic to something you can handle in the prescribed length.

- Brainstorm. Think about your topic. Approach it from different points of view. Get as many ideas together as you can before you begin to write.

- Decide on your thesis statement—what you are going to prove in your essay.

- Determine the three topics in your body. Go through the ideas listed in your brainstorming and organize them into the body paragraphs.

- Write an outline.

- Write your draft according to your outline. You may choose to write the body paragraphs before crafting your introduction and conclusion.

- Edit and polish your draft. Revise where needed. Make sure your writing is clear, concise, and correct.

- Use the spell checker and then proofread your draft.

- Print your final copy along with a cover page.

## *Check your essay*

- Do you have a clear, supportable thesis that is neither too broad nor too narrow for the length of your essay?

- Does your introduction lead your reader to your thesis statement and prepare the way for your essay?

- Are your ideas divided into separate body paragraphs that are logically arranged and do not overlap each other in ideas?

- Does each body paragraph start with a clear, supportable topic sentence?

- Do you support general statements with specific details or examples?

- Does your concluding paragraph begin with a restatement of your thesis?

- Does your concluding paragraph lead the reader out of your essay, perhaps explaining the "so what?" of your ideas?

- Have you made sure that your introduction and conclusion do not include points that support your thesis?

- Are your paragraph and sentence boundaries clear?

- Do you have variety in vocabulary and sentence structure?

- Are grammar and spelling correct?

- Is your essay in proper format—typed, double-spaced, with a cover page (see p. 225)?

## CHAPTER 6

# Types of Essays

All writing falls under the big umbrella of exposition, that is, exposing or explaining an idea, concept, or topic to the reader clearly and concisely. To this end, you, as a writer, can use a variety of rhetorical modes in an essay. For example, an essay on corporate sponsorship in public schools may include definition (to explain what you mean by "corporate sponsorship"), compare/contrast (to show the difference between kinds of sponsorship), and cause/effect (explaining what happens when corporations get involved in education). For learning purposes, we classify and isolate these modes for easier identification and for study.

You may also write a paper that particularly focuses on one technique. For example, if your instructor should ask you to discuss the worth of two types of equipment, you may want to use the compare/contrast method throughout the essay. Or, if your instructor should want you to debate an idea, you may wish to use the persuasive method to win your reader over.

If you are uncertain about which method to use, often the assignment topic or question will guide you. For example, a topic such as "Explain how the technology of communication has changed the modern world" suggests a process method. Other times, the way you phrase your thesis statement directs your methodology. A thesis statement such as "Corporate sponsorship in public schools undermines the values of the public educational system" indicates an argumentative essay.

As you read the essays, examine the structure. Look for the thesis statement and the topic sentence of each body paragraph. See how the ideas are supported. For some of the essays, we've included the outline or the brainstorming ideas to show you steps in the writing process.

# Illustration

An illustrative essay explains or shows something. It is, in a way, the most basic kind of essay. You can use examples and narration to illustrate your main ideas.

## Assimilation of immigrants

THESIS:

The rate of assimilation depends on the immigrants' background, individual qualities, and situation.

1. immigrants' background prepares them for their life in new country
   - language
   - education
   - similarity between their own culture and new culture
   - how much they've travelled and seen the world
2. each individual has certain qualities that makes him adapt well or not
   - attitude towards new culture
   - open-mindedness
   - willingness to learn
     - some qualities may be affected by age
3. the situation the immigrants find themselves is also important
   - existence of ethnic neighbourhood
     - immigrants don't need to interact to survive
   - education
     - if they are taking language classes
   - work situation
     - how much they come in contact with people
     - women who stay at home don't adapt as quickly

The modern world is a place of mobility where people travel around the globe with ease. They can learn about other countries through the mass media. Therefore, it is not surprising to see so many people willing to leave their homes and settle in new countries. The lives of immigrants are not easy, however, and some settle in their new homes more readily than others. The rate of assimilation depends on the immigrants' background, individual qualities, and situation.

The immigrants' background prepares them for their life in new country. If they already speak the language of their new country, they will assimilate quickly. Immigrants with more education can more easily understand their new situation. They can use reference sources like libraries to help them learn about their new country. Furthermore, those who come from a culture similar to the one in their new home adapt more easily. For instance, an American will adapt to life in Canada more quickly than a Japanese person will. Finally, immigrants who have experience travelling tend to be more open-minded and accepting of new places and cultures.

In addition to their experience, individuals have personality traits that determine how quickly they adapt to their new home. One personal characteristic is the attitude towards the new country. Immigrants who are genuinely interested in the culture of the new country adopt its ways easier. Open-mindedness is also an important quality. Immigrants have to be willing to learn new things. This may be affected by their age. As a rule, younger immigrants have the personal qualities that enable them to adapt more quickly.

Other factors determining the rate of assimilation are those that describe the situations the immigrants find themselves in. The existence of an ethnic neighbourhood affects immigrants' interactions. For example, Chinese immigrants who live in Chinatown will likely live within their own culture and use their own language more than Chinese immigrants who live in a small town with no Chinatown culture to fall back on. Immigrants taking language classes are taught about their new home and therefore adapt more easily. Another factor is the workplace. Some immigrants use their native tongue at work or have a job where they do not come in contact with people very much. Women who stay at home, for example, may adapt more slowly than their husband and children.

Immigrants gradually adapt to their new home at varying rates, and some never feel comfortable in their new land. However, they can all make important contributions to their new country. Moreover, their children grow up as citizens of a country their parents may never have quite accepted.

# The use of the Internet

Although many people think the Internet is a new business invention, the network actually started with military computers during the Cold War. It was seen as a way to keep communication open in the event of nuclear attack. Universities were added to the network, and scientists used it to communicate with their colleagues all around the world. In the 1990s it spread to businesses and individual homes. The Internet has now become indispensable for people all over the world.

Communication has been revolutionized with the Internet. E-mail is faster than regular mail, less expensive than long-distance phone calls, and more convenient than playing telephone tag. Unlike faxed documents, text sent as e-mail messages can be edited and searched. Moreover, UseNet newsgroups allow people to discuss issues and ask questions of experts. In the process, they are making friends and starting relationships with e-mail "pen pals." The Internet is facilitating communication with people in different countries, enabling them to learn more about different cultures and different points of view. We are seeing a revival of letter writing as people tap out their messages and send them around the world.

The Internet is also used for entertainment. Instead of passively watching TV, people are surfing the World Wide Web, choosing what they want to see and interacting with their computers. Online text is enhanced with audio and video segments. People are also using communication as entertainment, socializing on chat lines and maintaining e-mail correspondence. They can pursue their hobbies with information on the Web and even express themselves by designing their own home pages.

Above all, the Internet provides an invaluable source of information. Companies advertise their products and services on web pages, saving printing costs with online catalogues. Software companies offer upgrades that can be downloaded from the Net. Moreover, electronic publishing is flourishing in e-zines (electronic magazines). Although online texts are not as easy to read as paper resources, full text databases offer superior searching capabilities. For example, a search engine can pinpoint a Shakespearean quote in seconds. Most importantly, on-line information is more up-to-date than any print source could be. During the Atlanta Olympics, competition results were offered on the Internet before newspapers and television could report them.

Thus, it is not surprising that more and more people are using the Internet for communication, entertainment, and information. The Internet is actually in danger of being a victim of its own popularity, as phone lines are being overburdened with web surfers. However, technological advancements, such as data compression and service over television cables, are being developed to provide this vital service.

---

### ASSIGNMENTS

1. Explain the job opportunities in a specific field.

2. Using examples, show how kinds of cars fit the personalities of the drivers. Or show how pet owners resemble their pets physically and psychologically.

3. With extended examples, show how commercials on TV have seduced you into buying products you don't really use or don't need.

4. Illustrate how being the first born, middle child, or "baby" in the family affects a child. Or, explain how being the male or female child in the family affects parental expectations, affections, and responsibilities towards that child.

5. Using examples, show how waiting on tables can be a useful skill to have in dealing with the public.

# Classification

Another type of expository writing is classification, where the writer categorizes something, describing different types. For example, an essay might explain different types of computer programs: word processors, spreadsheets, and databases. Vehicles could be divided into cars, vans, and trucks. People could also be described according to different categories: by the job they do or according to their personality type. In the work world, you may have to write a classification for product and job descriptions.

# Language teaching methods

OUTLINE

Three basic approaches to language teaching: grammar-translation, audio-lingual, communicative

1) grammar translation

- used with Latin and Greek
- memorize grammar rules
- parse sentences
- translation
- reading literature

2) audio-lingual
- based on behaviourist psychology
- habit formation
- drill and practice
- language labs
- native language of learners not used

3) communicative approach
- understanding is important
- minor errors overlooked
- curriculum decided according to students' needs

One of the most difficult educational tasks that adults undertake is learning a second language. Children learn languages seemingly effortlessly, while adults struggle with vocabulary, sentence structure, and pronunciation. Teachers have long looked for the perfect way to ease the way to fluency in a second or foreign language. The change in language teaching methods can be seen in three schools of thought that have dominated language schools this century: grammar translation, audio-lingual methods, and the communicative approach.

The traditional grammar translation method focuses on the written language. It is well suited to the study of classical languages such as Latin and Greek, once considered essential to a good education. In this method, students memorize grammar rules and parse sentences to examine the structure. They also translate passages and read the literature of the language. This method, however, does not produce people who are capable of speaking the language fluently.

As the world's peoples travelled and migrated, it was recognized that schools needed to produce graduates who could speak a language, not just read and translate it. The theory of behaviourism in psychology stressed habit formation in learning, so language schools favoured drill and practice. With advances in technology, students were introduced to language labs and tapes. In audio-lingual methods, teachers were not supposed to speak in the students' native language in an effort to reproduce the way that people learn their first language. Teachers used pictures and mime to get meaning across to beginner students.

The recognition that speaking a language involves more than parroting learned phrases resulted in the development of communicative approaches. In these approaches, it is recognized that communication is paramount and understanding is fundamental. Minor errors in grammar and pronunciation can be overlooked with the emphasis on getting meaning across. Curriculum is determined by student need. For instance, hospital workers would concentrate on learning medical vocabulary.

Grammar translation, audio-lingual, and communicative approaches are three basic types of language teaching methodology. Other methods may take elements from these approaches. All recognize that learning a second language takes hard work and practice.

## ASSIGNMENTS

1.  Describe different kinds of supervisors, tourists, students, employees, salespeople, or babies.

2.  Categorize and explain the different tasks performed in a specific job. For example, receptionists may greet people (in person or on the phone), keep track of appointments, and do paperwork.

3.  Classify different types of housing or accommodations.

# Process

An explanation of how something is done is process description or analysis. You may be called upon to describe process in a science or technology course. Business writing also requires process writing—to explain a plan of action, for instance.

Writing an effective process analysis requires an understanding of step-by-step progression. Each step may have to be explained carefully, so that readers understand the reason for that action. Some processes have many small steps, while some have a few basic stages.

We differentiate between process description and instruction. Instructions tell the reader what to do; they are usually written in the second person (*you*) and include commands (e.g., "check your answer"). Instructions are often written as lists of steps rather than as developed paragraphs. Recipes, for example, are sets of instructions. Process description is usually written in the third person (e.g., "students take several tests") and may include the passive voice. A biology textbook contains many process descriptions. Some prose may be a mixture of process and instruction. On the other hand, some processes (like biological and geological processes) can never be written up as instructions. An explanation of how a plant grows is process, while an explanation of how to plant a garden is instruction. Child language development is process, and teaching a child to read is instruction.

One common problem in the process essay is shifts in person. Students start with the third person and then switch to *you* and give commands. Here is an example, followed by a correction:

> Computer buyers must first determine their needs. They should understand what they need a computer for. A very fast machine is required to process graphics in games and design applications. However, if you are just doing word processing and accessing the Internet, you do not need a top-of-the-line machine. Make a list of the type of programs you will use. Talk to people with similar needs.

**Correction**

> Computer buyers must first determine their needs. They should understand what they need a computer for. A very fast machine is required to process graphics in games and design applications. However, if they are just doing word processing and accessing the Internet, they do not need a top-of-the-line machine. Computer buyers should make a list of the type of programs they will use and talk to people with similar needs.

To write a process essay, you should first write down all the individual steps. Start these steps with a verb form so that you will not lose your focus. For example, the car buying process includes

> determining the buyer's needs
>
> deciding on a budget
>
> reading ads
>
> talking to salespeople

test-driving a vehicle

making a deal

If you write a paragraph describing the relative merits of sports cars and mini-vans, you are no longer describing the process. You can include this point as an example of determining buyer's needs, but stay focused on the purpose of your essay.

After you have a list of steps, you can group them into different stages for separate paragraphs. For instance, buying a car can be broken down into three stages: planning, shopping, and making a deal.

Make sure that you describe the process adequately and do not just pick out three individual steps to describe. For example, one student described the process of getting married in this way: "When people get married, they must take pictures, have a party, and go on a honeymoon." While these are three steps in the process of getting married, they do not hang together logically. A better thesis statement would be "Arranging a wedding is a process of fulfilling legal requirements, organizing the ceremony, and planning the reception."

# Finding a job

BRAINSTORMING:

- figuring out job goals, skills, talents
- writing a résumé: listing education and employment history, writing descriptions of job duties
- arranging references
- networking: asking friends and co-workers about jobs
- visiting an employment centre or agency
- visiting the library for research on companies
- looking in the help wanted or careers section in the newspaper
- calling and visiting possible workplaces
- writing cover letters
- sending out résumés
- going for an interview—preparation, being interviewed, follow-up

Job hunting is a task that people face several times in their lives. They face it with trepidation because it is so vital yet so difficult. However, the task seems more manageable when it is broken down into some basic steps.

Before job seekers actually start looking for a job, they must determine their skills, talents, interests, and goals. These are encapsulated in the résumé. In writing résumés, people are defining themselves as workers. They must have a clear idea of what kind of job they want in order to tailor the résumé and to write the summary or objective statement. They gather information to detail their employment and education history. Job duties must be described succinctly and accurately, stressing accomplishments. Job hunters must also think of any other skills they have, such as the ability to work with certain computer software.

After they have finished putting together their résumé, job hunters must find out about positions available. Networking is an important first step. They should let friends and acquaintances know they are looking for work because many positions are not advertised. Using whatever connections they have may gain them a foothold they might not otherwise be able to get. The next step is visiting employment centres to see job postings and to get valuable tips for job hunting. People can also read the help wanted or careers section in the newspaper and on Internet job sites. They should also use the library to consult resources such as business directories.

All this preparation leads to actually contacting and meeting potential employers. Job seekers can answer newspaper ads with cover letters and résumés. Internet ads may require sending or posting an electronic résumé. After having identified likely companies from business directories, applicants can make cold calls to personnel offices and follow up by sending in their resume. When they are called in for an interview, they move on to another step in the job hunting process. Job hunters must make sure that they make a good impression, answering questions well and presenting a good appearance.

Following these steps makes the job hunt less formidable. Looking for a job is never easy but, with a positive attitude and good preparation, job seekers should be able to find the position they want.

# From novel to movie

The movie industry is always looking for new material. Screenwriters are busily concocting new plots for the voracious maw of filmmaking. In addition, producers buy up plays, true life adventures, and novels—anything that can tell a compelling story—and adapt them for the screen. Buying a novel, however, does not mean that they have a ready script. The process from book to film takes a number of steps.

The first step involves choosing the book and getting rights to it. Moviemakers try to get the jump on other producers by being the first to option the rights to a movie. Some have contacts in the publishing industry—scouts who are on the lookout for a novel that will make a good movie. Books that are plot-driven are more easily translatable to film than books that are heavy with description or internal musings. John Grisham novels, for example, are not considered great literature, but they are very popular and make great movies, such as *The Client* and *The Pelican Brief.* Once a potential book has been chosen, producers try to acquire the film rights. The money the author receives in exchange for these rights can range from a few thousand dollars to millions. Because this is so lucrative, some authors even write their books with movie-making in mind.

The next step is writing the screenplay, that is, converting the book into a filmable project. Prose must be translated to dialogue and stage directions. Moreover, a two-hour movie cannot handle too many subplots and characters. For example, the 1995 six-hour mini-series of *Pride and Prejudice* remained very faithful to the book, whereas an earlier two-hour production, starring Laurence Olivier and Greer Garson, reduced a number of minor characters and scenes. Still, what may work well on paper may not work on screen, so adaptors often must forgo fidelity for screen integrity. Sometimes a movie adaptation is so unlike the original (as *Simon Birch* is different from *A Prayer for Owen Meany*) that character names are changed and the movie credit says that the film was "inspired" by the book.

In the third stage, film producers choose the look of the film—the cast and settings. Although all movie-making demands these decisions, making a film from a book is a particular challenge. If it is a popular novel, the filmmakers must reconcile their vision with the many readers who have imagined the book in a certain way. Readers have an image of a character in their heads that may go beyond the author's description. The effort that went into casting the lead actors in *Gone With The Wind* is so legendary that a 1980 movie, *The Scarlett O'Hara War*, focused on the search for an actress to play the story's heroine. Imaginary settings in science-fiction novels used to be difficult to film, but directors can reproduce the images better now with special effects, especially computer graphics.

These are the steps that moviemakers must pay particular attention to when they adapt a novel for a film. The effort is well worth it, since the world of books offers a wide variety of plots and characters as fodder for moviemakers. Adapting material for movies is recognized as a valuable process, with separate Academy awards for adapted and original screenplays.

## ASSIGNMENTS

1. Describe a process involved in one of the jobs you have held. For example, if you worked in a restaurant, you could describe how the restaurant was made ready for the day's business.

2. Explain how a specific food gets from the farm to the table.

3. Describe one of the these processes: getting married, immigrating to a new country, preparing for a trip abroad, buying an expensive item such as a house or car, moving, or preparing for an examination.

# Cause and Effect

The cause/effect essay shows your abilities to reason and to foresee. Sometimes you will explore both causes and effects in an essay, and sometimes you will focus on just one aspect. If you are examining why something happens, you are exploring the causes or reasons for an event or a problem. If you only focus on results and what happens because of a situation, you are exploring effects. For example, you could write about the reasons people drink to excess, or about the effects of alcoholism in society.

Often chronology or logical sequence dictates the organization of your paper. For example, in a history paper about the causes of the War of 1812, you may want to show events by date that led to global conflict. Or, in a psychology or sociology paper, you may want to show step-by-step what happens when someone defies social norms.

# Why students fail

BRAINSTORMING:

- too much pressure
- work is too hard
- lack of organization, scheduling
- inadequate skills
- can't understand professors
- not used to doing work on their own
- don't know how to take notes in lectures
- lack research skills
- don't want to work hard
- some students are in the wrong program
- college is different from high school
- ESL students have language problems
- adults are not used to school work anymore
- outside distractions

Students pursuing a college education face a great challenge. They must acquire the skills they need for a specific job while adapting to a new kind of school. It is not surprising that failure and drop-out rates for college studies are high. Some students cannot succeed in college because of the environment, their inadequate skills, or their lack of motivation.

Students may fail if they cannot adjust to the college environment. In high school, students get direction from teachers, whereas in college they must fend for themselves. They are treated as adults—responsible for their own attendance and their own work. Moreover, college professors are subject specialists and are not trained in teaching methods. They lecture rather than teach, so students are required to take notes, read course materials, and seek extra help when necessary. Some instructors do not speak the same first language as many of their students, and their accents may be difficult for students to understand. Inadequate facilities, such as not enough computer labs, can put extra stress on students.

In addition, some students do not have the basic skills they need for college. Although all students are supposed to have Grade 12 or the equivalent, what they have learned can vary greatly. They may have barely passed their high-school courses, and so have poor math or language skills. They may not have covered enough of the material that is prerequisite for college-level courses. They may not have the study skills required to do academic work without constant guidance from teachers. Foreign students may have to cope with a completely different educational system as well as a lack of language skills. Adult students may have rusty study skills. For example, they may have forgotten how to write essays or how to take notes as the professor lectures.

Some failures can be blamed on the students' lack of drive and ambition. If students do not have clear goals, they may not be motivated to put in the long hours of work. Perhaps they are taking a program simply because of the career opportunities. For example, computer science attracts many students because of the good job prospects, but students may have no real interest in computers. They may not be prepared to put in the time and effort to successfully complete their courses. Sometimes the lack of motivation relates to a specific course rather than the whole program. For example, students in technical programs are forced to take an English course. If they fail to recognize its value, they may skip class and put in minimal effort. Even when students want to pass, they may lack the single-mindedness to keep on track in their studies. They may get sidelined by other temptations. For example, as young adults on their own for the first time, they may not be able to resist going out to a party instead of studying.

These shortcomings may result in failure in college courses. Only after they receive their transcripts or grades do some students realize the true costs of a college education. Therefore, students must enter college with their eyes open to possible problem areas. Failing college courses can set them back emotionally and financially and retard their entry into the workplace.

# Poor driving habits

Driving is a hazardous occupation and nothing makes it more hazardous than the actions of other drivers. Everyone makes mistakes sometimes, but bad driving habits cause more potential problems than occasional errors. Bad drivers tailgate, weave in and out of traffic, block traffic, and speed. Such poor driving is the result of the drivers' aggressiveness, carelessness, or stress.

Many bad drivers are overly aggressive. They want to go fast, and they treat other drivers as impediments. These are the drivers who tailgate, trying to force the car ahead to move faster. They also weave in and out of traffic, sometimes cutting other cars off, just to gain a few seconds in the race to their destination. Aggressiveness is also shown in a lack of courtesy to other drivers. Poor drivers do not like to yield the right of way. They may turn into traffic when there is not enough room, forcing other drivers to slow down.

Poor driving habits are also a result of carelessness. These habits may develop over time as people forget the good driving practices they were taught. For example, it is easy to forget to signal a right turn at an intersection. On highways, sometimes, drivers do not check the side mirrors or their blind spot before changing lanes. If they have driven many years without an accident, they may get overconfident in their ability. They may not slow down early enough on wet or slippery roads,  or they might miscalculate the distance needed to stop, or believe they have the quick reflexes to avoid an accident.

Pressure can also lead people to drive poorly. Modern society is fast-paced and people have to meet deadlines, get to work on time, and get home in time to meet other obligations. So they cut corners. Instead of stopping for the amber light, these drivers hit the accelerator and try to race through the intersection or to make that left turn just before the on-coming traffic moves. Traffic jams cause more stress. Drivers may take the shoulder lane to by-pass blocked highway lanes. In extreme cases, stress results in road rage and violent acts.

It is easy to see why people become bad drivers. However, these factors are not excuses. More driver education and a police crackdown are necessary to make the streets safer for all traffic.

# Perception of crime

Crime statistics say that the crime rate is down. Fewer violent crimes are being committed. Yet fear of crime dominates public opinion. It is necessary to understand both the causes and the effects of this fear.

People's fear of crime comes mostly from their environment. They look around them and see a world different from the one they grew up in. Canada's multicultural society brings very different people together. While this is, for the most part, a positive advancement, it also means that the more conservative people feel uneasy when they see people they don't really understand. The media fuel people's fear of crime. Horrible, insane acts of violence get more widely reported today than in the past. Because of these reports, people think that crime is much more prevalent than it actually is.

This fear of crime affects people personally. Augmented by the constant news reports of home invasions, carjackings and other violent crimes, they are afraid to walk outside at night. Many people believe there is a young offender around the corner, ready to mug them. Then, fearing for their own and their family's safety, they install more locks and security systems in their house. They drive rather than walk to the corner store. Instead of getting to know the neighbourhood, they become fearful of the surroundings. People harbour a dread that any day, any time, when they least expect it, they will be a victim of crime.

The inaccurate perception of crime also affects society. Cries for harsher penalties come from a public that fears the inevitable encroachment of disorder and breakdown of social structures. Young offenders convicted of minor misdemeanours and property crimes are given the status of bank robbers, rapists, and murderers. The sentiment towards the return of capital punishment, the death penalty, increases daily after each heinous crime is reported in the media. Statistics of decreasing crime rates are not believed while the sensational crime of the moment is taken as the norm. Voters demand that their political and legislative members tighten up the "loopholes" in the law and punish offenders. This means that criminals are treated harshly and are given no opportunity for rehabilitation.

The false perception of crime forms a vicious circle of cause and effect. People fear crime more than they should, but this in turn makes crime a more serious problem. It is the fear of crime that makes our society a more dangerous place, more than the actual crime itself.

| ASSIGNMENTS |
|---|

1. Take a recent event in the news and explain what caused it to happen.

2. What causes road rage, or air rage? What are the effects?

3. Imagine a disaster (such as a tornado, earthquake, or ice storm) hitting a major Canadian city. Explain what the effects would be.

# Compare/Contrast Essays

Comparing two things is a common academic exercise. A compare/contrast paper tests your ability to analyze, understand, and express your findings clearly. In the workplace, you may also have to write a comparison, to evaluate two proposals, for example.

Traditionally, a distinction is made where the word *compare* refers to similarities and *contrast* refers to differences. However, most of the time *compare* is used to indicate both similarities and differences, so your academic assignments usually just ask you to compare two things. It may be obvious from the topic whether you should be stressing similarities or differences. For instance, if you are comparing two things that seem more alike than different, such as two schools, you will focus on differences. On the other hand, if you are comparing two things that are mostly perceived to be different, like computer programming and writing an essay, you might focus on similarities. The instructor may clarify exactly what he or she expects. Generally, however, if your assignment asks you to compare something, you can write about similarities and/or differences.

Comparison essays must have logic and reason behind them. There is little point in comparing two such wildly different things as a book and a chair, for example, or other truly uncomparable things. The introduction and the conclusion often give the reason or the "so what?" for the comparison. For example, you may choose to compare two books on a similar theme, or two chairs to say which provides better seating for a certain purpose.

It is important to remember that you must make the comparison for the reader—you do the work. You cannot just describe A, then describe B, and conclude, "As you can see, A and B are very different."

Organization is very important in a comparison essay. You don't want to confuse your readers, so you keep the same order throughout a paragraph. The proper use of transition signals helps readers follow the comparison. Words like "however" and "on the other hand" show that you are going to talk about the second item being compared.

You should also strive to keep your comparison essay balanced, so that it talks about each item to the same extent. You don't want to write a long block of text on one item and then have nothing to say about the other.

Some of the comparison is implied. When you have a good topic sentence that tells the reader to expect comparison in the paragraph, you do not have to keep repeating comparison phrases. If your reader knows you are comparing A and B, and you say A is more expensive, the reader understands that it is more expensive than B, so you do not need to repeat "than B."

In order to draw similarities or differences, you use comparative adjectives and subordinate clauses. Here are some examples of comparison sentences, so that you can see the forms:

> Generators produce direct current—electricity that goes only one way along the electrical wires—whereas alternators put out alternating current—electricity that changes direction.

> Both mid-sized Pontiacs and Chevrolets have the same engine under the hood. Both cars share design features, as well.

> Like a banana or an orange, the tomato is a fruit.

> Unlike bacteria that attack the enamel of a tooth, gingivitis preys on the gum and causes swelling and discomfort.

> In terms of population, Toronto has more urban dwellers than Montreal.

> One major difference between comparison and exposition is that in comparison the writer must juggle two items at the same time as he is explaining, while in exposition the writer gives out information on only one thing.

## Structure

There are two basic methods of comparison: point-by-point and block. In a point-by-point comparison of A and B, you take one point and use it to compare A and B, and then move on to the second point. In a block comparison, you discuss A first and then discuss B. To make it easier for the reader, you keep the same order of points.

You can choose which method works best for your topic. The block method allows for more expansion or explanation of ideas. While point-by-point comparison can make the comparison clear, too much of it may make your readers feel as if they are watching a ping-pong match, going back and forth and back and forth. You can mix the methods in a comparison essay, with a point-by-point paragraph followed by a block paragraph, as long as each paragraph has structural integrity.

Point-by-point:

| Point 1 | – A |
| | – B |
| Point 2 | – A |
| | – B |
| Point 3 | – A |
| | – B |

Block:

| A | – Point 1 |
| | – Point 2 |
| | – Point 3 |
| B | – Point 1 |
| | – Point 2 |
| | – Point 3 |

## Point-by-point example

When Canadian students graduate from high school, they have the choice of two different kinds of post-secondary institutions: university or community college. One difference is that universities focus more on theoretical and academic aspects of learning, expecting students to continue their studies or to learn to apply the theories once they have mastered them. Colleges, on the other hand, prefer the hands-on, practical approach and prepare students directly for the work world. Secondly, the learning environment is different. Universities are usually older, with larger, separate campuses that form their own little world. College students are more likely to be integrated into the community and the business world. Finally, a university education is worth more. After spending thousands of dollars, university students earn a degree, with the right to use recognizable letters like "B.Sc." and "M.A." after their names. College students, however, pay less tuition and spend fewer years in school, but their diploma or certificate does not have as much prestige. While these are the traditional differences between colleges and universities, both institutions are changing and the distinction is blurring; colleges now attract university graduates in search of practical training for the job world, they are forming partnerships with universities, and they want to offer degrees.

Point 1: type of learning   – university (A)
                             – college (B)

Point 2: environment         – university (A)
                             – college (B)

Point 3: value        – university (A)
                      – college (B)


## Block example

When Canadian students graduate from high school, they have the choice of two different kinds of post-secondary institutions: university or community college. Universities focus more on theoretical and academic aspects of learning, expecting students to continue their studies or to learn to apply the theories once they have mastered them. Universities are usually older, with larger, separate campuses that form their own little world. In addition, a university education is more valued. After spending thousands of dollars, university students earn a degree, with the right to use recognizable letters like "B.Sc." and "M.A." after their names. On the other hand, colleges prefer the hands-on, practical approach and prepare students directly for the work world. They offer a different learning environment. College students are more likely to be integrated into the community and the business world. College students, moreover, pay less tuition and spend fewer years in school, but their diploma or certificate does not have as much prestige. While these are the traditional differences between colleges and universities, both institutions are changing and the distinction is blurring; colleges now attract university graduates in search of practical training for the job world, they are forming partnerships with universities, and they want to offer degrees.

A) university    – type of learning (point 1)
                 – environment (point 2)
                 – value (point 3)

B) college       – type of learning (point 1)
                 – environment (point 2)
                 – value (point 3)

# Comparison of transportation

Commuters in Canadian cities can often spend an hour or more travelling to work every day. Therefore, their method of transportation must be considered carefully. Travelling by car or by public transit are different in terms of cost, health, and convenience.

The costs of a car are not the same as those of transit. Car travel has a lot of hidden expenditures. Not only are there the expenses for gas, maintenance, and insurance, but also the cost of the vehicle itself and its depreciation. Commuters may also pay high parking fees and toll charges. Operating a car can amount to several thousand dollars a year. On the other hand, public transit users have only the fare to worry about. They can pay a couple of dollars for a single ride or buy a monthly pass, which gives them unlimited access. Moreover, some of the cost of public transportation is borne by the government, and therefore by all taxpayers.

Health and safety issues are different for the private vehicle and public transit. Individual cars are responsible for much of the carbon monoxide in our air, whereas travel by bus or train reduces the amount of exhaust going into the atmosphere. Car drivers must stay alert to avoid accidents, while bus passengers can trust their safety to a professional driver and to a larger, safer vehicle. People who rely on their car may not get as much exercise as commuters who must walk, or sometimes run, to bus stops. On the other hand, car drivers have their own environment, whereas bus passengers are in close contact with other people and therefore more apt to be exposed to germs and viruses.

Commuters must also consider comfort and convenience when they decide whether to travel by car or transit. Car drivers do not have to wait in line and deal with crowds. They can travel whenever and wherever they want. Their vehicle is their own little environment where they can listen to the radio or tapes, but they must stay alert to the traffic. Transit users, on the other, hand, may have to suffer the inconvenience of being packed like sardines into a bus or subway car. They are limited by bus routes and transit schedules. However, they can read, sleep or listen to portable stereos as they travel.

The differences between travelling by car and using public transit show that both have some advantages. If the transit schedule and route work to the commuter's advantage, the reasons to take a private vehicle diminish considerably.

# *Star Wars* versus *Star Trek*

George Lucas' *Star Wars* and Gene Roddenberry's *Star Trek* are the two space operas most recognized in North America for the last three decades. Fans of television and movies will instantly recognize these catch phrases: "May the force be with you" and "To boldly go where no man has gone before." Frequently compared, both are dramas about humans venturing in futuristic worlds; both use mind-boggling technology. Both have sparked fans to endless debates on which is better. *Star Wars*, I believe, is better than *Star Trek* because of the story telling, its characterization of aliens and heroes, and its more highly detailed, and thus more creative, universe.

The plotting is grander in scale and more exciting in *Star Wars* than in *Star Trek*. George Lucas draws from ancient myths and well known tales to tell the story of the Skywalkers. He draws on multiple sources—Saturday matinee cliff-hanging serials, romance literature, legends, and even the Bible—to craft an original story. The quest of a young idealist for adventure, identity, and destiny is archetypal. Young Luke Skywalker wants to become a great pilot and Jedi knight, like his father. The odds against him are as plentiful and diverse as there are stars and planets in the heavens. It has a black-and-white theme of good and evil that viewers can recognize and appreciate. *Star Trek*, on the other hand, is merely a new take on the theme of settling the American frontier, in this case, space exploration. An intrepid crew goes out into the wild but comfortable unknown. Captains Kirk, Picard, and Janeway are all constantly hampered by the Prime Directive of non-interference with underdeveloped societies. By the third time the USS Enterprise goes boldly out, themes become very redundant. A super computer has gone amok; a stellar peace treaty must be negotiated; a starship officer must end a romance with some alien beauty. *Star Wars* is a fun romp through a galaxy full of wonders, while *Star Trek* is a self-important show that never quite goes beyond self-absorption.

The villains in *Star Wars* are much more realistic than in *Star Trek*. In *Trek*, the evildoers dump their prisoners in faulty brigs, gloat over how and when the prisoners will die, and reveal far too much about their nefarious plots. All too often the nasty Cardassians and Klingons are reduced to caricature and farce. How long can a viewer retain a willing suspension of disbelief when the Klingons regularly flip-flop as evil foes and virtuous allies? In *Star Wars*, on the other hand, prisoners are interrogated, locked up, and have to be rescued to escape their dastardly foes. Darth Vader doesn't mince words with his captives; he just kills them after asking them some cursory questions. He beats up his own fellow bad guys; he cuts off Luke's hand without regret, proving that he is truly evil.

Although both have a large cast of fascinating creatures, *Star Wars* is far more imaginative than *Star Trek* because it is expansive and richly detailed. For example, in George Lucas' universe, there are eight-foot woolly Wookiees, crustaceous Calamari admirals, fur-ball Ewoks, sluglike Hutts, and monsters the size of asteroids; however, in Gene Roddenberry's future, there are only humanoid creatures such as antennaed Andorians, big-eared Ferengis, wrinkly-nosed Bajorans, and pointy-eared Vulcans. Certainly there are far-out aliens in *Star Trek*, such as the Horta and the Tribbles, but they are few and far between. On the other hand, in just one *Star Wars* movie, there is a multitude of wondrous creatures, like the Sarlacc and the Rancor. The galaxy in *Star Trek* is defined and parcelled off: this is Federation space; this, the Klingon Empire; this, the Alpha quadrant. The universe of *Star Wars* has no limit: the expanse between Coruscant and Tantooine stretches the imagination of the viewer.

*Star Wars* is clearly better than *Star Trek*. *Star Trek* just can't hold a lightsabre to *Star Wars* at all. Even an eighteen-year gap between movies has not killed the interest in *Star Wars*. In addition to the films, the stories live on in novels and children's stories. *Star Wars* has truly captured people's imaginations.

## ASSIGNMENTS

1. Compare two different jobs, schools, or cities.
2. Compare computer programming and writing an essay.

# Persuasion

In persuasion and argumentation, you must choose a position and support it. For example, you could argue either for or against a controversial issue, such as capital punishment. You must take a stand and not waffle from one position to the other, even if you are not totally convinced. For example, you may be able to see both the advantages and disadvantages of wearing school uniforms, but your essay must either be for or against. You state your position openly and clearly in the beginning of your essay.

As you go about supporting and proving your position, you should have reasonable, logical points. Deliberately or implicitly, your reader will be looking for flaws in your reasoning. Beware of generalizations and other logical fallacies. They weaken your position. After all, your argument is only as strong as your weakest link in the chain of ideas.

In argumentation and persuasion, you must think the idea through. Make sure that your arguments are practical and logical. For example, one essay argued that professional basketball players should be paid whatever salary they desire so that they would play better, and then went on to say that ticket prices should be lowered. This argument goes against basic economic laws.

Remember that there are many sides to controversial issues. There is no right answer, but there are well-thought out arguments.

## Common pitfalls in argumentation and persuasion:

1. arguing against the person rather than the views or opinions

   incorrect: That guy never got past high school. He looks like a football player. How can he know anything about genetically altered food?

   improved: Genetically altered fruits may have damaging health problems that will not show up for years. For Richard Applegate to recommend this path to solve food shortages is irresponsible.

2. making gross general statements or stereotyping

   incorrect: Squeegee kids have no ambition; I have often seen them doing nothing particularly useful but getting in the way of hard-working taxpayers who drive to work.

   improved: The Department of Welfare has recently reported that 15% of those on social assistance have difficulty in finding any kind of job once they have been out of the workforce for six months.

3. using a circular argument; that is, using the same word or meaning to prove the point

   incorrect: He is a studious student because he studies a lot.

improved: Two weeks into the new semester, Soraya has exceeded the reading requirement, spent at least three hours an evening in the library researching her assignment, and consulted her professors about her project by e-mail and phone.

4. giving faulty cause/effect; that one thing naturally follows the other

incorrect: Because the witch cursed him, he had a car accident.

improved: Because his mind was distracted by the old woman's curse and by his own inattention to the slippery conditions of the road, Joachim slammed on the brakes and his car slid off the pavement and into the ditch.

5. appealing to pity; that is, making someone feel sorry enough for you to let you win the argument

incorrect: If you don't let me pass this course, I will be so humiliated that I couldn't look my parents in the eye for the rest of my life. They will disown me, and then what will I do with my life?

improved: I realize that I have not paid enough attention in class this semester. However, personal problems, such as the break-up with my fiancé, and financial problems, such as having to work the midnight shift at a grocery store, have taken their toll on my studies. I hope you, Professor Hyde, might take them in consideration when you evaluate my performance in class.

6. making threats or using force

incorrect: If you don't let me win this argument about gun control, I'll give you a black eye and a broken jaw.

improved: My black belt in Kung Fu and Judo should be not an intimidating factor in this debate. My reasons for stricter gun control are logical and sound to all concerned.

7. hiding negative information; that is, not giving the whole truth in the matter

incorrect: The Ku Klux Klan give great open-air parties with large bonfires, camaraderie with purpose, and distinctive costumes. So join us today!

improved: Although secret societies, like the Ku Klux Klan, are trying to improve their image to the public at large, their views on racism, white supremacy, and violence to achieve their goals should not be ignored.

8. arguing by source; that is, a tainted source means the ideas are also suspect

   incorrect: She comes from a communist country, so her ideas can't be good.

   improved: Svetlana has studied poverty in Third World countries extensively and her solutions to child labour are sound.

9. appealing to popular sentiment or thinking; jumping on the bandwagon

   incorrect: Everybody is buying up Hassenfas stock, so you had better get some soon.

   improved: While the stock in Hassenfas is in great demand, it is dangerous to follow trends in such a volatile market.

10. presenting a false dilemma; an "either/or" choice

    incorrect: If you don't sign this contract with us to market your new invention, you will never see it produced and sold.

    improved: If Acme Inventions Incorporated cannot offer you a fair contract, you can always take your invention to its competitors or produce it yourself.

## Concession

Another important part of making a good argument is taking into account opposing views. If you do not tackle pertinent arguments presented by the opposing side, your argument will be weaker because the obvious opposing points will be in the reader's mind. If you should find that the opposition has a legitimate point, concede it. Concession is the art of saying, "Yes, but." However, you can downplay the other argument, as in this sentence: "Although computers are valuable tools for students, they may not be worth the resources that the school boards commit to them." Your point is in the main clause.

Here are some examples of concessionary sentences:

**Anti-smoking argument:** Even though smokers have the right to make choices about their own health, they do not have the right to poison others.

**Pro-smoking argument:** Although smoking is harmful, smokers should be able to make their own decisions about the risks involved.

**Pro-uniform:** School uniforms are expensive, but they are less expensive than the designer clothes many teenagers want. **Anti-uniform:** Despite the high cost of "in" clothing, students can be dressed in inexpensive, practical clothing for much less than the cost of school uniforms.

# The importance of studying history

THESIS:

History is an essential subject for all students.

1. people should know basic historical information
   - historical facts
     - some dates, a basic timeline of human events
   - can put other events into context
   - essential for every branch of knowledge
     - science, e.g. previous events: flu epidemic after WWI
   - to understand historical references in books, movies
     - e.g. Henry VIII
2. students can learn about peoples, cultures, places
   - seeing how things developed helps us to understand them
     - e.g. English language shaped by the Norman invasion
   - people are shaped by historical events
     - e.g. to understand Japan's industrial success, have to go back to WWII
3. "Those who do not know their history are doomed to repeat it." (Santayana)
   - through history we learn about horrors of war and genocide
   - learn about the mistakes that people have made so that we can avoid them
     - e.g. problems in communist system

As technology dominates our world, students are being told to concentrate on science and mathematical studies. Liberal arts subjects are falling out of fashion, as students feel that there are no jobs that require a knowledge of literature or history. This view is extremely short-sighted, however, because arts studies contribute to general knowledge. History, especially, is an essential subject for all students.

Basic historical facts are an essential part of human knowledge. People need to know when wars occurred, how countries were established, and who the main players were. All Canadians, for example, should know that their country was established in 1867, by an act of British Parliament, and that the first prime minister was Sir John A. Macdonald. Having an understanding of the basic timeline of human events helps put other events in context. Knowing that the American Revolution and the War of 1812 preceded Confederation, for example, explains how Canada came into being. History is important for every branch of knowledge. Epidemiologists study the great influenza epidemic of World War I to see how infectious diseases spread. Finally, knowing historical facts is important to understand references in books and movies. For example, the fact that Henry VIII had six wives is a point that helps people appreciate the irony in the Herman's Hermits song of the1960s, "I'm Henry VIII."

History is not just facts and dates; students can learn about peoples, cultures, and places. Understanding the cultural and social changes brought about by various invasions of Britain, such as William the Conqueror's defeat of King Harold in 1066 at Hastings, helps language students understand why English has so many words from old French. People are shaped by their history. The history of European involvement in Asia explains the diplomatic relationships even today. We can see how the American power in Japan after World War II influenced Japan's development as an industrial power.

The philosopher Santayana said that those who do not know their history are doomed to repeat it. History, then, is not mere knowledge, but lessons. We learn about horrors of war and genocide. The Holocaust is a constant reminder of "man's inhumanity to man." To forget it, to ignore it, or to dismiss it merely underscores Santayana's belief; however, to confront it, understand it, and learn from it may change the soul of humanity. Knowing the mistakes that people have made gives others a chance to avoid past pitfalls. For instance, people can develop better systems of government with an understanding of failed systems such as Soviet communism.

Knowledge of history is a vital ingredient of a good education. Students should receive instruction in history throughout their elementary and secondary school careers. These studies should include a thorough history of their own country, as well as knowledge about major civilizations. With this background knowledge, they will be better equipped to pursue career-oriented studies in post-secondary education.

# Spam

THESIS:

Spam is bad

1. content
    - selling junk
    - lies
    - pornography
    - criminal actions
2. bandwidth problem
    - telephone lines, too much traffic
    - slow web screen load
3. reverses the usual costs of advertising
    - spammers do not pay for messages
    - Internet users pay

Unsolicited junk mail is filling up our electronic mail boxes. We get messages telling us we can make thousands of dollars easily from home, or advertisements for illegal services and products: "Make money fast at home!" "Check out our website for hot chicks!" This type of commercial message is called "spam" after a tinned luncheon meat (spiced ham). Spam is the scourge of the Internet.

The content of spam messages ranges from useless to criminal. They try to sell products and services we do not need. They pretend that we have requested the information, or they apologize for intruding on us, but it is all a sham. They say we can be taken off the mailing list if we send a "delete" message in reply, but those requests do not work. In fact, they simply confirm for the spammer that the e-mail address is valid. The messages advertising pornography are read by minors; sometimes even their subject headings are obscene. The "make money fast" messages are often for illegal pyramid schemes.

Spam takes up a valuable resource—bandwidth. Internet communication moves along telephone lines, lines never designed for such traffic. Anyone who has ever sat in front of a computer waiting for a web page to load knows the frustration of slow electronic communication. More people are connecting to the Internet everyday, compounding the problem. Moreover, the messages being transferred are more complex—graphics take up more bandwidth than simple text messages. Downloads of video clips and program files are also huge and take a long time to transfer. The phone lines are overburdened with the legitimate uses of the Internet. Millions of junk e-mail messages clog up the lines, making service even slower.

Junk e-mail reverses the usual expenses of advertising. Businesses usually put some thought and care into their advertising because each flyer and each commercial cost them money. But spammers send their messages out indiscriminately to hundreds of thousands of addresses, and they do not pay anything more beyond their regular Internet service fee. Instead, the cost is borne by the Internet users, who have to take up valuable connect time downloading the messages and their own time to weed out and delete these messages.

Spam is clearly a serious problem on the Internet. It should be controlled because it damages the system for all of us. Internet Service Providers should close the accounts of spammers and block junk e-mail from reaching their customers.

# The dangers of computer technology

THESIS:

It is dangerous to rely on computers

1. machines and systems themselves are unreliable
   - bugs in software
   - poorly designed systems
     - Y2K
   - viruses, hackers
2. security and privacy at risk
   - all information stored in databases
     - personal profile can be made
   - everything that people do is monitored and recorded
     - workplace surveillance

3. over-reliance on machines
   - taken over human skills

     e.g. can't give out change if cash register is down
   - people think the machines are perfect
   - makes people impatient and less sociable

Computer technology dominates our lives. The machines store records, track financial transactions, and allow people to communicate more efficiently. It is hard to imagine any kind of modern business operating without computers. Indeed, this reliance on computers comes with many dangers.

Although the machines appear to work miraculously, any true computer user knows that the machines and the systems themselves are unreliable. System crashes can bring business to a standstill. As software becomes more complicated and more interconnected, the possibility of clashes increase. Programmers write millions of lines of code and cannot anticipate every possible situation, so software can never be bug-free. One of the best examples of poor design and lack of forethought is the Year 2000 problem, called Y2K: programmers used only the last two digits of the year to save computer space, and thus created a situation where computers would not be able to compute dates after January 1, 2000. Another problem that plagues computer systems is sabotage; hackers break into systems and malicious practical jokers create viruses.

The use of computers puts our personal security and privacy at risk. Confidential employment, financial, and health records are stored in computers without adequate safeguards. Every time people use credit and debit cards, records of their purchases are stored. Companies access and use this information (an activity called data-mining) to build personal profiles of buying preferences. This type of database is useful for targeting advertising. Moreover, everything employees do on their work computers can be monitored and recorded. Their employers can read their e-mail messages, time every keystroke, and see what Internet sites they visit.

Our over-reliance on computers and other machines weakens us personally. We lose some of our skills because we do not use them. Many store clerks, for example, are unable to make change without their cash registers telling them how much money is owed. Another problem is the belief that computers are infallible. Bureaucrats fall back on saying they are powerless because some procedure is prescribed by the machine. The hours spent on the Internet or on computer games take away from the time we have for social interaction. It is not surprising that computer nerds are considered anti-social.

Therefore, although computers empower us to do more than we have before, they can make us vulnerable. It is important for all computer users to be aware of the problems inherent in computer use. Implementation of the technology should take into consideration the potential dangers, so that people can use the machines to their benefit, not their detriment.

## ASSIGNMENTS

Take a controversial issue in the news today and argue either for or against.

## CHAPTER 7

# Writing a Summary

A summary, also called a précis or abstract, is a brief version of a much longer article, report, or story. It gives the reader the same main ideas as the original, but it leaves out specific details. You summarize when you tell your friends about the movie you saw or relate the important points in a lecture a classmate missed.

Summaries are common in both academia and business. Journal articles include abstracts to give readers an idea of what main points are covered. University students may have to write an annotated bibliography, explaining in a sentence or a short paragraph what is in a 300-page book. Business people are often called upon to summarize reports. An executive summary, for example, gives essential information to supervisors and managers. Readers may use a summary as a preliminary reading before they read the entire article or report.

When you are called upon to write a summary in school, your instructor is evaluating your ability to understand a reading selection, to distinguish main ideas from less important ones, and to paraphrase an author's words concisely. You cannot write a good summary if you don't understand a reading, so the first step is spending enough time reading and re-reading the article to make sure you understand it. Use a dictionary for words you do not understand.

Finding the main ideas is another important part of summarizing. Ask yourself about the author's intended audience and purpose to help you determine the message. The more you read and evaluate what you read, the more you will be able to identify the main idea of a text. For instance, you will see how some writers relate a story or anecdote to set up the main argument, as in Kurt Wiesenfeld's "Making the Grade" (p. 00). As you work through readings in class, you will be asked to determine the author's main point.

Summaries must be concise. You may have to work through your summary several times to eliminate unnecessary words. For instance, instead of saying a story is about "a seventy-year-old woman from China whose husband died" you could say "an elderly Chinese widow."

Your summary will probably be one paragraph, from 75 to 150 words, depending on the length of the original article. Your instructor may insist on a specific length to test your skills. The summary should be a developed paragraph, with the topic sentence identifying the article so that it is clear to the reader that the paragraph is a summary.

You may also be called upon to write one-sentence summaries, or summary statements. For a reading test question that asks for the main idea of the article, the answer is essentially a summary statement.

# Paraphrasing

Paraphrasing is putting someone else's words and ideas into your own words. To be able to paraphrase well, you must have a good vocabulary. You must realize, however, that paraphrasing is not just a matter of replacing words with synonyms. You have to think about what the author is saying and try to express the same point in the way you would normally say it.

**Excerpt from "Making the Grade":**

In a society saturated with surface values, love of knowledge for its own sake does sound eccentric. The benefits of fame and wealth are more obvious. So is it right to blame students for reflecting the superficial values saturating our society?

**Poor paraphrase:**

In a society full of superficial values, the respect for learning alone sounds odd. We can more easily see the good points of being famous and rich. Therefore, is it the students' fault that they have the same surface values as our society?

(This paraphrase is too close to the original. It is a "paraphrase by thesaurus" with synonyms substituted for the original words.)

**Poor paraphrase:**

It is not surprising that students reflect the superficial values saturating our society, where love of knowledge for its own sake does sound eccentric and where the benefits of fame and wealth are more obvious.

(In this attempt, the writer has just switched around the sentence structure, using too much of the original wording.)

**Good paraphrase:**

Our society values fame and wealth, not learning, so it is not surprising that students have those values.

# How to write a summary

1. Read the entire article or report all the way through to get the gist of it. Make sure you understand the main points of the article. If you have trouble understanding some of the article, re-read it using a dictionary.

2. Jot down the main ideas in your own words. Often the topic sentence of each paragraph will give you the main idea. Keep the ideas in the same sequence as the original.

3. Focus on main points and do not include specific details in your summary. Leave out examples, illustrations, biographical data, references to other works, and irrelevant information.

4. Paraphrase the words of the author. As much as possible, avoid copying phrases from the original article. Do not just take a sentence and substitute synonyms.

5. Write a developed paragraph from your notes, making complete sentences and joining related ideas. The paragraph should be coherent and use transition markers.

6. Make sure that your paragraph has a topic sentence that identifies the article and gives the reader an idea of what the article is about: "In 'A Hanging,' George Orwell talks about his experience witnessing an execution." You may also have to reference the article, giving the name of the publication where it appears, the date, and the page numbers.

7. Remember your reader. Someone reading the summary on its own should be able to understand the summary without having to refer to the original article.

8. Revise your draft. Check grammar, spelling, and punctuation. Proofread your final copy carefully before you submit it.

# Sample summaries

To illustrate good and bad summarizing techniques, here are summaries of two of the reading selections in Chapter 17.

## "Why My Mother Can't Speak English" (page 236)

**Poor summary:**

In this story the author talks about his mother getting citizenship. He explains why she wants to be a citizen and talks about the citizenship procedure. His mother has a problem and some difficulty getting her citizenship. But in the end she becomes a Canadian and everyone is happy. (49 words)

*This summary is too short and too vague. It doesn't give enough information. For example, the summary says the mother has a problem, but it does not say what the problem is. Moreover, the topic sentence does not identify the article by giving the title and author.*

**Poor summary:**

"Why My Mother Can't Speak English" is a story about an seventy-year-old Chinese woman. She is an immigrant living in Canada. After she reads the Chinese newspaper, she wants her citizenship because she thinks that the government will take away her pension. She asks her son, the narrator of the story, to help her get her citizenship. They go to the immigration office early. The son talks to his cousin for a while, and the cousin tells him how difficult it is for the old to accept change, especially learning a new language. Then the mother and the son meet the liaison officer, who asks why the mother never bothered to learn English after thirty years in Canada. Then the mother tries to bribe the person with *lai-shi*, but fortunately the son stops her and explains the cultural etiquette. As they return home, the son thinks back to the time when the father forbade the mother from learning while at the same time encouraging his employees to better themselves. The father didn't believe that the Chinese women should learn English. The mother believes that the father was afraid that if she learned more she would leave him. The son wonders why his mother would bring up all these pains and sorrows after the death of his father. Yet she still goes to the cemetery regularly. She thinks that she will not get her citizenship, but some months later she is called to an interview. When she sees that the citizenship judge is a woman, she thinks the judge will be prejudiced against her. However, the judge is quite kind and understanding. Much later, the mother is granted citizenship and she goes to the ceremony with her son. Afterwards, the son asks how she feels being a Canadian and she answers by talking about the old-age pension increase and the harvest festival in China. The story ends with the mother saying that she will go to visit her husband at the cemetery and tell him her good news. (341 words)

*This summary is too wordy and has too much detail.*

**Good summary:**

"Why My Mother Can't Speak English," a story by Garry Engkent, tells of an elderly Chinese woman and her quest for Canadian citizenship. The woman asks her son, the narrator of the story, to help her, but the obstacle is that she is unable to speak English even after 30 years in Canada. Although lack of opportunity, her husband's disapproval, and her age played a part, the son concludes that his mother was afraid of losing her identity as a Chinese woman and so did not want to learn English. At the end of the story, the mother is granted citizenship despite her lack of English. (106 words)

## "Making the Grade" (page 250)

### Poor summary:

In the article "Making the Grade," the author Kurt Wiesenfeld talks about a beginner mistake he made. He went to his office the day after final grades were posted. Some of his students went to see him, e-mailed him, or left him voice mail messages. They asked him to change their grades. There were worried about flunking out, losing their scholarships or losing their life. But the professor was unsympathetic and he didn't give them a second chance, so they failed the course, and it was all his fault. (90 words)

*This summary misses main argument of the article and focuses on only one part of the article, giving minor details. Unnecessary words such as "the article" and "the author" in the first sentence could be eliminated to keep the summary brief. Another problem is that some of the phrases are worded exactly as in the original text. Finally, the last sentence is opinion and does not belong in a summary.*

**Good summary:**

In "Making the Grade," Kurt Wiesenfeld argues that grades should indicate actual academic achievement. Some of his students asked him to change their final mark, not because they deserved a higher grade but because they wanted or needed it. These students' attitudes reflect society's consumer values, where money is more important than learning. However, Wiesenfeld shows that academic standards are important. Students may earn a degree with partial marks even when they have the wrong answer, but when these graduates go out to work, they could make fatal mistakes. Thus, society needs schools to maintain standards. (101 words)

## ASSIGNMENTS

Write a one-paragraph summary (approximately 100 words) of a newspaper or magazine article. You can use one of the readings in Chapter 17, one supplied by your instructor, or one you find yourself in the newspaper.

## CHAPTER 8

# Research Papers

A research paper is an essay that requires you to look up information and use it to support, expand, or explain your topic to the reader. Unlike an opinion paper wherein you express only your own thoughts or ideas on a given topic, a research essay demands that you expand upon the ideas with other people's views in order to give a fuller understanding of the topic.

College or university professors assign such papers for several reasons:

- to see whether you can find specific information, not just general knowledge on the topic

- to test your ability to digest the information and make sense of it for your readers

- to help you develop proper and practical methods of searching for information

- to give you practice in documenting and referencing information

- to help you expand your knowledge base on a given subject matter

- to develop further your skills in written communication

- to prepare you for senior courses or for the workplace where you may need these skills

- to teach you how to manage your time and work efficiently.

The research paper is important to the development of your writing skills. It is the next step, a more difficult level to master. You use the same basic writing process already outlined in this textbook, but you add some steps for the research.

A research paper takes time and should not be left to the last minute. One reason is that you may be frustrated in your search for information. For instance, all the books on your topic might be checked out of the library. You could have trouble with your Internet connection and therefore require more time to try again. You may have to refine your search techniques and seek help.

As in any essay, the first step is choosing a topic and brainstorming. Brainstorming before you do your research is useful. When you have put your own ideas down on paper, you will have made clear how much you already know about the topic and how much research you need to do. What you already know can be considered general knowledge and does not have to be referenced. Afterwards, you can go to the library, the Internet, or other sources to search for information. If you rush to your outside sources before you have written your own material, you may never know what is truly yours and what belongs to your sources.

After having written down all you know about the topic, consider how you will do the research. It is best that you have varied sources, such as magazines, books, web pages, and personal interviews. First, you must read more than you need to build up background information. Second, you must find relevant sources, reference them, and pay attention to accuracy and completeness.

As you research, take notes and document your sources. You must be able to identify the source of each note and quotation, citing author, title, publication information, and page numbers.

Because a research essay is usually a longer piece of work, editing becomes even more important than in a short essay. It is a good idea to let your writing sit for a day so that, when you revise and edit it later, you can look at it more objectively, with a fresh eye.

Here are a few pointers:

- Have a set of questions or items you believe you need to deal with. Go to your source with a purpose rather than a vague notion of what you will be researching.

- Begin with the simple source first before you embark upon the complicated. For example, a children's book or an encyclopedia article or frequently asked questions (FAQ) file on a website might give you basic information you need first.

- Be prepared to be frustrated with fruitless searches, but don't let that stop you from continuing.

- Always find and absorb more information than you need. Part of research is to increase your knowledge in the field.

- Skim and scan your sources. You don't need to read the entire article or book if you are only finding specific information. Skimming is a rapid reading of the entire book or article to find out what it says; scanning is a deliberate search for certain ideas or phrases in that source.

- Summarize your information, or paraphrase rather than quote directly. Often this method saves you time. Moreover, it helps reinforce other writing skills, such as diction, expression, and critical thinking.

- Be meticulous in documenting who said or wrote what, and in copying passages from your sources.

Some Don'ts in Research:

- Don't procrastinate. If you wait until the pressure of deadline is upon you, you may panic and rush your work, and do a sloppy job of it.

- Don't merely underline or highlight the information in a book or magazine. You waste time because you will have to go back and do the reading and the note taking.

- Don't photocopy copiously. You waste time and money.

- Don't think that by possessing a photocopy of the information that you have done the research. You still have to read it, digest it, and include it in your essay.

- Don't plagiarize; that is, don't copy someone else's words or ideas and call them your own. Plagiarism is a serious offence and the consequences can be dire.

# Note taking

Use 4" × 5" index cards or separate pieces of paper to record your information.

Always include the specific source of the information in the top of the card or page.

Always note the page where this information is taken.

Designate what is direct quotation and what is paraphrased or summarized.

After completing your research, you can organize these index cards in the form of an outline of your sources.

## FIGURE 8.1 Samples of Research Notes

Foot, *Boom, Bust & Echo 2000*

"Newspaper articles, media pundits, and even Statistics Canada often confuse Generation X with the baby-bust generation that followed it. Even as the millennium looms, the media are still calling Gen-Xers "twenty-somethings" although all of them have celebrated their 30th birthdays." (p. 26)

Foot, *Boom, Bust & Echo 2000*

Gen-Xers are accustomed to waiting in line for everything, from childhood to adulthood: from summer camp to part-time job. (pp. 27–28) paraphrase

# Quoting

Quoting is the direct copying of the phrase, sentence, or passage from the source into your essay. You must copy verbatim—even if the source has a typographical error or incorrect information, you cannot change it. To absolve you from being penalized for such mistake, you can add [*sic*] after the typo. For example, "Prime Minster [*sic*] Pierre Trudeau invoked the War Measures Act."

Quoting lends authenticity to your research. Readers feel secure and confident about your paper when they see that others support or augment your argument. They also come to expect quotations as evidence of your expertise or knowledge of the topic.

Your choice of quotable passages from your source must be apt. Quoting merely to pad the length of your paper is improper. Don't string together passage after passage of quotes. You must include your own words or explanation. Otherwise, your essay is merely raw data, and not a developed, synthesized paper.

Don't misquote; that is, you must not either carelessly copy or deliberately change the passage to suit your argument. Always double check your source for exactness in word and idea.

# Summarizing

Summarizing condenses a large amount of information. It is useful in research, in that you can gather a lot of material from different sources or just from one long source and reduce it to the essentials. For example, you have read three books on a topic and discover that all three texts say the same thing. You can then gather these sources and summarize them quickly. Remember, though, that you must still reference all the sources. See Chapter 7 for more information on summarizing.

# Paraphrasing

Paraphrasing is a method by which you put someone else's words into your own words, instead of quoting the source. You paraphrase when you summarize. You can also paraphrase to simplify the explanation for your readers. In addition, paraphrasing is useful when you want a smooth integration of source material with your own words and ideas. Remember, however, that you must give credit to the original author. You can find examples of paraphrasing in Chapter 7.

# Avoiding plagiarism

In research papers you talk about and quote different writers' ideas. However, if you copy words directly without quoting, or use individual ideas from another author, you cross the line to plagiarism, which is considered a form of cheating. The penalty for plagiarism ranges from receiving a grade of zero for the assignment or failing the course, to being suspended or expelled from the college or university. In the business world, the penalties are as severe. You can be sued for a great sum of money or lose your professional reputation.

You can avoid the charge of plagiarism easily. Be careful; use correct references. If you have found the information from a source, reference it in the essay, and document it in the bibliography. Note that when you paraphrase, or put someone else's words into your own words, you are required to reference the source. If you were to change a few words from a source, you are still using someone else's passage.

Some students have difficulty with the concept of plagiarism because of cultural differences. They may have been taught to write using the words of other writers as models. However, in Canada each professor expects students to hand in assignments written in their own words.

At times, some students may get in trouble for sloppy use of references. You can avoid this problem by diligently keeping track of your sources as you are researching your topic, and by conscientiously placing the references appropriately when you are writing your drafts.

# Choosing information sources

Not all sources are created equal. Successful research includes careful and strategic use of resources. For instance, you may want to start with broad introductions to a topic. An encyclopedia entry might give you the basic facts to start your quest. Then you can move to online sources, books, and journal articles.

You need to find sources that are current, readable, reliable, and complete. Always check the publication date of your source material and make sure that it is not out-of-date. For example, a biography of Winston Churchill written in the late 1940s would not contain the information that he served as Prime Minister of England again in the 1950s. A readable source is one that is at your level and well-written. Do not waste time trying to wade through obscure academic volumes, especially if you are doing only a general-level research paper. Reliability is an important issue for websites. While books from established publishing companies are carefully reviewed and checked, anyone can put up a website without knowing a lot about the topic. Check to see if the website is from a reliable institution such as a university. One way to make sure that your information is correct is to make sure it appears in several different sources; this is not foolproof, however. Completeness of information is also important and, again, checking more than one source is a safeguard against missing something important.

Using several different kinds of resources is important. Don't just stick to one or two books. Find diverse points of view. Read authors who are acknowledged experts in the field; they often have several publications on the same topic and are often mentioned in other books and articles. Try to find the most recent articles and books; use their bibliographies to find other books and articles.

Get to know the different Internet search engines and how they work. Each has search tips to make your job easier. You can use Boolean operators to narrow your field: "and" narrows a search by making the search engine look for more than one key word; "or" is used for alternative keywords; and "not" eliminates words from your search. For instance, if you wanted to find information on the python, you should add the word "snake" to eliminate hits on the Python programming language and the Monty Python comedy troupe. Your success depends on what keywords you use. Try to narrow the field by using a very specific keyword.

# Evaluating your information

Because there is so much information available, you may find it difficult to decide which is the better source or expert opinion, or to identify a proper source. While there is no fool-proof method, here are some suggestions:

- The writer is an acknowledged expert in the field.

- The publisher of the text or article is reputable.

- The information can be verified or authenticated with a different source or another source.

- Other writers have used this source to support their ideas or argument.

- As you go deeper into your research with other references, you find this source reliable.

- With online research, the source of the website is reliable. For example, if the article comes from a professor in the appropriate department from a reputable university, the information is more likely to be reliable, valid.

As you do more research projects, you should sharpen your skill in evaluating your information and sources. Develop that "sixth sense" in your feeling that information "has the ring of truth in it."

# Citation

Each of your references must be carefully documented. Some references are included in the text of your paper when you quote or refer to another work. The traditional style was to put these citations in footnotes. Now, however, they are more commonly found in parentheses. The word "footnote" is so established that some people use it even when they are actually referring to endnotes or citations in parentheses. In addition to the references within the text itself, there is a bibliography page at the end of your research paper. Here you include all the sources used, some of which you may not have directly referred to in your paper. You may cite online/Internet material, books, magazines, newspapers, CD-ROMs, and interviews.

We recommend that you document your references according to the style preferred by your institution. In a college or university, this may even vary from department to department, school to school. Essentially, do what the professors or your supervisors want. If they don't specify, choose the one the school prefers.

There are various ways to cite your sources of information. However, the three most popular are Modern Languages Association (MLA), American Psychological Association (APA), and the Chicago Manual of Style. Citation from Internet sources is varied. Because of the relative newness of the medium, you will find no standardized method of citation yet.

Accuracy, consistency, and completeness in referencing and in the bibliography are important.

## Referencing in the essay

When you quote a passage or incorporate ideas from a source, you need to show where you have taken the information. Generally, the citation immediately follows the paraphrase or quotation.

### MLA

The MLA style is preferred by humanities and arts faculties. Referencing in the essay is simple. In parentheses, you give the page number, if you have identified the author in the sentence. If you haven't included the author, then you will need to add the author's last name before the page reference in parentheses.

> According to Kurt Wiesenfeld, students see a college degree as merchandise, much as a consumer who pays for a toaster would. (250)

> Accordingly, students see a college degree as merchandise, much as a consumer who pays for a toaster would. (Wiesenfeld 250)

Here is an extended example of MLA documentation:

> Most Canadians know Laura Secord as a corporate icon for a chain of candy stores, and see her only as a delicate and elegant nineteenth-century ingenue in a cameo portrait. In 1913, Senator Frank O'Connor, a Toronto business entrepreneur, decided to use the picture of Laura Secord to promote his stores (Boulton, 53). The first portrait to grace the Laura Secord Candy Store chain was that of an elderly woman. That was the only

actual picture of the Canadian heroine left in existence. However, according to Stephen Smith, Laura became progressively younger and sexier with each make-over of her portrait in the stores. "The Laura who greets you in stores today is robust, a woman who looks to have been raised on a diet of red meat, wine, and beaches. This is a Laura to be reckoned with, a Laura of maraschino lips and manifest cleavage, a siren Laura to seduce the unsuspecting customer with the lure of Jellifruits." (266) The hard life of a pioneer woman becomes transformed into that of a high society lady who appreciates the finer things of life. Could the average Canadian imagine such a young beauty in fineries climbing over fallen logs, sinking ankle-deep in bogs, and scaling treacherous hillsides without breaking a fingernail, without some mud on her face? Would the Canadian consumers care about historical accuracy as they bite into a Laura Secord chocolate?

Boulton, Marsha. "Without a Cow, " in *Just a Minute: Glimpses of Our Great Canadian Heritage.* Toronto: Little, Brown and Company (Canada) Ltd., 1994, pp. 51-53

Smith, Stephen. "Like Raptor for Chocolate," in *Reader's Choice, Second Canadian Edition* by Flachmann et al. (ed.) Scarborough: Prentice-Hall, 1997, pp. 264-267

## APA

The APA style is preferred in social sciences, sciences, and technology. Referencing differs slightly from the MLA method. In parenthesis, you enter only the year of publication right after you have identified the author in the sentence. If you haven't included the author, then you will need to add the author's last name and a comma before the year reference in parenthesis. Authorless entries use the title (or part of the title) as reference.

According to Kurt Wiesenfeld (1995), students see a college degree as merchandise, much as a consumer who pays for a toaster would.

Accordingly, students see a college degree as merchandise, much as a consumer who pays for a toaster would. (Wiesenfeld, 1995)

Here is an extended example of APA documentation:

Laura Ingersoll Secord is an authentic Canadian heroine. She was born in Great Barrington, Massachusetts, (*Canadian Encyclopedia*, 1988). Her parents, the Ingersolls, moved to

Upper Canada after the American Revolution to take advantage of inexpensive land (Basset and Petrie, 1981). She married James Secord, a local merchant, and had five children. During the War of 1812, her husband was seriously wounded at Queenston Heights, and Laura went to the battlefield to find him. The Secords were forced to billet American troops, and Laura overheard the plans of Gyrenius Chapin, the American commander, to lead a surprise attack on the British under the command of Lieut. James FitzGibbon, (*Path*). Because of her husband's wounds, Laura decided to go herself to warn FitzGibbon. On June 22, 1813, she began her historic trek of 32 kilometres. Originally, she was accompanied by Elizabeth Secord, her sister-in-law. However, when Elizabeth faltered from exhaustion, Laura continued the journey herself. In late evening, she reached the DeCew house, where FitzGibbon was posted and, with the help of Indian allies, she was able to warn him. Assisted by the Mohawks and Caughnawagas, FitzGibbon routed the Americans at the Battle of Beaver Dams on June 24, 1813, (*Path*). The British commander attributed the victory to Laura Secord. Indeed, according to historians, Laura Secord risked her life and saved Canada from becoming American.

"A Path to FitzGibbon" Online.
<http://www.flarc.edu.on.ca/~olmc/secord/FitzGibbon.html> May 20, 1999.

Bassett, John and Roy Petrie. *Laura Secord.* Don Mills: Fitzhenry & Whiteside, Ltd., 1981.

Boulton, Marsha. "Without a Cow, " in *Just a Minute: Glimpses of Our Great Canadian Heritage.* Toronto: Little, Brown and Company (Canada) Ltd., 1994, pp. 51-53

"Secord, Laura." *The Canadian Encyclopedia*, 2nd Ed. Vol. 3., Edmonton: Hurtig Publishers, 1988, p. 1972.

## Chicago Manual of Style

The Chicago Manual may be used in high schools. However, it is generally considered to be an outdated and more complicated system.
Here is a brief example:

Accordingly, students see a college degree as merchandise, much as a consumer who pays for a toaster would.(1)

1. Kurt Wiesenfeld, "Making the Grade," *Newsweek* (June 17, 1996), p. 16.

# Bibliographies

All research papers must have a bibliography, or a list of the sources used in researching the topic. The bibliography page is always a separate page that follows the last page of the essay. You list your sources so that someone else interested in your topic can use your bibliography; so that a scholar might check and validate your information; and so that you give credit where credit is due.

All bibliographical data follow established patterns for articles, books, and Internet sources (with some variances).

## MLA

In listing your citations and research material, the MLA prefers that section to be called "Works Consulted/Cited."

Note the indentation for the second and subsequent lines of information.

### Books

Alphabetical order by last name of the author. *Title of book (in italics).* Place of publication: Publisher, Date of publication.

Gordon, Stuart. *The Book of Hoaxes.* London: Headline Book Publishing, 1995.
Walker, Barbara G. *The Woman's Dictionary of Symbols & Sacred Objects.* New York: Harper Collins, 1988.

If the authorship is unknown or unnecessary, then begin with the title of the book or article:

*The Canadian Encyclopedia.* 2nd ed. Edmonton: Hurtig Publishers, 1988.

### Articles

Alphabetical order by last name of the author. "Title of the article (in quotations)." *Title of periodical (in italics).* Volume and date. Pages.

Barber, John. "How isolation has bred our uncivil society," *The Globe and Mail.* (Saturday, Oct. 31, 1998), D7.

Gordon, Charles. "When bigger is not necessarily better," *Maclean's,* (Oct. 20, 1997), 11.

### Online sources

Alphabetical order by last name of the author or by "title of the article (in quotations)." *Title of the site* (underlined or italicized). The publication medium (online). Date of access. The electronic address.

"A Brief History of Laura Secord." *Laura Secord Homestead.* Online. May 18, 1999. <http://niagaraparks.com/historical/ls-history.html>

Muir, Elaine. "The Courage of Laura Secord." Online. May 18, 1999. <http://hal9000.wsdl.winnipeg.mb.ca/nnl/laura_s/lauhist.htm>

## APA

In listing your citations and research material, the APA prefers the section to be called "References."

Note that the first line is indented, and the second and subsequent lines are not.

## Books

Alphabetical order by last name of the author. Date of publication. *Title of book (in italics).* Place of publication: publisher.

Gordon, S. (1995). *The book of hoaxes.* London: Headline Books Publishing.

Walker, B.G. (1988). *The woman's dictionary of symbols & sacred objects.* New York: Harper Collins.

If the authorship is unknown or unnecessary, then begin with the title of the book or article:

*The Canadian Encyclopedia.* 2nd ed.(1988). Edmonton: Hurtig Publishers.

## Articles

Alphabetical order by last name of the author. Initials of given names. (Year of publication followed by date in parentheses). Title of the article without capitalizing all subsequent words. *Title of the magazine or periodical (in italics),* page references.

Barber, J. (1998, Oct. 31). How isolation has bred our uncivil society, *The Globe and Mail,* p. D7.

Gordon, C. (1997, Oct. 20). When bigger is not necessarily better, *Maclean's,* 11.

## Online sources

Alphabetical order by last name of the author. Initials of given names. (Year of publication followed by date in parentheses). Title of the article without capitalizing all subsequent words. The publication medium (online). The electronic address. Date of access.

A brief history of Laura Secord. *Laura Secord Homestead.* Online. <http://niagaraparks.com/historical/ls-history.html> May 20, 1999.

Muir, E. The courage of Laura Secord. Online. <http://hal9000.wsdl.winnipeg.mb.ca/nnl/laura_s/lauhist.htm> May 19, 1999.

## ASSIGNMENTS

1.  Select one of the documentation methodologies: MLA, APA, or Chicago. Choose a topic and find three different sources for that topic. For each source, cite a short passage from it, and paraphrase another. Reference each source, both quotation and paraphrase. Write up a bibliography, using the three sources of information.

2.  Using all three sources and information from the above exercise, write a paragraph. Select one of the documentation methodologies. Reference your sources in the paragraph.

## SUMMARY

# *Research checklist*

- Do you have a variety of sources—books, articles, web pages—by different authors and with different viewpoints?

- Did you accurately reference all quotations and ideas from other authors?

- Are quotations clearly marked with quotation marks or as indented blocks?

- Are your citations accurate and complete? Do they follow an approved style?

- Do you avoid excessive quoting?

- Is your essay formatted correctly and does it include a title page and a bibliography page? (see page 225 for formatting guidelines)

- Is your essay concise and clear?

- Did you check for spelling and grammar mistakes?

## CHAPTER 9

# Oral Presentations

Because oral presentations are so important in the work world, many college English courses include speaking activities. You may be asked to participate in group discussions or present a topic to an audience; you may deliver an impromptu talk or a formal speech.

In general, oral presentations follow the structure of good writing: a beginning, a middle, and an end. In other words, you tell the readers what you are going to tell them (the subject or topic), actually tell them (supporting ideas), and tell them what you have told them (the conclusion). Like writing, an oral report makes ideas and information accessible and clear to the audience.

Moreover, like an essay, a presentation must be carefully planned. First, consider your audience and purpose. For example, on the topic of the fairy tale Sleeping Beauty, you would not go into a psychological and sexual analysis to a group of children, but you probably would if you were talking to college students taking child psychology. Secondly, choose a topic of interest. "How to buy a home computer" may not be as interesting to a group of computer-science students as to a gathering of parents. Thirdly, do your research. Even a simple topic like "How we celebrate Chinese New Year" can be enhanced with information from books on the significance of customs or through an interview with older relatives to show how customs have changed.

In some ways, oral presentations are different from written documents. Instead of someone reading your words, you have an audience in front of you listening as you deliver your words. Thus, you have the opportunity to gauge your listeners' reactions as you see their facial expressions. This visual contact gives you immediate feedback. If your listeners don't seem to understand something, you can ad lib an explanation or spend more time on the concept.

Your delivery is critical. Even if the speech is read or memorized, it should sound relatively natural. You modulate pitch and tone, so that your delivery has a rhythm and flow. A flat, monotone delivery puts listeners to sleep.

Body language is an important part of your presentation. For example, your posture tells your audience how relaxed you are. Stand straight but not stiff, and don't slouch. Looking confident makes you feel confident. Don't fidget: Watching a speaker shift from foot to foot or shuffle paper is distracting.

You must make eye contact as much as possible with your listeners. Don't look at just one person or at just one part of the room—it will make other members of the audience feel left out. In some cultures, making eye contact with people is considered rude, but in North American culture a failure to make eye contact makes the speaker look untrustworthy.

Before you deliver your speech or presentation, rehearse until you know the content and have a definite flow in your delivery. Rehearsing is preparing both mentally and physically. Check the pronunciation of unfamiliar words and names, and practise them so that you do not stumble over them. The more confidence you develop as you practise, the less nervous and distracted you will be when the actual presentation is at hand. You can practise your speech with family or friends, or in front of a mirror. You can tape your presentation so that you can evaluate your voice quality.

Try to relax. Many people fear public speaking, but the more relaxed you are, the more successful your speech will be. The better prepared you are, the more confident you will feel.

The protocol for an oral presentation differs from the conventions of an essay. You should have prefatory remarks, such as acknowledging your audience ("Good afternoon, ladies and gentlemen.") In an essay you should never say, "Today I am going to tell you about. . ." but this kind of opening style is expected in speeches.

Unlike the oratorial style of the 19th century, which favoured long, complex rhetorical devices, a more conversational style is common today, even in business presentations. The degree of formality depends on the situation and the subject matter. For example, a speech on deaths caused by medical mistakes should be given in a more formal tone than a talk on finger painting as a relaxation technique. You will probably have a chance to hear others' presentations before you are called upon to do one yourself. Theirs should give you an idea of what works and what doesn't.

You can get more tips about public speaking on the Internet. You can even read and listen to sample speeches. Try searching for "public speaking" and "oral presentations."

# Equipment

For your presentation you might use equipment and props, such as blackboards, whiteboards, photographs, overheads, computer graphics, and handouts. It is important to use these aids effectively. For example, you should never just read aloud what you have written on overheads or in handouts. Do not make your audience wait while you cover the blackboard with notes. Use the whiteboard to write down proper names or words your audience may not know. Don't get carried away with the bells and whistles of your software and ignore the content. If you give your audience a book or picture to pass around, they will be distracted and not give your speech full attention. Visual aids are important, but they must be used effectively.

# Evaluation

In assessing your performance, your instructor will probably pay attention to content, delivery, body language, and audience rapport.

Content is not simply a matter of giving out information. Your instructor will be looking at how well you have researched your topic and how well you explain your ideas. Some of this will be revealed in audience questions. The amount of interest in your topic can usually be determined by the reactions of the audience: Are they paying attention or looking bored?

Delivery can make or break a presentation. Your instructor might sit farthest away from you to make sure your voice carries far enough. You may also be graded on your pronunciation: Your accent does not have to be perfect, but your words must be comprehensible. You will also be judged on how natural and relaxed you sound.

Body language reveals much about you to the audience. Your instructor will observe how you stand in front of the class as you talk. The involuntary movements or gestures you make with your hands, face, and feet may distract your audience. Gazing at the ceiling or staring down at the floor instead of making eye contact gives the impression that you are talking at, rather than to, your audience.

Finally, the way you answer questions from the audience is an important part of the presentation. Your instructor wants to know how well you can field questions. Make sure you understand exactly what is being asked and address it directly.

Your instructor may give you an evaluation checklist to help you prepare your presentation. We have included one at the end of this chapter. Knowing the elements that are the focus of evaluation can help you prepare and deliver your presentation.

# The importance of the audience

The audience is a vital part of an oral presentation. It defeats the whole purpose if there is no audience—speakers need the experience of facing other people and of interacting with them. For the audience, listening to speeches is an important learning opportunity. As a listener, you can learn what makes a successful presentation as you evaluate your classmates' work. You also learn from the content of the talk. To be a good listener, be attentive and don't disrupt a presentation by coming in late or by talking to your classmates. Ask useful questions.

# Improving your speaking skills

While it seems that some people are born with the gift of gab and the ability to address a group eloquently, everyone can improve with practice. If you have a fear of speaking in public, start small by participating in class discussion and asking questions in class. Look for opportunities to speak, such as discussion groups and debating clubs. You can join organizations such as Toastmasters, where you learn about public speaking and participate in a variety of speaking activities, such as small group discussion and impromptu talks.

If English is your second language, you may have to force yourself to find opportunities to speak English. Don't spend all your time talking with family and friends who share your native language. Some schools have ESL conversation clubs.

You may feel self-conscious about your accent and pronunciation, but one of the advantages of living in a multicultural society is that people are generally used to hearing English spoken with a foreign accent. There is no real stigma attached to having an accent; however, comprehensibility is vital. Concentrate on making your pronunciation understandable.

SUMMARY

# *Preparing an oral presentation*

1. Choose a topic you are comfortable with and one that will be interesting to your audience.
2. Research the topic.
3. Decide on the main message of your speech.
4. Organize your points and write an outline.
5. Practise and edit your speech. Make sure it fits time constraints.
6. Write your outline on index cards.
7. Prepare audio-visual aids (overhead transparencies, computer slides, or handouts). If you plan to use the blackboard or a flip chart in the room, decide what you need to write.
8. Rehearse.

# *Evaluation checklist*

- Is the presentation easy to hear and understand?
- Is the intonation pleasant to listen to—not flat or monotonous, but not overly emphatic either?
- Is the presenter's posture good—neither slouching nor standing too stiffly?
- Does the presenter sound relaxed?
- Does the speaker make eye contact with the audience?
- Does the speaker use gestures appropriately?
- Does the presenter speak fluently?
- Does the presentation sound natural—or is it read aloud or overly memorized?
- Did the speaker introduce himself and his topic?
- Is the topic interesting and informative?
- Are the speaker's points clear and easy to follow?
- Is the talk well organized?
- Are the speaker's grammar, use of vocabulary, and pronunciation correct?
- Are important names, dates, and figures written on the board, on an overhead, on the slide, or in a handout?

# Beyond Academic Writing

After you graduate from school, you will rarely be called upon to write an essay. Prospective employers might ask you to write one to demonstrate your writing ability and communication skills when you apply for a job, but other opportunities to demonstrate your essay-writing ability will be few and far between, unless you become a professional writer. Nevertheless, the skills that you develop as you learn to write a good essay will always be useful to you. Mastering the paragraph and the essay gives you the groundwork to build upon as you move to the work world.

Learning to write well gives you more than the ability to put words on a page. It develops your ability to think clearly, concisely, and precisely. You learn to organize ideas logically and coherently. It gives you the capacity to research and analyze, to persuade and compare, and to express yourself. It even makes you appreciate language and the art of communication. In short, the act of writing develops your thinking skills.

In this chapter we show how academic writing relates to other kinds of writing, such as business letters and reports. You will find that writing a well-structured report is not very different from writing an essay. Content, clarity and conciseness are important in all kinds of writing.

## Business letters

Time is money to business people, so they like letters and memos to be clear and concise. They want to know from the first paragraph what the letter is about. If, for example, the matter would be better resolved by another person in the company, they can redirect the letter. In effect, the first paragraph of the business letter is like a thesis, giving the main idea.

# FIGURE 10.1 Sample of a Business Letter

100 Saddleback Road
Edmonton, Alberta
T6E 4I8

April 12, 2001

Ferdinand Winters
Videos Galore
109-82nd Avenue
Edmonton, Alberta
T8N 3R5

Dear Mr. Winters:

I am applying for the position of cashier/assistant manager at Videos Galore, advertised in *The Edmonton Journal* today.

My previous work experience fits your requirements. As cashier/server at BurgerLords, I know how to use computerized cash registers and how to deal with cash and credit cards. In addition, I have learned how to handle all kinds of customers in a professional manner. At All-Nyter Convenience Shoppe, I had the opportunity to manage the entire store by myself during the graveyard shifts.

I have been taking part-time courses at Edmonton Business College, and I am almost finished earning a business diploma. I am trained in accounting and am familiar with most of the popular software packages.

In addition, I have been an avid fan of classic films, music videos and other contemporary movies since I was ten years old. Over the years, I have accumulated as much knowledge of the cinema as some critics and movie reviewers on television. This knowledge, I believe, can be quite useful in your store when customers come and ask for suggestions or suitability of the rentals.

My résumé is enclosed. I am available for an interview, and I can supply references. I look forward to hearing from you.

Sincerely,

Siobhan Jones
enc.: résumé

There are many kinds of business letters. Large corporations use mass distribution of letters to inform customers of new products. With the help of technology, now such "junk mail" can be personalized. Other popular uses of the letter are the application, in which you can apply for various jobs and positions, and the complaint letter, in which you voice your concern or disapproval of a product or service. You may even wish to write to your member of parliament either in support of or against government policies. Moreover, you may feel strongly enough about an issue that you would write to a newspaper's editorial page.

Business-letter style varies from culture to culture. In Asian cultures, for example, you might read a business letter that starts with a personal introduction. You might find that the writer never comes to the point and goes about elliptically in the entire letter. The North American method, however, is direct, straightforward, and lean. Its premise is that the reader should not have to waste time and effort in deciphering the writer's message.

Paragraphs tend to be relatively short in business letters. Ideas should be organized so that each paragraph has one main idea. In a job application letter, for example, experience could be in one paragraph and education in another.

# Memos

The word *memo* is short for *memorandum,* or a brief written message to remind you and others of what has been discussed or what will be done in the near future. It can be as brief as a few scribbled words or as long as several typed pages. It can be informally or formally written, but usually short ones are informal and longer ones are formal. While a business letter is written to someone outside the company, the memo is a piece of internal communication within a place of work.

Like all business writing, a memo must inform with the fewest number of words. In short, it is like a telegram: brief, to the point, clear (see Figure 10.2).

FIGURE 10.2    Sample of a Memo

---

| MEMO |
| --- |
| **To:** Suneel Nair<br>**From:** Allyson Pip<br>**Date:** June 1, 2000<br>**Subject:** Computer training<br><br>Now that the new software packages have been installed and tested, we can extend the training program. I posted the schedule of workshops in the staff room. I have asked anyone who cannot make the scheduled times to contact you. Keep a list of names and workshop requests. If there is enough demand, we can add workshops. If not, you and I could fill in gaps with personal tutoring.<br><br>Thanks.<br>Allyson |

# E-mail messages

E-mail (electronic mail) is like a written conversation. It is informal and the recipient often uses bits of the sender's message in the reply. E-mail messages look very much like memos.

Some people want to take short cuts when they send e-mail messages. They use no capital letters—or, even worse, all capital letters—and improper punctuation, such as ellipses instead of commas and periods. However, e-mail messages are easier to read if they follow conventions and use proper form (see Figure 10.3).

Just because an e-mail message is less formal than a business letter on letterhead stationery, it does not mean it should not follow conventions of language. As teachers, we have received many e-mail messages from students asking us to reconsider failing grades on English courses; these messages are often written with poor grammar, spelling, and punctuation—not pleading well for their case at all.

New formatting options allow senders to use different fonts, choose "stationery" as backgrounds, and include graphics and audio clips. Despite the trappings, an e-mail message is primarily to communicate something, so the rules of good writing (content, clarity and conciseness) still hold.

## FIGURE 10.3    Sample of an E-mail

---

**From:** hfenton@howdy.ca
**Date:** January 24, 2002
**To:** lvernicky@howdy.ca
**Subject: Report**

Here's the report you wanted. We can use it as a basis for the project report, but the specifications will be completely out of date.


>
lvernicky@howdy.ca wrote:
>
>Harcourt,
>
>Could you send me a copy of that Barclay report you mentioned in the meeting yesterday? >Thanks.
>
>Lucinda

 Barclay.doc

Name: Barclay.doc
Type: Microsoft Word Document (application/msword)
Encoding: x-uuencode

---

Another consideration that applies to electronic communication is the use of the previous message in the text of the reply. While the previous message can serve as a good reminder of what the original sender said, keep your message clearly distinguishable from the text of the old message. You might also want to edit the quotes so the new e-mail message does not become too long.

The word *e-mail* itself is controversial. It is new to the English language, so different forms exist: E-mail, e-mail, and email. After a while, one form will emerge as the standard. In the meantime, choose which form you like and be consistent. E-mail, like mail, is considered to be an uncountable noun, so it is more proper to say "many e-mail messages" rather than "many e-mails." However, many people choose the shorter form and this is will probably be considered acceptable by all except the strictest grammarians. The word is also becoming a verb, so someone might ask you to "e-mail me."

# Reports

Business reports are closer in style to academic essays than to letters and articles. Most reports are formal in language and structure. They have a set pattern, depending on the company's preferences. They may include

  title page

  summary or abstract

  table of contents

  introduction

  subtitles

  recommendations

  conclusion

  appendices

  documentation

Reports can be as short as a few pages or as long as several volumes. For example, Canada's royal commission inquiries often exceed 1000 pages. Whether you must produce a lengthy or short piece to inform a CEO, the writing style is quite formal, just as in academic writing.

The summary is an important part of any report. It gives a brief but comprehensive overview of the content. For upper management, this summary is often the only page read; therefore, this portion of the report must be concise and informative. Your ability to condense information is critical.

# Journalistic articles

Newspaper and magazine articles are organized differently than essays. Because they are printed in columns, paragraphs are short to aid readability. In other words, these forms of writing do not have developed paragraphs. News reports begin with the five W's—who, when, where, what, and why—in the first two or three short paragraphs. Thereafter, the news item gives details, quotations, and accounts. It does not have a conclusion because the editor determines the column length and may lop off paragraphs at the end to make it fit the available space.

News stories tend to follow a spiral pattern. The headline tells the main idea in a few words. Headlines are in telegraph style—they lack articles and full verb forms. Then the first paragraph or two tells the story again in few words. The rest of the story tells the story again, this time adding details. Readers can just read the headline or the beginning. They can stop reading when they think they know enough, and they will usually not miss anything vital.

Magazine articles are different. Unlike the news item, the magazine article does have an introduction and a conclusion. A common opening to magazine stories is to tell a personal story, and then to move on to the general facts. This method catches the reader's interest by tapping into the average reader's experience or feelings. Titles are often provocative as well. Magazine articles offer more analysis and exploration of a topic than news stories do.

Although many of the reading selections in Part III are from newspapers and magazines, they are not news stories. Many of them are op-ed (opinion and editorial) pieces, which are like personal essays. You can compare those readings to current news stories that show the spiral organization.

# Brochures and pamphlets

Brochures and pamphlets promote a business or disseminate information. They vary from glossy booklets to simple, folded pieces of paper. For example, the federal, provincial, and municipal governments publish brochures and pamphlets to inform the average citizen about government services and programmes. During elections, candidates running for office will distribute information and ask for voters' support with pamphlets and flyers. Similarly, companies use brochures to advertise products and services.

Because the space is limited, the writing must be concise. Bulleted lists are common. For sales brochures, the language must be descriptive and enticing in order to sell the product. In other words, this type of writing is very different from academic writing. Writers need special skills to produce good advertising copy.

# Newsletters

Like brochures and pamphlets, the newsletter is a popular method to dispense information. It is inexpensive and easy to distribute. School principals use newsletters to inform parents about upcoming events. Pharmacies now include helpful information along with prescription drugs, explaining side effects and dosage. Fan clubs have always depended on the newsletter to keep members up to date about their favourite musician, movie star, TV personality, or author. Activist groups bring public awareness to their particular special interests.

The ability to explain things clearly and concisely will come in handy for newsletter writing. Ideas must be effectively organized.

## A S S I G N M E N T

Collect samples of the documents mentioned in this chapter and bring them to class. In groups, compare the kinds of messages. Discuss the format, organization, and language used. How are these documents similar to and different from academic essays?

# PART 2

# Tools

## CHAPTER 11

# A Word about Grammar

Grammar is, believe it or not, a contentious issue. Instructors argue about how to teach grammar, what terminology to use, and even whether to teach it or not. Complicating the issue is the fact that some students know nothing about traditional grammar rules yet write well. Native speakers may be unable to tell you what transitive verbs are but they can use them correctly in a sentence. On the other hand, some ESL students ace grammar tests but cannot apply their knowledge to their writing.

Grammarians seek to explain how a language works, but language is self-regulating. Languages exist just fine without grammar rules written down. This does not mean that you can ignore any rule you don't like. Language depends on mutually agreed upon conventions. In the book *Through the Looking Glass*, Humpty Dumpty tells Alice, "When *I* use a word…it means just what I choose it to mean—neither more nor less." However, if you act like Humpty Dumpty, you risk a breakdown in communication or making a poor impression professionally or socially.

Another problem is that there are different varieties of English and different ideas of what is correct. In school and work, you are expected to write in standard English. However, in speech you use dialect forms and a conversational style that might "break" traditional grammar rules. We discuss the question of style in Chapter 13, but the issue of correctness goes beyond difference in style. Language is not black and white; sometimes the answer to "Is this correct?" is "It depends."

You also have to contend with different terminology used in different textbooks. For instance, the present progressive tense is the same as the present continuous. The small words in phrasal verbs (like the *up* in "listen up") might be called prepositions, adverbials, or particles. We have used traditional terminology in this book because it is what most students have been exposed to. However, we recognize that it may not be the best way to describe English.

Languages constantly evolve and change. There was never a pure and perfect form of any language. What is considered right and wrong can change over the space of a few years. For example, the use of progressive tenses in English has increased over the last two or three hundred years. In Shakespeare's play *Hamlet* (written in 1603), Polonius sees Hamlet reading and asks, "What do you read, my lord?" Today, it would be more likely for him to say "What are you reading?" Grammar books written fifty years ago might caution against using progressive tenses for verbs like "think" and "wonder," yet this usage is becoming more popular. Another change in grammar is the form of questions. English speakers used to say sentences like "Saw you the girl?" instead of "Did you see the girl?"

What this means for you as a student is that you may get conflicting advice. What you have been taught in one English course may differ from what you are taught in another. However, English teachers agree on more than they disagree on, so this is a minor problem. The best rule of thumb is to go with whatever your current instructor says. Your instructor may even disagree with some of the advice we give in this book. It's the same situation in the work world: You will find supervisors who have different ways of doing things, and you must adapt to and follow your current supervisor's preferences.

And sometimes the best advice is "don't sweat the small stuff." In other words, don't worry about knowing all the grammar rules. If you can't tell the difference between a gerund and a participle, it does not really matter as long as you can write correct sentences with gerunds and participles. We tell you the difference so that, if you are having a problem using them correctly, you can better understand what the problem is. And if you are an ESL student trying to get a grip on the complexities of English usage, you should concentrate on major areas, such as sentence structure and the correct use of verb tenses, and give less attention to minor, but problematic, areas such as article use. An incorrect article will usually not make your sentence incomprehensible, but an improper verb tense can make it difficult for the reader to understand your meaning. This does not mean that you should just ignore the rules for article use, just that you should not worry yourself into a panic over them. Much of the usage is idiomatic, and you will gradually get a better sense of articles.

# Contentious grammar rules

Some of the most commonly quoted grammar rules are actually contentious, or just plain wrong. People refer to rules they may have learned in school without realizing that they no longer apply. Here is what you should know about these common "rules."

## Don't end a sentence with a preposition.

While there are some sentences that sound awkward if they end with a preposition, this rule is not really a rule of English. This "rule" was established in the 18th century, when grammar books and dictionaries were being written for English, and some scholars used Latin as a model. English, however, is a Germanic language, and does not have Latin-style sentence structure. For example, English has phrasal verbs, such as "get up." Even though some will argue that the word *up* is not really a preposition (see, we warned you grammar was complicated), sentences with phrasal verbs might require that the preposition appear at the end. So, don't go to awkward lengths to try to follow this "rule." The most famous rejoinder to this rule is attributed to Winston Churchill: "that is the type of nonsense up with which I will not put" (which would more naturally appear as "the type of nonsense I will not put up with").

## Don't split an infinitive.

Splitting an infinitive means putting words between the *to* and the base verb form. One of the most famous examples of breaking this "rule" is in the introduction to *Star Trek* shows: "to boldly go where no one has gone before." Again, the basis of this "rule" is Latin, which has one-word infinitives, so the problem does not appear. You don't have to worry about following this rule at all. If you write a sentence where an adverb seems to fit best in the middle of the infinitive, use that structure.

## Don't start sentences with co-ordinate conjunctions: *and, or, but, yet, so.*

Here's a rule that we've broken often in this textbook. Some teachers will be quite fussy about this rule, while others will not care at all. If you are writing in formal, academic English, it is best to avoid starting sentences with co-ordinate conjunctions. These sentences give writing a conversational tone. However, if you are writing in a more casual style, go ahead and start a sentence with *and, but,* or *so.* But don't do it too often.

### Don't use *hopefully* as an adverb describing the whole sentence.

Some grammarians don't accept sentences such as "Hopefully, it won't rain." The argument is that a person can be full of hope, but a subject like *it* can't hope. However, it is very difficult to get around this construction. "I hope it won't rain" does not quite give the same meaning. "It is hoped that it won't rain" is awkward. Our advice is to ignore this rule. You probably won't use "hopefully" very often in academic writing anyway.

### Don't use "it is because" or "it is when."

The formal grammar rule says that copula verbs like *to be* should not be completed by a subordinate clause. This rule seems destined to change because almost everybody speaks with these types of sentences. We ask our students not to do this in their academic writing, however. ESL students, especially, seem to over-use this structure, perhaps to avoid writing a complex sentence. Instead of writing "Michael is sad. It is because his dog died," write "Michael is sad because his dog died."

### Don't start a sentence with *because.*

We've never seen this rule in a grammar book, but some of our students have told us they were taught this. We conclude that some teachers tell students this so that they will not write sentence fragments that start with *because.* However, sentences that start with *because* are correct, but sometimes awkward, as long as they have a main clause. A sentence like "Because the propane tank was empty." is incorrect because it is an incomplete sentence. However, "Because the propane tank was empty, we couldn't start the barbecue." is correct.

### Don't use *their* with singular subject.

You will often hear people saying sentences such as "Everyone should bring their umbrellas." This is considered incorrect because *everyone* is singular while *their* (the possessive pronoun) is plural. However, "Everyone should bring his umbrella" sounds sexist even though it is grammatically correct. "Everyone should bring his or her umbrella" is awkward. While we caution our students to avoid this structure in academic writing, we acknowledge that this form is on the verge on being accepted. It has also been around for a long time, showing up in the works of 19th century writers like Jane Austen and Charles Dickens.

# Common grammar problems

Even though there are some "rules" of English that are not really rules at all, we can identify several problem areas in students' writing. The common errors pointed out by teachers include problems with

- non-sentences (fragments)

- run-on sentences, including comma splice

- mistakes in agreement (subject-verb and pronoun-antecedent)

- shifts in person, tense, or number

- faulty parallelism

- mistakes in forming plurals, possessives, and contractions

Incomplete sentences (fragments) and comma splices (two sentences joined by a comma) are grammatically incorrect, but some writers use them for effect in less formal styles of writing such as magazine articles. Academic writing should contain proper, complete sentences, so we include these structures as errors.

In addition to these common errors, ESL students have a few other problem areas that are not usually found in native speakers' writing:

- incorrect verb forms and use of tenses

- wrong prepositions

- misuse of articles: *a, an, the*

- incorrect parts of speech

- mistakes in idiomatic English

Some of these problem areas are examined in Chapters 14 and 15.

# Dictionaries and usage and style guides

Dictionaries tell you more than just correct spelling and meaning. They give a lot of grammatical information, such as the part of speech for each entry and irregular forms. Dictionaries for ESL learners generally give more grammar guidance and show how the word is used in a sentence.

Usage and style guides are other handy reference tools. Even professional writers and language teachers often consult such books. *The Ready Reference Handbook,* Canadian Edition, by Jack Dodds and Judi Jewinski (Prentice Hall Canada 1998) is one such usage guide that you may appreciate having on your bookshelf. It goes into more detail than textbooks on writing, like this one, can.

# Using a grammar checker

Word-processing software often includes a grammar check feature in addition to the spelling checker and thesaurus. The problem with using a grammar checker is that you must know something about grammar rules and terminology to get some benefit from it. If you are not sure of what you are doing, a grammar checker may do more harm than good. Of course, the irony is that most people who know grammar rules don't need and don't use computerized grammar checkers.

The other problem is that language is so complicated that computers do not do grammar very well. Some of the suggestions that grammar checkers make are completely wrong. Even with all the incredible advances in computer hardware and software, machines still cannot process natural language as well as humans.

Grammar checkers are good for some things. For example, if you use too many passive constructions, the check will help you to spot them. If your sentences are fairly straightforward, the computer program may pinpoint errors.

If you find a grammar checker useful, use it. But don't expect it to solve your grammar problems for you and don't expect it to always be right. You have to rely on your own knowledge and judgement to accept or reject the suggestions made by the grammar program.

| S U M M A R Y |
| --- |

## *How to improve your grammar*

Writing in acceptable standard English takes practice and knowledge of how the language works. Some errors in writing are due to sloppiness and can be easily corrected. Students have to be aware that written English demands more precision and careful use of language than spoken English.

For ESL students, however, grammar is much more complicated. Students must move beyond translating from their native language to being able to produce sentences in the correct English idiom. This takes many years of familiarity with the language.

- Read an article or book for the way it is written, with an eye on grammatical structures.

- Review marked essays carefully. Pay particular attention to grammatical errors you regularly make and correct them.

- Review your knowledge by perusing a grammar handbook occasionally. It may not be exciting reading, but it is certainly useful.

- Use resources such as grammar checkers, dictionaries, and usage guides.

- Teach someone who has even less knowledge of grammar. Teaching forces you to learn, know, and apply the rules so you can help someone else improve. For instance, native speakers have to really think about their language when they try to explain rules and usage to an ESL student.

## CHAPTER 12

# The Words We Use

Words are the writer's tools. The larger your vocabulary, the more you can control shades of meaning. Moreover, you can use synonyms, words that mean almost the same thing, to vary your wording and make your writing more interesting. For example, in this paragraph we used both *words* and *vocabulary*—two synonyms. *Vocabulary*, unlike *words*, is an uncountable noun and therefore not generally used in the plural.

Because of its history, English has a huge vocabulary at the writer's disposal. After the invasion of 1066, England was ruled by French-speaking Normans, and for many years French and English were used side by side. As a result, many French words came into the English language, practically doubling its vocabulary. For instance, the word *help* is Anglo-Saxon (old English) while *aid* is from old French. It is not surprising to find that the names of animals (*cow, calf, sheep*) are English, while the names of the meat (*beef, veal, mutton*) are of French origin; after all, Anglo-Saxon was the language of the farm, French was the language of the castle where the meat was prepared. Even grammar was complicated by this influx of French. English has two ways of expressing comparative adjectives: the *-er* ending and the use of *more*, which is like the French construction *plus* + adjective.

In the 17th century, English also started getting a large number of words from Latin and Greek. Many technical words are based on these two classical languages. For example, the word *television* is from the Greek word *tele* meaning "far" and the Latin word *video* which means "I see." Moreover, this same word, like many based on Latin and Greek, is found in several European languages, as in the French *la télévision*.

Some dictionaries give the etymology of words, telling you whether the word is from Latin, Greek, or Old English. Like all history, etymology is useful knowledge because it helps you see relationships between words. The more connections you have in your brain, the easier it is to understand new information. For example, if you know that the ending *-phobia* is from the Greek word for fear, you can see the connection between words like *claustrophobia* (fear of enclosed places), *agoraphobia* (fear of public places), and *hydrophobia* (fear of water). Thus, whenever you encounter a new word that ends in *-phobia*, you have a vital clue to its meaning.

A C T I V I T Y    **12.1**

Look at the following word groups and identify common roots. Try to figure out what the words mean. Use your dictionary if necessary.

biology, psychology, geology, numerology, graphology, etymology

biology, biography, autobiography

psychology, psychoanalysis, psychosomatic

geology, geography

# Connotation and denotation

Words have layers of meaning. A word may mean the same as another word, and have the same denotation, but have a different connotation or implied meaning. For example, a thin person may be called *thin, skinny, slim, slender, gaunt, lean, scrawny,* or *emaciated.* All these words have the same denotation but different connotations. While *thin* is a fairly neutral adjective, *slim* and *slender* are considered positive words. On the other hand, it would be insulting to refer to someone as *skinny* or *emaciated.* Connotation also depends on the context and how the word is used in a sentence.

Dictionaries include the connotation in the definition of some words. Check your dictionary to see if it marks words as "derogatory," "offensive," or "pejorative." These terms mean that a word is very negative—so use it carefully.

Connotations change over time. A *bachelor* is an unmarried man and a *spinster* is an unmarried woman, but *bachelor* has a much more positive connotation than *spinster.* Since *spinster* is now considered an insulting term, it is rarely used except in legal terminology.

Be aware of a word's connotation when you write. Sometimes a more neutral term is more appropriate than a stronger word. For example, the word *kill* is less accusatory than the word *murder.*

In groups, decide whether the following words are positive, negative, or neutral. Sometimes the connotation depends on context, so you may not always agree with your classmates.

thrifty, stingy, economical, frugal, conserving, generous, spendthrift

aggressive, self-assured, arrogant, confident, proud, pushy

# Idioms

An idiom is an expression, a group of words that has a different meaning than the words have individually. In other words, the figurative meaning is different than the literal meaning. For example, the meanings of the individual words *kick* and *bucket* do not apply to the expression *kick the bucket*, which is an idiom meaning "to die." A similar idiom with the same meaning is *bought the farm.* These idioms are not polite expressions, in contrast to euphemisms, which are nice or polite ways of saying something. It would be polite to say your grandmother "passed away," but not to say she "kicked the bucket." Of course, the meaning of the term depends on the context. The speaker might actually be referring to someone actually kicking a bucket or buying a farm.

The words *literal* and *figurative* are easy to remember and distinguish if you associate *literal* with "letter by letter" (and thus, word by word) and *figurative* with a figure or picture—the idea of the expression as a whole.

Some phrasal verbs are idiomatic. For example, *hang up* is not idiomatic when we refer to clothes being hung up on pegs, but it is an idiom when we refer to someone's fears, as in "She was hung up over the possibility of failure."

Idioms are more common to speech than writing. They are less standardized, so they vary from dialect to dialect. The more idioms you have in your prose, the less formal it is. As a writer, you have to use idioms carefully when you write in more formal styles. If there is a standard term that can be used instead of the idiom, use it.

If you speak English as a second language, you probably want to learn more idioms. One way is just to pay attention when you read or listen to English. Dictionaries usually include idioms, but you can also use an idiom dictionary for a specialized list. Moreover, there are ESL books specifically devoted to idioms. You can also find idioms on the Internet (try "idioms" as an initial search term).

**A C T I V I T Y**    **12.3**

Discuss the following idioms, comparing literal and figurative meaning. Try to find a more formal way of saying the same thing.

Don't <u>beat around the bush</u>.

He's <u>in deep water</u> now.

That <u>rings a bell</u>.

It happens <u>once in a blue moon</u>.

I have <u>a bone to pick with you</u>.

That argument <u>doesn't hold water</u>.

I can <u>kill two birds with one stone</u>.

He's just <u>a wet blanket</u>.

It's a <u>dog-eat-dog</u> world.

She's just <u>pulling your leg</u>.

# Slang

Slang is language that belongs to a particular group—like teenagers or jazz musicians—and goes in and out of use very quickly. For example, something good might have been described as "the cat's pyjamas" in the 1920s, "groovy" in the 1960s, "awesome" in the 1980s, and "bad" in the 1990s. Slang also varies according to region. Australian English, for instance, has very different slang words than Canadian English.

Slang is part of group identification and can sound "wrong" when used by someone who is not a member of the group. For example, a middle-aged man who tries to talk or dress like his teenage son may be ridiculed. In the same way, it sometimes sounds odd when non-native speakers use slang expressions. Moreover, it is easy to use a slang term inappropriately. So ESL students should avoid using too much slang.

Slang changes so fast that it is impossible to keep up with it. Dictionaries of slang are rapidly out-of-date, but they are good to show you the history of a slang term. Try looking for glossaries of current slang on the Internet. Use the word "slang" as an initial search term.

Some slang terms survive and move into informal language. The words *kid* for a child and *buck* for a dollar, for example, have moved into common usage and are now considered informal rather than slang.

You should not use slang in academic, business, or technical writing. Even in creative writing, use slang judiciously.

---

### A C T I V I T Y   12.4

Collect some examples of current slang. Teenagers should be able to supply words used to say something is good or bad, for example. The Internet has lists of slang words for different fields, such as hacker slang. Watch out for words that have more than one meaning. Here are some slang terms to get you started:

chick

doofus

geek

dude

hottie

stud

# Jargon

We use the word *jargon* to refer to technical vocabulary or words belonging to a certain profession. Medical terminology like *ICU* for Intensive Care Unit and *primagravida* for a woman in her first pregnancy is considered jargon. Lawyer's jargon is sometimes called "legalese." Sometimes jargon becomes part of the regular vocabulary. Computer terms like *input* and *output*, for example, are now part of everyday English.

The word *jargon* has a negative connotation because it is often incomprehensible to most people. If you have too much jargon in a document, it will not be understood by non-professionals, or laypeople. However, using jargon in a document intended only for professionals is acceptable. If you are writing a memo to co-workers, you would use the jargon of your profession, but not if the memo were intended for a more general audience. The term "jargon" is also used to describe language that is unnecessarily complicated, such as bureaucratic language.

Here are some common examples of jargon. Identify each as a computer, legal, or medical term. If you don't know the meaning, check your dictionary.

contusion

indictment

interface

ISP

I.V., intravenous

keyboarding

laceration

plaintiff

RAM

subpoena

# Using a dictionary

All students need a good dictionary, preferably more than one. Some students use a pocket dictionary to carry around with them and a larger, hardcover dictionary as a better reference tool to use at home. You may have a dictionary on your computer, but it may not always be accessible. Small electronic dictionaries can be handy but they also have limitations. If you prefer machines, make sure that they give as much information as the book form, and keep in mind that some schools do not allow electronic aids to be used for tests and exams.

Dictionaries also vary as to the information they give. Some dictionaries are encyclopedic; they include proper names of people and places. Some dictionaries include etymological information that shows where the word comes from. You can also find dictionaries of slang or idioms.

ESL students often use bilingual dictionaries which translate words from their native language to English. While these dictionaries are good to start with, advanced students should use an English dictionary. Bilingual dictionaries keep students translating from their native language, instead of thinking in English. Moreover, these dictionaries may not explain usage. It is better to get an English dictionary designed especially for ESL students; they are sometimes called learner's dictionaries. These books usually give more grammatical information and have clearer explanations than regular English dictionaries. Bilingual dictionaries can be used as back-up for spelling checks and as memory aids.

Make sure your dictionary is up to date. Check the date on the copyright page (the back of the title page), and look for the date of the edition, not the reprint.

If you need to buy a new dictionary, ask your instructor for a recommendation. Much depends on personal choice, however, so test drive your dictionary in the bookstore by looking up several words. Compare a few dictionaries to see which one has clear definitions, preferably with example sentences, and which one gives grammatical information. Make sure the dictionary is easy to handle and the print is legible.

Watch out for poor quality dictionaries. For example, although the name "Webster's" has a long history in dictionaries, it is not a registered trademark—anyone can write a dictionary and name it a "Webster's." We have seen some terrible bilingual dictionaries in use among our students. One remarkable one had "Illusterated" (a spelling error) in large letters on the cover, as well as many spelling mistakes inside.

Do not use unfamiliar words in your writing unless you are sure of the exact meaning. Sometimes two words have a similar meaning, but they cannot be used in the same situation. If you find a word in a thesaurus or a bilingual dictionary that you want to use, check the meaning in a regular dictionary.

Become familiar with your dictionary. Read the introduction to know what kind of usage guidelines your book gives you. Learn the abbreviations used. Check out the pronunciation guide and make sure you understand the symbols.

## ACTIVITY 12.6

In class, look up the following words in your dictionary. Compare the information in your dictionary with the entries in your classmates' dictionaries. Look for usage notes saying whether a word is slang or derogatory. Check the pronunciation guide. Decide which dictionary is the best based on your results.

bimbo

chaos

flip out

freedom

nerd

per diem

perestroika

serendipity

triskaidekophobia

Trojan horse

# How to use a dictionary to check spelling

If you can't spell a word, how can you look it up in the dictionary? Good question. It's not easy, but you can use some techniques to help you.

The most important thing to concentrate on is the beginning of the word. Don't worry about the ending. This also holds true when you use electronic spelling aids, including spell checkers in word-processing programs. Sound out the beginning of the word and try different possible spelling combinations to look up the word. For example, if the word starts with an "f" sound, try *ph* as well as *f*. Look for the base form of the word: the verb without the ending, the singular of a noun.

You can also use other kinds of dictionaries and word lists. If you are having trouble with the spelling of a fairly common word, use a smaller dictionary, like a pocket dictionary. You'll have fewer words to look through. If English is your second language, you can use your bilingual dictionary to find the spelling of a word by looking for the translated word. Special dictionaries called misspeller's dictionaries are helpful for some cases. These books contain common misspellings, but they do not have full definitions. Some grammar and usage books include a list of commonly misspelled words, as we do at the end of this chapter. If you are looking for the spelling of a specific technical term, try looking in a book or an article where the word is likely to be used.

Always read the definition to make sure you have found the right word. Check the part of speech. The dictionary should show you how to spell different forms of the word, like plurals or different tenses, if they are irregular.

ACTIVITY    12.7

For practice in looking up words to find the correct spelling, have your instructor or a classmate say aloud some words that you may be unfamiliar with. Figure out a probable spelling and look up the word in the dictionary. Some suggested words for your instructor can be found in the Answers section.

# Spelling

Unlike languages such as Spanish and Polish, English spelling is not an accurate guide as to how a word is pronounced. For instance, the letter combination *-ough* has several pronunciations as shown in these words: *cough, through, bough, enough.* Some people argue that the spelling of English words should be simplified, but spelling reform creates other problems. For example, pronunciation can vary by region. Also, spelling by pronunciation would not show the relationship between words. For example, the relationship between *sign, designation,* and *signature* would be lost if we changed the spelling of the letters *sign* to reflect the pronunciation.

English spelling does have a system, but it is a complicated system. Some words even have more than one acceptable spelling. Some complications occur because pronunciation has changed since the spelling of a word was established. Some silent letter combinations once had a distinct pronunciation. For instance, the *gh* in "night" used to have a harsh h-like sound, as in the German word *nicht.* When Old English was first written down, it had sounds that were not adequately covered by the Roman alphabet. Moreover, English has borrowed words from many different languages; these words may retain a non-English spelling.

Words that have come to English from Greek are generally easy to recognize because of the letter combinations used to represent Greek letters, which are from a different alphabet. *Ph* is used for the Greek letter phi, *ch* for chi, *ps* for psi, and *th* for theta. A *y* in the middle of a word can also indicate a Greek word, since it usually stands for the Greek letter upsilon. The word *psychology,* for example, shows this spelling pattern; its etymology shows that it means the study of the mind or spirit. Think of other words that use these two roots: words that contain *psych* are generally related to the mind, and words that end in *-ology* mean the study of something: *psychiatrist, psycho, biology, zoology.*

The pronunciation of *ch* varies in English because of different word histories. Old English words, like *church,* generally have the "tch" sound. Words from Greek, such as *Christmas* and *chronology,* use a "k" sound for *ch.* Recent French borrowing, like *chef* and *champagne,* use a "sh" sound.

You don't have to become an expert in English etymology to understand spelling. However, understanding patterns will make you a better speller (and Scrabble player). And it's comforting to know that English spelling isn't completely chaotic (a Greek word).

# Some basic spelling rules

1. Double the final consonant before you add the suffix, or an ending to a word.

   *travel + l + er = traveller*

   *travel + l + ed = travelled*

   *begin + n + ing = beginning*

2. Drop the silent *e* at the end of a word before you add suffix that starts with a vowel.

   *live + able = livable*

   *argue + ing = arguing*

   *use + age = usage*

   Exceptions: changeable, noticeable

3. Keep the silent *e* at the end of a word when you add a suffix that starts with a consonant.

   *improve + ment = improvement*

   *use + ful = useful*

   *live + ly = lively*

   Exceptions: argument, truly

4. Change *y* to *i* before you add a suffix, except for endings starting with *i*.

   *spy + es = spies*

   *lively + er = livelier*

   *beauty + ful = beautiful*

   Exception: spying

5. Write *i* before *e* except after *c*, or when the vowel sound is "ay" (such as *weight* and *neighbour*).

believe, receive, reign

Exceptions: caffeine, codeine, protein, species, weird

## Using a spell checker

Word processing software often includes a spell checker, which checks the words you have written against a list of words stored in its dictionary. A spell checker is good for catching typographical errors, but it cannot be used as the only check for spelling mistakes. If you type a homonym (such as *too* when you mean *two*), the spell checker will not catch the mistake.

Spell checkers often flag words that are not spelling mistakes. For example, their word lists do not usually include many proper names, and even if they do, the spelling of names can vary. You can easily add words to your program's dictionary, but be sure not to add incorrectly spelled words.

A spell checker can help you find typographical errors, or typos, and some spelling mistakes. The biggest danger is relying on the computer program. You cannot assume there are no spelling mistakes because the program did not flag any words. Moreover, if your software does flag some words, it doesn't mean they are wrong. It also does not mean that proposed alternatives are right. Check a dictionary if you are unsure.

Before you hand in a piece of writing, always run it through the spell checker, but proofread it yourself as well.

## Canadian spelling

Generally, Canadian spelling is a mix of British and American spelling. For example, many Canadians write *colour*, instead of the American *color*, but they also write *tire*, unlike the British *tyre*. Spelling may also vary from province to province, under the influence of different education systems.

Generally, both American and British spellings are recognized in Canada. (American spelling diverged from British spelling when Noah Webster published his dictionary in 1828.) Accustomed to reading both, Canadian writers have some choice in their spelling, but they are generally advised to be consistent. For example, if they write *colour*, they should also use *neighbour* and *favour*.

Here are some of the common spelling variations:

| British | American | Canadian |
|---------|----------|----------|
| centre | center | centre |
| cheque | check | cheque |
| colour | color | colour |
| criticise | criticize | criticize |
| dialogue | dialog | dialogue |
| defence | defense | defence |
| grey | gray | grey |
| kerb | curb | curb |
| manoeuvre | maneuvre | manoeuvre |
| moveable | movable | movable |
| programme | program | program |
| traveller | traveler | traveller |

## How to become a better speller

While spelling errors appear to be a rather minor problem, they play an important part in how your writing is judged. A few spelling mistakes may be excused as typographical errors, but readers cannot respect a writer whose work is riddled with spelling errors, especially since such mistakes are relatively simple to fix. When there are too many mistakes, readers become distracted or even confused.

Always check spelling before you hand in a piece of writing. Use a dictionary and the spell check feature in your word processing software. While your work should be clean before you hand it in, your spelling does not have to be perfect in your first draft. Some students let their concern for spelling hamper their writing. For example, they avoid using some words because they are unsure of the spelling or they stop the flow of ideas as they look up words. You can leave your spelling check until the end of the process. As you improve your spelling, your first attempt will be correct more often.

Improving your spelling takes attention and work. You have to look for patterns, learn the rules, and memorize exceptions. English spelling is systematic. It is a complicated system, but it can be learned. Make your own spelling list. Use a notebook to keep track of words you have trouble spelling. If a spelling mistake is noted on your work, be sure to look up the correct spelling and copy it out. Writing the word out several times helps you to remember it. Most misspelt words are the ones commonly and frequently used. You probably have only 25 to 50 words in your vocabulary that you have trouble with, so you can simply memorize the correct spelling.

# Using a thesaurus

A thesaurus is a book giving synonyms, which are words that have similar meanings, and antonyms, which are words that have opposite meanings. Sometimes these books are simply called dictionaries of synonyms and antonyms. Your word processor may also have a thesaurus function.

The word *thesaurus* comes from the Greek word for "treasure," and it's true that a good thesaurus is invaluable. A thesaurus can nudge your memory to help you think of another word to use. But don't just grab one of the words your thesaurus suggests. Make sure you know the meaning (including connotations) and how to use the word.

## ACTIVITY 12.8

Use a thesaurus to look up synonyms and antonyms for the following words:

bare

do

foolish

hot

nice

power

rich

road

situation

walk

# Wordiness

One reason a good vocabulary is important is that it can help you cut down wordiness in your writing. Wordy writing is, simply, writing that has too many words. Students who lack vocabulary sometimes use a long phrase to explain what they mean instead of an apt word or two. Circumlocution, talking around an idea, adds to the length of your document, making it harder to read and understand. As we said in Chapter 1, all good writing is concise. No one wants to read unnecessary verbiage.

**E X E R C I S E    12.1**

Replace each of these phrases with one word that means the same thing.

1.  woman whose husband has died

2.  man who is throwing a party

3.  person who is paid to drive a car for somebody

4.  elected official who runs a city

5.  person who heads a large corporation

6.  woman who owns apartments and rents them out

7.  reference book giving synonyms and antonyms

8.  move to a new country

9.  walk in a leisurely manner

10. people who are invited to a party

**S U M M A R Y**

## *How to improve your vocabulary*

1. Read.

2. Read a lot.

3. Read a variety of materials.

4. Pay attention when you read.

5. Look for patterns in words, such as common roots.

6. Use a dictionary when necessary.

Some readers go to their dictionary as soon as they see an unfamiliar word. This approach, however, is not recommended because it breaks the flow of your reading. Usually, you can guess the meaning of the word from the context. If you understand the general idea, even if you do not know the meaning of every word, read on. Turn to your dictionary only when the unfamiliar word is repeated often or when you can't understand the meaning of a paragraph without knowing the word.

Some people enjoy doing vocabulary exercises and follow a regimen of learning new words. If you like doing this, fine. You can buy books such as Barron's *504 Absolutely Essential Words* for practice vocabulary exercises. But the best way is to learn words from reading because you will see them in context, not in isolation.

# List of commonly misspelled words

| | | | |
|---|---|---|---|
| a lot | answer | brilliant | conqueror |
| absence | apology | bureau | conscience |
| academic | appearance | business | conscientious |
| accidentally | appropriate | cafeteria | conscious |
| accommodate | Arctic | calendar | convenient |
| accomplish | argument | category | criticism |
| accumulate | arithmetic | cemetery | criticize |
| achievement | arrangement | changeable | curiosity |
| acknowledge | association | characteristic | dealt |
| acquaintance | athlete | chosen | decision |
| acquire | athletic | column | definitely |
| address | attendance | coming | descendant |
| aggravate | audience | commitment | description |
| all right | bachelor | committee | desperate |
| almost | basically | comparative | develop |
| although | beginning | competitive | dictionary |
| amateur | believe | conceivable | dining |
| analyze | benefited | conference | disagree |

| | | | |
|---|---|---|---|
| disappear | guard | occur | receive |
| disappoint | guidance | occurred | recognize |
| disastrous | height | occurrence | recommend |
| dissatisfied | humorous | original | reference |
| eighth | illiterate | pamphlet | religion |
| eligible | imaginary | parallel | repetition |
| eliminate | imagination | particularly | restaurant |
| embarrass | immediately | pastime | rhythm |
| emphasize | incidentally | performance | schedule |
| entirely | incredible | permissible | secretary |
| entrance | indispensable | perseverance | seize |
| environment | inevitable | phenomenon | separate |
| equivalent | infinite | physically | sincerely |
| especially | intelligence | politics | succeed |
| exaggerated | interesting | practically | success |
| exhaust | irrelevant | precede | surprise |
| existence | knowledge | precedence | temperature |
| experience | laboratory | preference | thorough |
| explanation | legitimate | preferred | tragedy |
| extraordinary | license | prejudice | transferred |
| extremely | literature | preparation | tries |
| familiar | maintenance | prevalent | Tuesday |
| fascinate | manoeuvre | privilege | unanimous |
| February | marriage | probably | unnecessarily |
| foreign | necessary | proceed | usually |
| forty | nevertheless | professor | vacuum |
| fourth | noticeable | prominent | villain |
| friend | obstacle | pronunciation | weird |
| government | occasion | quantity | whether |
| grammar | occasionally | quizzes | |

## CHAPTER 13

# A Question of Style

Spoken English encompasses a wide range of dialects and accents. Sometimes the difference is so great that two people who speak different dialects of English have trouble understanding each other. Accents, idioms and slang can vary greatly from one region to another.

These variations are not as evident in writing because most prose is in what is considered Standard English. You may see dialect differences in the dialogues of novels and short stories where the author tries to show the spoken language. Informal writing often contains more idioms and slang, which can vary from region to region. You also see some spelling differences when you compare books produced in Great Britain and in the United States. Otherwise, much of written English is standardized, especially in formal writing.

In addition to regional differences, all writers have their own individual style. Some favour elaborate sentence structure and long words while others use a casual style. Moreover, people write in different styles, according to the situation. While a conversational style can be used in a letter to a friend, a more formal style should be used in a business letter.

Even within this textbook you will see a range of styles at work. Our advice and explanations for students are written in a semi-formal style, while most of the sample paragraphs and essays are more formal, less personal. The readings in Part III are also in a variety of styles. Conversational English is common in works for a general audience, such as newspaper articles.

As students, you should develop a simple, concise writing style and be able to write in formal, standard English as modelled in the sample paragraphs and essays. Students who have only conversational English at their command may have trouble with the written communication required in the workplace.

# Speaking and writing

Spoken language is different from the written form. What you say in conversation is never written in exactly the same way. Therefore, it is impossible to learn to be a good writer without reading a lot. You must learn the forms and structures common to written expression in written, not spoken, English.

When you talk to someone, you get immediate feedback from your audience. You can tell, for example, whether someone understands what you are saying from the person's expression and comments. With written English you do not get this response. Your writing has to stand on its own; you cannot follow the document around and make sure each reader understands what you have written.

Therefore, written expression is generally more precise than spoken English, and longer, more specific words are preferred over general, vague words. For instance, when you speak to someone, you can say, "Hand me that thingamagig over there." With the aid of gestures and context, you can get your meaning across. Imagine, however, written instructions that tell you to "attach the thingamagig to the round thing."

Spoken English uses contractions. You say "I don't want to go" instead of "I do not want to go." Indeed, in relaxed speech, the phrase becomes "I don't wanna go." Words like *wanna, gonna,* and *kinda* are written in dialogues to show spoken forms, but these words should never be used in standard writing. Moreover, contractions should not be used in formal writing, but they are common in semi-formal and informal styles.

Sometimes you may make mistakes when you try to write the way you speak. For example, the contraction "should've" sounds like "should of" so you may write "I should of known better" instead of "I should have known better."

Slang is part of spoken language and is found in dialogues and informal writing. Slang expressions are usually only popular for a short time and are rarely used in writing. For instance, 1960s slang like "groovy" sounds out of place today. Moreover, slang varies greatly from region to region, so slang is not part of the standard language.

Often you break or bend rules of grammar when you speak, but these rules are more strictly adhered to in writing. For instance, you may say "it is because" or use the singular "there's" with plural subjects. These constructions are ungrammatical; both phrases would be considered incorrect in formal writing.

Generally, you use shorter sentences, including many non-sentences, and simpler words when you speak. However, in an essay, too many short sentences and simple words sound juvenile. While you do not want to go to the extreme of using only long sentences and big words, you should make sure your writing shows some degree of sophistication.

**Spoken English:**

- Do you wanna go to the show tonight?
- Nah. I'm kinda tired. How 'bout we rent a video instead?
- Um...okay. What're you in the mood for?
- Hmm. Let's see. Last time we saw that Jackie Chan movie you wanted to see. Guess it's my turn to pick one.
- Sure. Anything you want. A chick flick it is.
- Just because I don't wanna see something violent, doesn't mean we're gonna be watching a chick flick. How 'bout that new Harrison Ford movie?
- Sounds great. And I'll pick up a pizza, too, 'cause I don't feel like cooking.

**Written version:**

Last night I was too tired to go out, so my husband and I opted for a video rental and a take-out pizza. We had seen an action adventure film the last time, so we decided to get the new Harrison Ford movie.

# Standard and non-standard English

English is spoken all around the world in many different varieties. Variations may range from a slight difference in accent to completely different dialects. Regional varieties include British, American, Canadian, Australian, Singaporean, Jamaican, and Indian English. Some varieties have grown where English is used as a second language and have incorporated elements from other languages.

Despite differences in accent and some expressions, most people use a more standardized form when they speak to people who come from other regions. For example, we once had an office mate who spoke a lovely, but almost incomprehensible to us, variety of Jamaican

English, which we heard only when she was speaking on the phone to someone else who was Jamaican. Her speech with us was standard English, with a slight Jamaican accent.

Standard English is the variety of language that would be understood by most speakers of English and accepted as correct by educated speakers. Most writing is in Standard English. There are slight variations; for instance, in this book we use Standard English, but with Canadian spelling.

Some varieties of English are grammatically different than Standard English. For example, in Black English (sometimes called Ebonics), the sentence "He be gone" is perfectly grammatical. Students who speak a dialect of English that is very different from standard English may have difficulty writing, so they are sometimes placed in ESL classes. These students are actually English as a Second Dialect (ESD) learners.

In academic, business, and technical writing, you are expected to use standard English. Most of the prose you read is in standard English. You hear non-standard varieties spoken, but rarely written.

Here are some examples of non-standard English, along with the standard forms:

| **Incorrect:** | **Correct:** |
|---|---|
| I ain't got none. | I don't have any. |
| She was a wantin' to go. | She wanted to go. |
| They be scared. | They are scared. |

# Informal and formal style

North American society is moving towards more informality. This is evident when business people use first names instead of calling someone by a title, like *Mr.* or *Ms.*, and last name. Business dress is also getting less formal. Sports jackets may be worn instead of formal suits; some companies have "Casual Fridays"; and people working from home rarely dress up.

Writing is undergoing a similar change—a move to a more relaxed and casual style. Business letters of the past had set polite phrases such as "I am in receipt of your letter dated January 24th."

The use of the pronoun *one* to mean people in general has been replaced by *you* as a general pronoun.

One must look both ways before one crosses the street.

You must look both ways before you cross the street.

However, in academic writing, this use of *you* should be avoided because it is informal. One way to deal with this problem is to recast the sentence with third person forms.

People must look both ways before they cross the street.

In addition to being used for people in general, *you* is used when you are addressing someone—as we, the writers of the book, address you, the students and teachers using this text. Therefore, using *you* in writing can be somewhat confusing.

Informal writing mirrors spoken language in its use of contractions, slang, and idioms. It is relaxed and casual. For instance, in informal style, you may start sentences with subordinate conjunctions such as *and, or, but, so,* mirroring spoken style. In formal writing, this practice is considered incorrect although it is becoming more common.

Your dictionary may use the tag "informal," "colloquial," or "conversational" to show words and expressions that should not be used in formal writing. Check your dictionary to see what term is used.

Even though writing styles tend to be less formal than in the past, you should be able to write in a fairly formal style. It will be important in your academic and work career. Because informal writing is similar to spoken English, you may find it easier to produce. However, you should write in formal English for the situations where informal writing is inappropriate, just as you would be prepared to wear a suit where blue jeans would not be proper. Informal writing is generally used in personal letters, advertisements, and popular fiction. Formal writing is more common in business letters, reports, legal documents, academic writings, and essays.

There are degrees of informality. It is not just a question of formal versus informal. Just as clothing can vary in formality from blue jeans, to dress shirt and pants, to sports jacket, to suit, to tuxedo, writing style can vary from a very casual style in a letter to a friend to increasingly more formal styles in business situations.

For the writing assignments in this book, we expect semi-formal or formal writing style. Your instructor may allow a more casual or personal style.

Here is an example of a paragraph written in conversational style, followed by one in formal language:

Well, you know, kids sometimes do stuff just to give their folks a hard time. You can never tell what they're gonna do. It's because they do things just to make their parents mad. So sometimes they do the opposite of what the folks expect. Like, I had a friend who would even go so far as do something her parents wanted her to do, like clean up her room, just so's she could keep 'em off guard. It was like it was a battle zone or something. The kids just wanna show that they aren't gonna be controlled by their parents.

**Formal style:**

Teenagers' actions are often calculated to annoy and bewilder their parents. The parents often cannot predict what their children will do because the children deliberately try to go against their parents' expectations. For example, a daughter might clean her room, not in a desire to please her parents, but in a strategy to keep her parents confused.

## E X E R C I S E    13.1

Match the informal expressions with the more formal ones:

| | |
|---|---|
| 1. He chickened out. | a) She was just barely able to get in. |
| 2. Let's do lunch. | b) He paid ten dollars. |
| 3. She just squeaked in. | c) He became scared and did not follow through. |
| 4. It was one of those things. | |
| 5. He popped the question. | d) She'll investigate it. |
| 6. Been there. Done that. | e) He asked her to marry him. |
| 7. She's a no show. | f) She did not come. |
| 8. She'll check it out. | g) Let us meet for lunch sometime. |
| 9. He'll fix the grub. | h) He will fix the meal. |
| 10. He paid ten bucks. | i) I have already experienced what you are now experiencing. |
| | j) It was one of those unfortunate incidents. |

# Personal and impersonal writing

When you use pronouns like *you* and *I*, you are talking directly to the reader. Sometimes this personal style is appropriate and sometimes it is not. Lab reports and technical writing are rarely personal, so passive voice may be used in this type of writing.

You should be able to produce impersonal writing as well as personal writing. Whether you write a personal or an impersonal essay often depends on the question or topic. For example, "Why would you like to get married?" calls for a personal response, whereas "What are the benefits of marriage?" calls for an impersonal essay.

Do not over-use "I" in your essays. You can express your own opinion without stating "I think" or "in my opinion." Almost every piece of writing expresses the writer's thoughts, unless it reports someone else's ideas, as in a summary. If you say "the work week should be shortened" in an essay, the reader knows that that is your opinion, unless you attribute it to someone else, as in "Many people think the work week should be shortened."

Students in English courses are often asked to write personal essays. In our courses, we ask students to produce impersonal essays because we find that our students have not had enough practice writing impersonally and that they need to develop this skill for the work world.

---

### SUMMARY

## *To make your writing more formal*

- Use third person (not *I* or *you*).

- Do not use slang; avoid idiomatic expressions.

- Do not start sentences with subordinate conjunctions: *and, or, but, so.*

- Do not use contractions, or shortened forms like *gonna* and *kinda.*

- Do not use conversational expressions, such as *let's, OK* or *well,* to start a sentence.

- Use precise vocabulary, not words like *thing* and *stuff.*

- Use some long, complex sentences that show levels of meaning, rather than mostly short, simple sentences.

## CHAPTER 14

# Grammar Troublespots

This chapter highlights a few areas where students often make grammatical errors. Some of these areas are especially problematic for ESL students. You may use this chapter as a quick review of troublespots, or you may go directly to a specific section in order to help you with one of your writing problems. Use the exercises to see how well you understand the point. If you need more detailed information, or make several errors in the exercise, you should consult a dictionary, grammar book, or usage guide. Incorrect sentences are marked with an asterisk (*).

## Parts of speech

The different parts of speech are defined in Chapter 2. A noun is the name of a person, place or thing. A verb can tell the action or describe the state or feeling of something. Adjectives describe nouns, while adverbs describe verbs or adjectives. While these are the basic distinctions, the English language is not so straightforward. Nouns, for example, can sometimes function as adjectives in a phrase such as "computer store."

Students sometimes use the wrong part of speech in sentences. It is important to be able to distinguish words such as *succeed* (a verb) and *success* (a noun) and be able to use both words properly.

You can identify parts of speech by their meaning, by their position in a sentence, by prefixes and suffixes, and by their similarity to other words. In your dictionary, the second piece of information (after pronunciation) given for a word is its part of speech designation. These are usually abbreviated (n., v., adj., adv., conj., prep.). Pay attention to these tags when you look up unfamiliar words in the dictionary.

Common noun endings: *-ence, -ion, -ism, -ment, -ship, -ity, -age, -ian, -hood*

Common verb ending: *-ize*

Some verbs are formed from nouns with an *en-* prefix (*enable, entrust*) or a *be-* prefix (*befriend, becalm, begrudge*)

Common adjective endings: *-able, -ent, -ible*

Adverbs that are formed from adjectives usually end in *-ly*

Sometimes the present and past participles are used as adjectives. For example, we have the verb *arrange* and the noun *arrangement;* the past participle *arranged* (as in *arranged* marriage) is used as an adjective.

## E X E R C I S E   14.1

Fill in the missing word forms in the following chart:

| NOUN | VERB | ADJECTIVE |
|------|------|-----------|
| admiration | | |
| | | advisable |
| | believe | |
| | compete | |
| | | developmental |
| | differ | |
| | | enjoyable |
| | function | |
| necessity | | |
| | | provable |
| | reason | |
| | succeed | |

## EXERCISE 14.2

Choose the correct part of speech to complete the following sentences:

1. I feel **comfort/comforting/comfortable** when I visit their home.

2. He is a **violence/violent** man.

3. The **difference/different** between the two stories is the ending.

4. She was **succeed/success/successful** in her new career.

5. Is there a new **develop/developing/development** in the case?

6. He asked her to **define/definition/definitive** the problem.

7. It's the **repeat/repetition/repetitive** of the command that caused the problem.

8. She told me to take a deep **breathe/breath** and **relax/relaxation/relaxing**.

9. He is very **protect/protection/protective** of his family's privacy.

10. The child-care centre is a **necessity/necessary/necessarily**, not a luxury.

# Parallel Structure

When you put ideas in a series and join them with *and*, you must ensure that what is being joined has the same grammatical structure. To check for parallel structure, look to see what the *and* is joining.

> *He tried calling,
>
> > e-mailing, and
> >
> > to go to her house.

**Correct:**

> He tried calling
>
> > e-mailing, and
> >
> > going to her house.

Whether you join whole clauses, phrases, or single sentences, each section must fit the sentence:

> He prepared the meal, she washed the dishes, and then they went out.

He prepared the meal, washed the dishes, and went out.

He prepared lamb, squash, and rice for dinner.

## EXERCISE 14.3

Rewrite the following sentences to correct the errors in parallel structure:

1. The host's job is to greet guests, introduce them to others, and making everyone feel comfortable.

2. Instead of watching television, the children amused themselves by singing, play games, and telling stories.

3. A voter must understand the election issues, listen to all the local candidates, and then he must cast his ballot on election day.

4. Eating nutritious foods, exercising, and sleep at least eight hours a day will make you feel better.

5. She speaks with ease and confidently.

6. The government stopped the housing project because of the recession, there was no private sector investment, and changing policies.

7. Full-time students today suffer from these hardships: they have responsibilities to their family, no time to study, and the teachers are hard on them.

8. Fear of the unknown, the fact that the media hype the Y2K problem, and distrust in the political leaders are all valid reasons for millennium paranoia.

9. The causes of longevity in some people are they eat properly, they live modestly and their forefathers all have lived long lives.

10. Part of the building code states that during construction, the site must be inspected regularly, that inspectors must work independently of the builders, and enforcing all rules to ensure safety.

# Articles

The proper use of the articles *a, an,* and *the* is one of the most difficult areas to master in the English language. Native speakers use articles correctly without really thinking about them, but the rules are complex. Moreover, many cases are idiomatic.

The basic rule is that you use the definite article *the* when you are talking about something specific that you already know about. The indefinite article *a* or *an* for singular nouns is used in the sense of "one." For plurals, no article is used for this indefinite sense. Use an indefinite article the first time you mention something, but then use the definite article with the noun when you refer to it again.

> We bought a new armchair. We put the chair in the living room next to the piano.

> *After the chair is mentioned, it can be referred to as "the chair." Since people usually have only one living room, the definite article is used. "The piano" is the specific piano the people own, so the definite article is used.*

*An* is used instead of *a* if the word starts with a vowel, in pronunciation not in spelling. For instance, we say "an hour" because the *h* is silent, but we say "a hair-do." We say "an umbrella" but "a university" because the first sound in *university* is more of a *y* sound than a vowel. If you need to use an indefinite article before an acronym or abbreviation, use the pronunciation as a guide.

> a master's degree, an M.A.

> a NATO agreement, an NYPD officer

Uncountable nouns do not take an indefinite article. These nouns include abstract qualities, such as *beauty* and *intelligence,* and mass nouns, such as *water* and *sand.* You can read more about uncountable nouns in Chapter 15.

When the name of the type of school comes first, we use a definite article. We say "the University of Toronto" but "York University."

Country names that have a word like "republic" usually take a definite article. For example, the name "the Republic of China" needs an article, but "China" does not. Other examples: the U.S., the United States of America; Canada, the Dominion of Canada; the U.S.S.R, the United Soviet Socialist Republic, Russia.

## EXERCISE 14.4

Fill in the blanks with the correct article—*a, an,* or *the*—or leave them blank if no article is necessary:

The shape of _____ Canadian houses follows both fashion and lifestyle changes. Attics and third storeys were popular in _____ first half of _____ 20th century. In _____ 1960s bungalows became popular. Today, buyers want _____ residence with several bathrooms, _____ large family room and _____ practical kitchen. Another change is the garage attached to _____ front of _____ house. It used to be separate and behind _____ main building.

Verandas were popular when people actually sat there on _____ summer evenings and talked to passers-by. After many years of _____ houses designed away from ____ street, ____ verandah is making ____ come-back. Patios and _____ decks in ____ back-yard extend recreation and entertaining space for _____ home-owner. Finished basements give children _____ playroom and teenagers ____ recreation room for _____ parties. In _____ next century Canadians will see ____ smart houses wired to respond to their owners' commands.

# Pronouns

Pronouns like *she, they,* and *it* must refer to a specific noun. In grammar terminology, this noun is called the antecedent. The reader must be able to identify who or what the pronoun means.

> <u>Bob and Tomas</u> investigated the complaint. <u>They</u> talked to the <u>woman</u> who made the 911 call. <u>She</u> said that <u>a man</u> had shouted for help but that <u>she</u> could not see <u>him</u>.

> <u>Peter</u> was unable to contact <u>his daughters</u>, so <u>he</u> left <u>them</u> a <u>message</u>. <u>They</u> had trouble understanding <u>it</u> so they tried to call <u>him</u>.

It is a grammar mistake to use a pronoun that does not have a correct antecedent:

> *<u>The company</u> wanted to expand, so <u>they</u> bought the adjoining property.

> *The word* they *is a plural pronoun and cannot refer to the singular noun* company.

Another problem is the third person singular pronoun: *he, she, it.* English does not have a word that can mean "he or she." Grammatically, *he* and *his* are the correct pronouns in the following sentences:

> Each person should bring his book.

> When a student registers for the supplemental course, he should bring his I.D. card.

However, many people object to the *he* pronoun because it excludes women. Some people try to get around this problem by saying "he or she." This is grammatical, but it is awkward and should be avoided, especially if it has to be repeated many times. Even worse is to use a slash between the pronouns; there is no word *he/she* in English.

In speech, people often use *they* forms with singular antecedents even though it is ungrammatical:

Everybody can use <u>their</u> own worksheet.

Each person should bring <u>their</u> luggage.

This usage has a long tradition and has been noted in the works of such famous writers as Jane Austen. Nevertheless, it is considered ungrammatical, and most English teachers will mark it as an error. However, some accept it, and that acceptance is growing. We advise our students to use plural forms (such as "students" and "they"), so that they do not become mired in awkward or ungrammatical pronoun use.

Another pronoun that gives writers headaches is *you*. *You* can refer to the reader, but it can also refer to people in general. It is best to avoid using second person in academic writing because it is a confusing reference and because it gives the prose a conversational tone. In the past, *one* was used to refer to people in general, but the words seems stilted and unnatural now. It is best to use third person plural references such as "people," "students," and "workers."

We had to face pronoun usage decisions when we wrote this textbook. We decided to use *we* and *you* to give the book a more personal tone when we offer advice. Sometimes we refer to writers or specific groups of students in more general terms, and for this we used the third person.

Another common error is a switch in pronouns. Students may start out with reference to *we*, then use *they*, and switch to *you*.

**E X E R C I S E  14.5**

Correct the pronoun switch problem in the following paragraph:

Immigrants can improve their language skills in many ways. First, we can use the media by listening to the radio, watching TV, and reading the newspaper. If you read the newspaper every day, you can learn about important issues and improve your vocabulary. The library is a useful facility for immigrants because they can find information about the local area, as well as get books, magazines, videos, and audiotapes. An immigrant can also take continuing education courses. These courses do not have to be language classes. If he interacts with English-speaking people, he will improve conversation skills. We need to take advantage of opportunities to practise English.

# Verb Tenses

Chapter 2 introduced the verb tenses of English. Here is a quick review of the main uses.

## Present events

To express general facts, you use the simple present tense, as in this sentence. To describe actions that are occurring now, as in this clause, use present continuous. To express past ideas that are relevant to the present, use the present perfect tense or present perfect continuous.

> The earth is round. The sky is blue. Astronomers are people who study stars.

> I am studying sign language at night school.

> Jack has been in Canada for six years.
> *This means that he still lives here, in contrast to "Jack lived in Canada for six years."*

## Past events

Actions that happened in the past and are complete are described with the simple past tense. Actions that took place over a period of time are expressed with the past continuous. Actions that occurred before another past action are in the past perfect.

> I tried to learn how to play the bagpipes, but I stopped taking lessons.

> Naomi was cleaning up the mess when her supervisor walked in.

> He had studied Arabic for several years before he went to Egypt.

## Future events

The simple future with *will* can be used for most actions that will take place in the future. The present continuous and *going to* also express future actions. The difference in meaning is slight.

> The band will travel by bus to Halifax.

> The band is travelling to Halifax by bus.

> The band is going to take the bus to Halifax.

## E X E R C I S E  14.6

Fill in the blank with the correct tense of the verb in parentheses:

1. Yesterday we _____ (walk) along the beach and _____ (collect) sea shells.

2. While I was _____ (cook) supper, the phone _____ (ring) three times.

3. Next week I _____ (go) to Prince George for a conference.

4. Mary-Anne _____ (be) an epidemiologist. She _____ (analyze) health statistics. She _____ (work) for the department for ten years.

5. I _____ (forget) my notebook, but I _____ (think) Helena _____ (have) a copy of those questions too.

6. They _____ (start) the company in 1995. After five years they _____ (want) to expand, but the expansion never _____ (happen). Today the company _____ (be) not much bigger than when they _____ (begin), but they _____ (make) a good income nevertheless.

7. He usually _____ (take) the seven o'clock train, but yesterday he _____ (have) to accompany his sister, who _____ (want) to leave earlier.

# Tense Shift

Sometimes writers get careless and change a verb tense inappropriately. It's not just a matter of telling about past events in the past tense and current events in the present tense. For instance, we often use the present tense to describe the contents of books and articles. Even though Shakespeare lived 400 years ago, we say "Shakespeare tells a tragic story of two lovers in *Romeo and Juliet*."

As part of your editing and proofreading, make sure that you have used verb tenses logically. If you change verb tense, there should be a good reason for that change. For instance, you can be arguing that a law should be changed using the present tense, but you may tell a story or anecdote in the past tense.

Remember that the tense you use often in essays is the simple present tense. It is used for general facts.

**E X E R C I S E    14.7**

Correct the tense shift errors in the following paragraph:

One of the worst disasters of the 20th century was the Halifax explosion. On December 6, 1917, at 8:45 a.m., the *IMO* collided with the French ship *Mont Blanc* in Halifax harbour. The *Mont Blanc* is a munitions ship carrying tons of explosives. The collision caused the explosives to ignite. About 20 minutes after the collision, the French ship explodes in a huge boom that is heard as far away as Prince Edward Island. More than two-and-a-half square kilometres of Halifax is levelled, and the force of the explosion was felt many miles away. A tidal wave was created and fires spread through the city. More than 1600 people died and 9000 are injured. It was a terrible time for the thousands left homeless because they have to endure a December blizzard with no proper shelter. The Halifax explosion was the largest non-nuclear manmade blast in the world. It was dramatized in Hugh MacLennan's novel *Barometer Rising*.

# Verb Forms

When you look up a verb in the dictionary, you see the base form. This form is the infinitive without the *to* and it is used to make the simple present tense. Here are some base forms of verbs: *do, make, be, find, run, sleep, talk, seem, believe*. The base form is used to form the simple present tense, and the present participle with the addition of *-ing*. Chapter 10 reviews some of the spelling rules used to form different verb forms.

If the verb is a regular verb, it is easy to form the simple present tense:

|  | **singular** | **plural** |
|---|---|---|
| 1st person | I talk | we talk |
| 2nd person | you talk | you talk |
| 3rd person | he/she/it talks | they talk |

The only complication here is the *-s* ending on the third person singular. This ending is very difficult for many ESL learners to produce, both in speech and writing, and sometimes even to hear. Leaving the *-s* off in writing is one of the most common errors among ESL students.

The base form of the verb is also used to make the present participle, the *-ing* form used in continuous tenses and as gerunds and participles.

do, doing

make, making

be, being

find, finding

run, running

sleep, sleeping

talk, talking

seem, seeming

believe, believing

The other principal parts of the verb are the simple past form and the past participle. For regular verbs, both forms are the same, with an *-ed* ending: *walk, walked, walked.* Some verbs have an *-en* ending for the past participle: *taken, hidden.* Most dictionaries list the principal parts of the verb for irregular verbs.

Check your verb form. After modal verbs such as *can, could, should, might* and after the auxiliary *do,* the simple form of a verb is found. After the auxiliary verb *have,* the verb form is always the past participle (the *-ed* form of regular verbs). After the auxiliary verb *to be,* two possible verb forms are found. If the verb is in a progressive tense, the *-ing* form will be used. If the verb is in the passive voice (see page 193), the past participle (the *-ed* form of regular verbs) is used. This holds true even when there is more than one auxiliary verb used:

I should have been taking care of the plants.

| AUXILIARY | VERB THAT FOLLOWS | USED FOR | EXAMPLE |
|---|---|---|---|
| have | past participle (*-ed* ending for regular verbs) | perfect tenses | I have seen it before. |
| be (am, is, are, was, were) | present participle (*-ing* form); past participle (*-ed* ending for regular verbs) | continuous tenses; passive voice | He is leaving now. The umbrella was forgotten. |

| AUXILIARY | VERB THAT FOLLOWS | USED FOR | EXAMPLE |
|---|---|---|---|
| will | base form (infinitive without *to*) | future tenses | He will go now. |
| do | base form (infinitive without *to*) | emphasis; negatives; questions | I did call him. You did not finish. Did he see them? |
| modal verbs (can, could, may, might, should, would, etc.) | base form (infinitive without *to*) | express possibility, probability, conditions, etc. | They can walk there. She might be late. I would ask first. |

EXERCISE 14.8

Pick the correct form of the verb in the following sentences:

1. I should have **be/been/was/being** more careful.
2. The students were **apply/applying/applied** for summer jobs all week.
3. Angelica can **go/going/gone/went** to university next year.
4. The players could **have/having/had** been traded easily.
5. I am **wait/waiting/waited** for an acceptance letter from the college.
6. Marshall might have **want/wanting/wanted** to go too.
7. Having **finish/finishing/finished** the report, they were **clean/cleaning/cleaned** out the files.
8. I do **know/knowing/knew** the answer.
9. They could not **understand/understanding/understood** the problem.
10. Sylvie and Kyoko will be **take/taking/took/taken** the children to the baseball game.

# Passive Voice

English sentences can be in the active or the passive voice. In active sentences, the grammatical subject performs the action of the verb. In the passive, the grammatical subject is acted upon. For example, in the last two sentences, the former sentence is in the active voice, the latter is in passive. The passive voice is formed with the verb *to be* and the past participle. The doer of the action is shown with a *by* phrase.

Here are some examples. The first sentence of the pair is in the active voice; the second is passive.

> A burglar broke the window.
> The window was broken by a burglar.

> They elected him leader of the party.
> He was elected leader of the party.

> The company developed the Insta-Peel in 1987.
> The Insta-Peel was developed in 1987.

The passive voice is more difficult for the reader to comprehend, so the active is preferable. For this reason, computer grammar checkers flag passive constructions, and writing teachers warn against them. However, the passive cannot be avoided completely. It is useful when you want to emphasize the action that was performed and to de-emphasize, or ignore altogether, the doer of the action.

> Someone built the Parliament Buildings in 1866.

> The Parliament Buildings were built in 1866.

The passive may be used in technical writing. Lab reports, for example, are often in the passive.

> The water was poured into the beaker.

> NOT: I poured the water into the beaker.

The passive voice is sometimes used in bureaucracies to minimize blame and responsibility. However, this practice is not condoned.

> We did not check the shipment for contaminants.

> The shipment was not checked for contaminants.

Usually, a passive sentence that needs a *by* phrase is better rewritten as an active sentence.

## EXERCISE  14.9

Rewrite the following sentences from the passive to the active voice. If there is no noun or pronoun that can serve as a subject, choose one that fits the sentence meaning.

1.  The essay was corrected by a tutor in the Writing Centre.

2.  The proposal was put together by our new development team.

3.  The dance was well performed by the children.

4.  The CEO was arrested for conspiracy.

5.  The landlord did not listen to his tenants, and they were soon evicted from the housing complex.

6.  She was trained to keep the books for the company.

7.  The award ceremony was held in the gymnasium.

# Modal Verbs

Modal verbs such as *should, could, may, might, must,* and *would* are auxiliary verbs, also called helping verbs. They are always followed by the base form of the verb. They are used with another verb to express ideas of possibility, obligation, and ability. Modal verbs can be confusing, especially since the same verb can be used to express different ideas. Usually the meaning is made clear by the context.

Our team should win now that the Jets have been eliminated.

*(probability)*

You should quit smoking.

*(giving advice)*

Ability: *can, could, be able to*

The past tense of *can* is *could* when it is used to describe ability. Since there is no future form, use *be able to* to express future ideas.

I can speak French fluently.

He could run a marathon when he was in high school.

After this course, I will be able to work as a lifeguard.

I was able to do a hundred push-ups easily, but now I'm out of shape.

Permission: *can, may*

Using *can* to ask for permission is considered incorrect by some grammarians, but it is so widely heard that arguing against it is fighting a losing battle.

May I have another book, please?

Can I borrow your pencil?

Possibility and probability: *could, may, might, should*

It might rain tomorrow.

It could rain tomorrow.

If you turn it around, it may be easier to open.

He should have received the package by now.

Obligation and necessity: *have to, must, should*

My doctor told me that I must quit smoking.

You should call him again.

I have to wait for my cousin.

Condition: *would*

If I had a million dollars, I would buy a mansion.

If he could swim faster, he would enter the Ironman competition.

Wants, preferences: *would like, would rather*

Would you like a cup of coffee?

I'd like to take a break now, please.

He'd rather play golf.

## E X E R C I S E  14.10

Fill in the blanks with appropriate modal verbs:

1. I _____ meet with the president to discuss that. (necessity)

2. You _____ drink several glasses of water every day. (obligation)

3. _____ I borrow that book for a few days? (permission)

4. I _____ speak French fluently, but now I've forgotten so much of it. (past ability)

5. If I had the time, I _____ join the parent council. (condition)

6. He _____ type 70 words a minute. (ability)

7. This project _____ take more time than we anticipated. (possibility)

8. I really _____ go now. (obligation)

9. _____ you like to visit our Vancouver plant? (want)

10. Anyone _____ improve writing skills with practice. (ability)

# Participles and infinitives

Verbs can be followed by other forms of verbs—participles and infinitives. These can be very confusing, especially to ESL students, because the main verb determines whether the next verb form should be in the *to* or *-ing* form. Therefore, you have to learn the structure along with the verb. A good dictionary should tell which form is required, so, if you're not sure, look it up.

Note the forms in these example sentences:

He pretended to be a member of the executive.

I am learning to ride a unicycle.

I forgot to take down his I.D. number.

The class is practising writing a letter.

We are considering giving him another chance.

I can't face taking that driving test again.

In some sentences, an object appears before the infinitive:

I'll help the students to organize their materials.

Some verbs take both forms, each giving the sentence a different meaning:

We stopped to talk.
*(We stopped what we were doing in order to talk.)*

We stopped talking.
*(so we were no longer talking)*

The *-ing* form is used after prepositions:

> You should check the spelling and grammar before handing in the essay.

## EXERCISE 14.11

Fill in the blank with the infinitive or the *-ing* form of the verb in parentheses:

1.  It seems _____ (make) no difference.

2.  I expect _____ (finish) by noon.

3.  I can't imagine _____ (be) a firefighter.

4.  Don't miss _____ (see) that movie.

5.  I hope _____ (see) you soon.

6.  Laura refused _____ (take) on the extra assignment.

7.  They're always talking about _____ (learn) _____ (speak) Japanese.

8.  He won't admit _____ (write) that memo.

9.  I would like _____ (avoid) _____ (call) another meeting.

10. She's interested in _____ (learn) to fly a helicopter.

# Sentence fragments and run-on sentences

A sentence requires a subject and a verb. A sentence fragment, sometimes referred to as a non-sentence, is incomplete. It may lack a subject or a verb. Some fragments are a clause or a phrase without a main clause. Some writers occasionally use sentence fragments deliberately, for effect. However, this usage gives the prose a conversational style. Academic writing should contain complete sentences.

Here are some examples of fragments:

*The commercialization of education.

*TV in the classroom, opening the way for other advertising.

*Because students should be brought up to be good citizens, not consumers.

*At the insistence of the Minister of Education.

To fix a sentence fragment it is necessary to determine what is missing. Look for a main subject and verb. Remember that an *-ing* verb is not a complete verb without a helping verb. Make sure there is a main clause in the sentence.

The commercialization of education should concern everyone.

TV in the classroom opens the way for other advertising.

This goes against the accepted values of education because students should be brought up to be good citizens, not consumers.

At the insistence of the Minister of Education, the contract was not signed.

A sentence that does not stop where it should is a run-on sentence. These can take different forms. A comma splice, for example, occurs when a comma separates two independent clauses. Sometimes the run-on contains no punctuation between the two clauses. An overly long, but grammatical, sentence may also be referred to as a run-on.

Here are some examples of run-on sentences:

*They decided to defer the motion, the president adjourned the meeting.

*The committee had to be reformed some of the members were reassigned to other departments.

*The chair was not pleased with the lack of progress therefore he brought in his own assistants to help with the project.

*Although the project was important to the firm, it was not recognized as such by the CEO so he kept giving the group members other work that he felt was more important, so that they could not work on the project, and then the momentum was lost, so they had to start from square one again, but it became a vicious circle because the CEO looked at the lack of progress as a reason that the committee should be disbanded even though he was the one who was unwittingly sabotaging their work by his incessant demands, so it was no wonder that the chair was very frustrated.

You can fix run-on sentences by dividing them into separate sentences or by using a conjunction or semi-colon to join them.

**Correct:**

They decided to defer the motion. The president adjourned the meeting.

After they decided to defer the motion, the president adjourned the meeting.

They decided to defer the motion, and the president adjourned the meeting.

They decided to defer the motion; the president adjourned the meeting.

EXERCISE 14.12

Correct the run-ons and fragments:

1. The win, a first for the premier, who became the leader of the party two years ago.

2. The New Democratic Party (NDP) has always had strong union support it opposes the domination of big business.

3. Right wing refers to conservative values which embrace free enterprise, left wing believes in aid for the disadvantaged and in radical government intervention.

4. The reason being that more women prefer entrenched social programs to tax rebates.

5. Running on empty promises and disinformation. Both candidates are bound to lose the election.

6. The voters split the vote between the two established parties, they inadvertently let the third-choice party come from behind to form the next government.

7. "Corporate welfare bums," an expression first coined by David Lewis, leader of the national NDP, in the 1970s.

8. The Bennet buggy was a horse towing a car without an engine, the Diefendollar was a Canadian dollar worth 98 cents American.

9. William Lyon MacKenzie King, the Liberal prime minister during WW II, who secretly used a crystal ball and a talking dog to help him develop national policy.

10. Sir John A. Macdonald was an alcoholic, he won two elections and weathered monumental scandals virtually unscathed.

# Prepositions

Prepositions are little words that can be very confusing for second language learners. The basic meanings of the different prepositions are generally straightforward. It's easy to understand the difference between *on the desk* and *in the desk*, for example. But prepositions get complicated when they are used with verbs. For example, we *rely on* but *believe in* someone. Sometimes the preposition is actually part of the verb, as in phrasal verbs, sometimes called two-part verbs, such as *dress up* and *sleep in*. Certain adjectives also require certain prepositions. For example, we can be *proud of* but *content with* something. If English is your second language, you have to learn this idiomatic use of prepositions. A good dictionary will tell you which prepositions go with which verbs and adjectives.

## E X E R C I S E  14.13

Fill in each blank with a preposition:

1.  I don't agree _____ her plan because we can't depend _____ the schedule.

2.  He is always late _____ meetings.

3.  She is known _____ her use _____ vivid colours _____ her paintings.

4.  That university is located _____ a small town, so it dominates the economy.

5.  I am opposed _____ raising tuition fees.

6.  Are you acquainted _____ Dr. Patel?

7.  Terry Fox will always be remembered _____ the courage he showed _____ cancer.

8.  This textbook is suitable _____ a first-year class.

9.  She is familiar _____ the new methodology we are using.

10. Harold is qualified _____ the managerial position.

# Phrasal verbs

Phrasal verbs are two part verbs that are completed by a preposition such as *by, for, in, up,* or *with*. In this construction, the second word is not considered a true preposition because it is actually part of the verb, and it is sometimes referred to as an adverb, a prepositional adverb, or a particle. To simplify matters, we will just call it a preposition.

I <u>looked up</u> the word in the dictionary.

I looked up the road but I could see no sign of the car.

In the first sentence, *look up* is a phrasal verb. In the second sentence, the verb is *look,* and *up* is part of the prepositional phrase *up the road.* Phrasal verbs are usually listed in the dictionary under the main verb.

Phrasal verbs are often idiomatic. In other words, the combination of preposition and verb means something you wouldn't expect if you looked at the meaning of the words individually. Grammar rules will not help you learn these two-part verbs; you have to learn them as separate vocabulary items.

You can look for patterns. For example, the particle *up* often adds the idea of "completely" to a verb. Compare these pairs of examples:

He tore the registration form.
He tore up the registration form.

I have to get dressed for the party.
I have to get dressed up for the party.

Phrasal verbs are an important part of spoken English, but sometimes they can be replaced by less colloquial verbs in academic writing. For example, you might use the word *distribute* instead of the phrasal verb *hand out.* This does not mean that you cannot use phrasal verbs in your essays. You will often find that they are the best expression to describe an idea.

## EXERCISE 14.14

Fill in the correct preposition to complete the phrasal verbs in the following sentences:

1. I get _____ early in the morning and go jogging.

2. We can't put _____ this work any longer. We can't miss this deadline.

3. They need another income just to get _____.

4. Her work always stands _____ . She's the best in the field.

5. All the papers burned _____ in the fire, and the computer files were not backed _____.

6. Do you want to go _____ tonight?

7. They held a lottery for the residence rooms, and I lost _____.

# Singular and plural

Some grammar mistakes seem to stem from a lack of understanding of, or attention to, the basic concept of singular and plural. When we talk about more than one item, we need the plural form. Be careful to add the -*s* to plural nouns. For nouns that end in *s* or an *s* sound, -*es* is the usual ending of plurals: *boxes, buses, churches.*

Not all words that end in -*s* are plural. Possessives are formed with an apostrophe and *s*; they are not plurals in themselves, but possessives can be made with plural nouns: *the students' responsibility.* Verbs that end with *s* (*walks, listens, reorganizes*) are not "plural." They are, in fact, used for the third person singular in the simple present tense.

Some plurals are not formed with an *s*. Irregular plurals include *mice, teeth, people,* and *criteria.* If you think a word may have an irregular plural form, check your dictionary. Another exception is the plural of odd forms like letters which require an apostrophe before the *s* to make them more readable: *A's and B's.*

Uncountable nouns cannot be made plural. See Chapter 15 for more on these words.

---

## EXERCISE 14.15

Correct the errors in the following sentences:

1.  There is many way for people to conserve resources and cut pollution in their everyday activities.

2.  People can walk or bike to work to get exercises.

3.  A women's place is in the boardroom.

4.  How many cup of coffees and teas can he carry in one hands?

5.  Childrens' program are only on Saturday.

6.  He lost both of his front tooth.

7.  The deer run around free in the park, where the childrens often catch a glimpse of them.

8.  There are three men and seven woman working on the project.

9.  That instructor give the most homeworks of all the instructor.

10. Most of the athlete prefers to train in the morning.

# Subject-verb agreement

In a sentence, the subject must agree or match up with the verb. A single subject takes a single verb; a plural subject a plural verb. Otherwise, the reader may become confused. Usually, the error occurs when you forget what the true subject of the sentence is.

> *One of the oldest Canadian paintings now hang in that gallery.

> One of the oldest Canadian paintings now hangs in that gallery.

In this example, the true subject is "one"; therefore, the verb should be "hangs." (To find the true subject, cross out prepositional phrases. See the examples on page 37.)

---

**E X E R C I S E** **14.16**

---

Correct the errors in the following sentences. (Not all sentences contain errors.)

1. The students in the band gets time off from class to rehearse.

2. Sad movies and books makes me cry.

3. Star Wars is my favourite movie.

4. The fact that he disrupted the meeting is irrelevant.

5. Deer are plentiful in this area, and skunks is a nuisance.

6. Many people wants to live in a warmer climate.

7. Each of the students want to take the make-up test.

8. The people who lives in the surrounding area complain about the noise.

9. While many people applied for the job, it will be given to the person who have been with the company the longest.

10. If Jack really want to go to Kitchener, I can take him next week.

## CHAPTER 15

# Usage of Troublesome Words

This chapter has explanatory usage notes based on common errors we have seen in student writing, including ESL errors. Words with similar patterns are grouped together.

Each of these sections begins with incorrect sentences marked with an asterisk (*). Correct these sentences after you have read the explanation of the error. You can find the corrected sentences in the Answers section.

## agree, develop, happen

*Accidents are usually happen when people are not paying attention.

*The professor was develop this theory last year.

*I am agree with this theory.

*It is happen when I opened the door.

With these verbs, students sometimes use the verb *to be* when it is not necessary, or they form the passive voice incorrectly. Study the correct sentences below and then correct the errors above.

**Correct use:**

The accident happened because I was going too fast.

I happened to see him on his way to work.

He agreed with the approach but thought we should change the schedule.

Jane and Maria have agreed to host the conference.

The program was developed with the co-operation of the Ministry of Education.

He said we should just wait to see what develops.

## a lot

*Alot of students have trouble with this course.

*There is allot to be thankful for.

The expression "a lot" creates a lot of problems for students. First, it is properly two words, not one. Spell checkers sometimes suggest the word "allot" as a correction for "alot," but that is an entirely different word that means allocate or distribute. Secondly, you should not be using "a lot" in your academic writing because it is an informal expression. Use *much* and *many* instead.

**Correct:**

She is absent a lot of the time.

She is absent much of the time.

A lot of people attended the meeting.

Many people attended the meeting.

He helped me a lot.

He helped me greatly.

## although, even though, though

*Although, he studied very hard, but he couldn't understand the theory.

* He applied for the engineering program. Although he didn't meet the requirements.

*Even though he was late. He came into the meeting.

*Even she knew the answer, she didn't put up her hand.

*Although* is a subordinate conjunction. As such it joins two clauses. It should not be followed by a comma. *Even though* is used in the same way but it is stronger in meaning than *although*. *Though* is a short form, used in conversational English. The main clause should not start with *but; although* already carries that meaning and using *but* is redundant, saying the same thing twice. *Even* cannot be used alone to mean *although* (See the entry for *even* below.).

**Correct:**

Although the company has had many setbacks, Milo decided to sign the contract.

Even though Amanda suffers from bronchitis, she continues to smoke.

Jack decided to hire her although she had been in trouble with the law.

## computer

*Computer has changed the world.

*I want to study computer.

*Computer is very useful for essay writing.

You may encounter problems with the noun "computer" if you forget that it is a countable noun and refers to the machine itself. It is not an abstract noun. It can be used as an adjective to describe courses or other activities.

**Correct:**

I need a new computer.

Computer science is the most popular program at the college.

The computer is the most important invention of the late 20th century.

Computers have changed the way students do assignments.

He is studying computer programming.

## easy, convenient, difficult, hard

*I am difficult to learn English.

*He is easy to do math.

*He is convenient for the meeting.

*When they find something different, they will be difficult to accept it.

*If I live on my own, I feel difficult to finish all the housework.

These adjectives are sometimes incorrectly used to describe people. The more common constructions have something as the subject or use an "it" subject, called a non-referential subject.

Algebra is easy, but calculus is difficult.

It is easy to travel into the city by bus.

That day is not convenient for any of us.

It is more convenient for me to meet you there.

It is hard to understand him.

These adjectives can be used to describe people, but in a different way than shown in the sentences above.

He is a hard man to get to know.

Mrs. Jamal is an easy marker.

To avoid the problems shown in the incorrect sentences, you could also use the adverb form—*easily, conveniently*—or the noun—*ease, difficulty, convenience.* No adverb exists for *difficult.* Although the synonym *hard* can sometimes be used for *difficult, hardly* does not mean "in a difficult or hard way."

I learn languages easily.

I have always been able to learn math with ease.

She has difficulty with the programming language.

## e.g., etc., i.e.

*The program includes many arts courses, e.g. English, philosophy, and history.

*The program includes many arts courses, e.g. English, philosophy, and history, etc.

*In the Ancient Civilizations course, we study Greece, China, Rome, and so on, etc. ...

Latin abbreviations are often used in English, especially in short form note taking. Here are the common ones:

| Abbreviation | Latin | English equivalent |
|:---:|:---:|:---:|
| e.g. | exemplum gratis | for example, such as |
| etc. | et cetera | and the rest, and so on |
| i.e. | id est | that is |

Do not use these abbreviations in your essay writing. You should use English expressions. These abbreviations are handy to use in note-taking, but should not be part of your prose writing.

The program includes many arts courses, such as English, philosophy, and history.

When you are giving examples, use *such as* for a list within a sentence, and *for example* when you are giving a whole sentence as an example.

He likes scientific studies, such as biology and chemistry.

He likes science. For example, he took biology and chemistry last year.

Do not use *etc.* at the end of a list of examples. When you use an expression like *such as* or *for example,* you are already telling the reader that you are not giving the complete list, so *etc.* is unnecessary. Another way to do this is to use the word *include,* which tells the reader there are others.

The program includes English, philosophy, and history.

Another way to avoid using *etc.* is to use wording like this:

The program includes English, philosophy, history, and other arts courses.

In academic writing, you should avoid *and so on* (an informal expression) and ellipsis points (...), as well as *etc.*

## even

*Even he has the money, he will not go.

*He couldn't do the work even he spent hours on it.

*Even she was tired, she agreed to do the work

*Even* is not a conjunction. It is an adverb that is used with some conjunctions to intensify them. Without a conjunction, the sentences are incorrect.

Even if he were rich, he would not drive a Mercedes.

The exam was fair even though many of the students failed.

Even when he comes in at six o'clock, his boss is not satisfied.

I like him even when he is acting foolish.

*Even* can be used to emphasize other parts of a sentence:

Even Amelia couldn't figure out that math problem.

He did even worse on the next test.

Even now I can't think about seafood without feeling sick.

## interesting, boring, confusing, exciting (and other participles describing emotions)

*I am interesting in computer studies.

*I am boring during the holidays.

*I am confusing about this grammar rule.

*If they are boring, let's get out some games.

*It's my first trip to Newfoundland. I am very exciting.

The words used to describe emotions can be confusing in English. Sometimes we need to use a participle, an adjective formed from a verb. A common ESL error is to use the present participle (the *-ing* form of the verb used as an adjective) to describe people when it is the passive participle (the *-ed* form) that is meant. A person is more likely to want to say "I'm bored," not "I'm boring."

These errors with the participle stem from the verb used to make it. Verbs describing emotions can follow two basic patterns: In one, the person experiencing the feeling is the grammatical subject of the sentence. In the other, the person feeling the emotion is the direct object of the verb. Even verbs that have a similar meaning may not follow the same sentence pattern:

I fear bats.
*The person is the subject of the sentence*

Bats frighten me.
*The person is the object of the sentence*

Children enjoy surprises.
*(the person is the subject)*

Surprises delight children.
*(the person is the object)*

The problem shows up when ESL students try to use the participles of verbs that follow the second pattern. They do not realize that these verbs need a past participle (*-ed* form) to describe the person. Because the person experiencing the emotion is the object of the original verb, a passive construction must be used to describe the person. If you go back to the verb, you can see that the passive must be used to describe the person:

Stamp collecting interests me.

Stamp collecting is interesting.

I am interested in stamp collecting.

Shopping bores me.

Shopping is boring.

I am bored with shopping.

This grammar lesson confuses me.

This grammar lesson is confusing.

I am confused by this grammar lesson.

Thus when you have verbs that follow this pattern, you describe the person with the *-ed* form and the thing (stamp collecting, shopping, grammar lesson) with the *-ing* form.

Here is a list of verbs that generally take the person as the object:

| | | |
|---|---|---|
| amuse | excite | offend |
| annoy | fascinate | please |
| bore | flatter | puzzle |
| bother | frighten | reassure |
| charm | horrify | relieve |
| confuse | impress | satisfy |
| delight | insult | scare |
| depress | interest | shock |
| disgust | irritate | surprise |
| disappoint | mislead | thrill |

Here are some example sentences:

I am interested in taking the introduction to anthropology course.

Anthropology is interesting.

The kids are excited about their uncle's visit.

That roller coaster is exciting.

Ning is bored with the exercise.

That movie was so boring that I almost fell asleep.

She was surprised that they threw her a party.

The results of the exam were surprising.

He is relieved to have passed all his courses.

Elizabeth was impressed with his credentials.

E X E R C I S E  **15.1**

Choose the correct word to fill the blank in the following sentences:

1. It is **surprising/surprised** that he has never been out of the country.

2. That horror movie was the most **frightening/frightened** one I have ever seen.

3. I was very **confusing/confused** when I saw his filing system.

4. That advertisement is **misleading/misled**.

5. The long winter season can be **depressing/depressed** for many Canadians.

6. I was **insulting/insulted** when he told me how much he thought my work was worth.

7. That part of the course was poorly **understanding/understood**.

8. She was **exciting/excited** when she heard the news.

9. The employees were **reassuring/reassured** when the new owners offered to keep them on.

10. They are **interesting/interested** in taking another course.

## its, it's

\*Its a shame they can't go on the trip.

\*I can't understand it's purpose.

\*Its beginning to look as if he did it on purpose.

\*The company lost its' credibility when the scandal broke.

Confusing *its* and *it's* is probably the most common error in English, for all writers. You can see this mistake everywhere, in newspaper articles, on signs, and in books. Sometimes the mistake is just a typographical error or simple slip-up. Some people, however, do not understand the difference between the two forms.

*It's* is a contraction for *it is* or *it has*:

It's time to go now.

It's been a long time since we've seen each other.

Remember that in formal academic writing, you should avoid using contractions.

*Its* is the possessive pronoun, "meaning belonging to it." If you remember that *its* is like *his*, you should be able to avoid putting an apostrophe after *it* for the possessive pronoun.

The dog was wagging its tail.

Travelling has lost its charm now that I have to do it for a living.

There is no word *its'* (with the apostrophe after the *s*).

## many, most, almost, much

*Most of people like dancing.

*Not only one but almost immigrants were homesick.

*The most difficulty the immigrants face is homesickness.

*Much people drink coffee.

*Almost* is an adverb that means "very nearly."

I almost missed the bus. (but I didn't miss it)

I spent almost a month in Hong Kong. (a little less than a month)

*Many* is an adjective, with *more* the comparative form and *most* the superlative.

I have many contacts.

Jessica has more contacts than I do.

Amil has the most contacts.

You can say "many people" or "many of the people," but you cannot say "many of people." The same holds true for *most*. You need to use *the* with *of* because you are specifying a group.

Many people enjoy country music.

Many of the people in our club enjoy country music.

Most of the books in the library were damaged.

Most of the information was found on the Internet.

*Much* is used with collective and uncountable nouns.

Much of the work was completed beforehand.

I don't have much time.

## suppose

*I suppose to go to that meeting.

*I supposing they will be late.

The verb *to suppose* has different uses in English. The verb means *to think* or *assume.*

I suppose she will be attending the conference.

Do you suppose we will need more food?

It is used in the passive voice to show an expected action:

She is supposed to win the music award.

They are supposed to have the plan ready by next week.

In the past tense, it is used for an action that did not happen, but was expected.

He was supposed to meet us here at noon. (but he didn't)

## used to

*We have to get use to it.

*I use to live downtown.

*But I still cannot used to live here.

Another troublesome verb form is *used to.* One problem is that it is sometimes misspelled as *use to* because of the pronunciation; the "d" sound drops out next to the *t.* The other problem is that there are two different expressions using *used to,* in addition to the regular verb forms of *use:* one refers to a past action; the other means *accustomed to.*

The verb *to use* is a transitive verb: It takes a direct object. This object becomes the subject in a passive sentence. *Used to* for a past action is always followed by the base form of another verb. To show the meaning "being accustomed to something" the verb form used to is preceded by an auxiliary verb of *to be* and is followed by a gerund (*-ing* form) of another verb. Note the different structures and meanings in the following examples:

I still use my electric typewriter sometimes.

This key is used to open the front door. (passive voice of the verb *to use*)

I used to smoke. (a past action)

He used to drive long distances in his last job. (past action)

I'm used to people recognizing my name. (I'm accustomed to it)

He's used to driving long distances. (He is accustomed to it)

# Countable and Uncountable Nouns

*I have too many homeworks to do.

*Where can we get the informations?

*You can get advices at the counselling centre.

*I value an honesty in an employee.

*I must do many researches to answer that question.

*That company produces good softwares.

Uncountable nouns are also called mass nouns or non-count nouns. They cannot be made plural and cannot be used with the indefinite articles *a* and *an*. They cannot be used with words like *many* and *few*, instead, use *much* and *little*.

Uncountable nouns include liquids and gases (*water, air*), things that are in very small pieces (*sand, rice*), and abstract qualities (*beauty, truth*).

Here are some examples of nouns that are usually uncountable. To further show you the difference between countable and uncountable, we have also listed some examples of related countable nouns.

| **Uncountable** | **Countable** |
| --- | --- |
| advice | a piece of advice, an opinion |
| bread | a loaf of bread, a slice of bread |
| cloth, fabric | a piece of cloth, a bolt of fabric |
| clothes, clothing | an article of clothing, a shirt, jacket |
| damage | |
| equipment | a tool |
| furniture | a chair, table, bed |
| information | |
| luggage, baggage | a bag, a suitcase |
| mail | a message, a letter |
| money | a coin, a bill |
| news | a news story or article |
| paper | a sheet of paper, a piece of paper |
| research | a study |
| software | a program |
| water | a glass of water, a bucket of water |
| work | a chore, a job, a task |

Although coffee, like all liquids, is an uncountable noun, people often refer to "a coffee," as in "Would you like to go for a coffee?" This is actually an ellipsis, where words are left out, for "a cup of coffee." It has become such an accepted expression that even tea drinkers might ask a friend to "go for a coffee."

Note that *e-mail* is often used as a countable noun. This usage would be considered a grammatical error by purists, because mail is an uncountable noun.

I received five e-mails.

Here are some sentences showing how uncountable nouns can be used:

I asked him for information about the company.

She's designing some new software to track the packages.

I need some new clothes for my business trips.

The printer is out of paper.

The water tastes funny.

# Commonly Confused Words

Here is a list of commonly confused words that sound the same or similar. If you are unsure of the difference in meaning, look them up in the dictionary.

| | |
|---|---|
| accept, except | conscience, conscious |
| advice, advise | coarse, course |
| affect, effect | cite, sight, site |
| all ready, already | desert, dessert |
| a lot, allot | does, dose |
| aloud, allowed | hear, here |
| are, our, hour | hole, whole |
| ascent, assent, accent | incidence, incident |
| bare, bear | its, it's |
| break, brake | later, latter |
| buy, by | knew, new |
| choose, choice, chose | know, no, now |
| complement, compliment | loose, lose |

| | |
|---|---|
| man, men | than, then |
| passed, past | their, there, they're |
| patience, patients | though, thought |
| peace, piece | to, too, two |
| personal, personnel | threw, through |
| plain, plane | weak, week |
| principal, principle | wear, were, where, we're |
| presence, presents | weather, whether |
| quiet, quite | which, witch |
| right, write, rite | who's, whose |
| scene, seen | woman, women |
| stationary, stationery | you're, your |

## EXERCISE 15.2

Circle the correct word:

1. **You're/Your** supposed to use this once a **weak/week**.

2. It **does/dose** not seem **right/rite/write** that **woman/women** are not **aloud/allowed** to join the club.

3. He will **accept/except** all the **advice/advise accept/except** for the part about not borrowing money from his brother-in-law.

4. **Wear/Were/Where/We're** are we going this evening? I want to know **which/witch** jacket to **wear/were/where/we're**.

5. I'm **to/too/two** full. I can't possibly eat any **desert/dessert**.

6. She **complimented/complemented** me on my **choose/choice**.

7. The **principal/principle** of the high school said that they could not operate under those **principals/principles**.

8. In your essay, you have to **cite/sight/site** the Internet **cites/sights/sites** where you found that information.

9. **Their/there** are many people asking **weather/whether** the meeting will go on as scheduled.

## CHAPTER 16

# Punctuation, Capitalization, and Format

## Final stops

Most sentences end with a period. Some end with a question mark or an exclamation mark. These marks are used because the reader needs to see clear sentence boundaries in order to comprehend the text.

The question mark (?) indicates to the reader that a sentence is a question, or an interrogative sentence. Essay writers sometimes pose rhetorical questions in order to pique the reader's interest and then go on to give the answer.

What if we were to challenge the belief that the earth is round?

Use rhetorical questions rarely. They lose effect if they are used too often. Also, be sure to use question marks only with true questions, not with reported questions.

What should the government's role be?

He wondered what the role of the government should be.

The exclamation mark (!) is used after emphatic or surprising statements.

The whole class failed the test!

In academic writing and other formal styles, exclamatory sentences are rare. They make your writing more conversational, so avoid using exclamation marks.

You will sometimes see sentences end with ellipsis points (...) to mean "and so on" (often in e-mail messages and Internet posts, for example), but this is poor writing style. It gives the impression that the writer is indecisive and is letting his voice just trail off. Do not end sentences with ellipsis points. The only time you should use ellipsis points is to show that you have omitted some text in a quote.

"The ellipsis, like any other punctuation mark, has defined functions."

"The ellipsis...has defined functions."

Periods are also used with some abbreviations. These include words that are shortened, such as *Nov.* for *November*. Acronyms are abbreviations that are pronounced like words, such as *NATO* (North Atlantic Treaty Organization) and *AIDS* (Acquired Immune Deficiency Syndrome). Acronyms and initialisms, such as *RCMP* (Royal Canadian Mounted Police) and *ESL* (English as a Second Language), are commonly written without periods now. Abbreviations of place names like *U.S.* (United States) and *B.C.* (British Columbia) and university degrees such as *M.A.* (Master of Arts) and *B.Sc.* (Bachelor of Science) are written with periods. If you do not know whether to use periods or not, consult a dictionary.

# Commas

The comma sets apart clauses, items in a series, and extra parts of the sentence, such as interjections and appositives. Sometimes comma use depends on the writer's style and preference.

A comma is used before co-ordinate conjunctions, like *and, or, but, so,* and *for* if the conjunction introduces a full clause.

I asked him to send me a copy of the report, but he forgot.

He wrote to his parents, and he asked them to forgive him.

He wrote to his parents and asked them to forgive him.

After clauses and phrases, a comma is needed to tell the reader that the main clause of the sentence is coming. A comma is not necessary when the subordinate clause comes second because the conjunction serves to signal the beginning of the next clause for the reader.

When she became department head, she streamlined many of the processes.

She streamlined many of the processes when she became department head.

If I had more data, I could put together a computer simulation.

I could put together a computer simulation if I had more data.

Note how the following sentence is difficult to read without the comma:

> While running the car should be in neutral.

> While running, the car should be in neutral.

When items are listed in a series of more than two items, commas are used to separate them. The comma before *and* is optional, but be consistent in your usage; this serial comma is commonly used in British English, but not in American English.

> He brought ham, potatoes, bread, and cheese for lunch.
> (OR: He brought ham, potatoes, bread and cheese for lunch.)

> She is studying economics, French, and political science.

A comma is generally used after transitional adverbs such as *however, moreover,* and *therefore* when they are at the beginning of a sentence, and before and after these words if they are in the middle of a sentence.

> Therefore, the best action is to combine the two departments.

> Phyllis, however, does not endorse that plan.

Another use of the comma is to separate appositives, a group of words modifying or defining a preceding noun, from the main structure of the sentence. (For example, the definition of *appositives* in the preceding sentence is separated from the rest of the sentence by commas.)

> The rocket, sleek and majestic, seem to hover in the sky.

> The principal, a graduate of the University of Toronto, counselled students to go to a large university.

One of the trickier aspects of comma use is in relative clauses, because commas change the meaning of the sentence.

> The students, who failed the test, had to stay after school.

> The students who failed the test had to stay after school.

In the first sentence, all the students failed and all had to stay after school. In the second sentence, only those students who failed had to stay after school. Grammatically, the first sentence has a non-restrictive relative clause, while the second sentence has a restrictive relative clause. You can test whether or not to put commas by deciding whether eliminating the clause changes the meaning of the sentence. In the first sentence, eliminating the clause does not change the meaning of the sentence, so the clause is surrounded by commas.

Commas should not be overused or abused. For example, a comma is not used to separate the subject and the verb, as in this sentence:

> *The part of the test that dealt with matrices, was difficult to understand.

Some people say that you should use a comma where you pause for a breath when you read a sentence aloud, but using this as a guideline may cause you to overuse the comma and make a grammatical error.

# Apostrophes

Apostrophes are probably the most misused piece of punctuation. You may see signs and publications with apostrophes incorrectly used before the *s* of a plural, or even the *s* ending of the third person singular verb.

An apostrophe indicates possession, as in *John's house*. If the noun is plural with an *s*, the apostrophe is used alone: *my parents' car*. This is usually the same for words and names that end in *s*. Writers may add an *s* if it is pronounced with another *s*: *Charles' computer, James's tuba*.

An apostrophe is also used to show dropped letters in contractions. In words like *don't* and *shouldn't* the apostrophe replaces the *o*.

Normally, the apostrophe is not used to indicate the plural form. It is only used before the *s* of a plural if the word would be confusing without it, like with some abbreviations, acronyms, letters and numbers: *T.A.'s, 5.9's*. Consult usage guides and dictionaries if you are unsure whether an apostrophe should be used. Sometimes both forms are acceptable.

## EXERCISE 16.1

Correct the following sentences where necessary:

1. In the 1960s, the Baby Boomer's came into their own.

2. I got all As and Bs on my report card.

3. The childrens' room was a mess.

4. You should'nt believe his' story. He's always stretching the truth.

5. It's time we looked at the Smith's place. It may be what were looking for.

6. She always want's to outdo her sister.

7. The Sheridan's decided to return to the farm.

8. The mens and ladies restrooms are downstairs.

9. The students were looking for more poster's for the library walls.

10. Susans aunt is visiting from Prince George.

# Quotation marks

When you are quoting someone else's words, you use quotation marks at the beginning and end of the section. In English, quotation marks are at the top of the line and curve to face the quote.

> In Shakespeare's *Hamlet*, Polonius advises, "Neither a borrower nor a lender be."

Do not use direct quotation if you are not giving the exact words of the other speaker. Indirect or reported speech is the preferred form.

> People often ask me if I am related to the royal family.
> NOT: People often ask me, "Are you related to the royal family?"

Quotation marks are also conventionally used for titles of poems and stories; the titles of longer works are italicized or underlined.

> You can read "Why My Mother Can't Speak English" in the anthology *Many-Mouthed Birds*.

# Dashes and hyphens

The dash shows the interjection of extra or helpful but not essential information in a sentence. Often it is used to clarify an earlier idea or point.

> The two office clowns—you know, Bill and Joe—were at it again with their practical jokes.

Because the hyphen is found on a regular keyboard, writers tend to use it as a dash. However, parenthetical dashes—used to set apart extra information—are properly em dashes with no space between them and the words. Typewritten documents use two hyphens to represent the dash; these are replaced by an em dash when the document is typeset. Unlike the hyphen, dashes have to be inserted as special characters. Your word processor probably allows you two kinds of dashes, the em dash (the wider one, the width of an "m") and the en dash (the width of the character "n"). The em dash is used for parenthetical dashes, and the en dash is used with numbers: *1993–1997*. The hyphen is used to separate parts of a word: *co-operate*.

The hyphen is used in compound words and to split a word to fit two lines. (Avoid splitting a word as much as possible. It makes the sentence more difficult to read.) Some noun compounds, such as *on-coming, lieutenant-general,* and *Mr. Fix-it,* are written with a hyphen. Some words can be written both with and without hyphens: *left-overs, leftovers.*

# Parentheses

Parentheses (round brackets) are used for extra information in a sentence. For example, you might give the definition of a word in parentheses, as in the preceding sentence.

> Last year, the members of Mothers Against Drunk Drivers (MADD) campaigned to have stiffer sentences for convicted drunk drivers.

> All the charts and statistics (see attachments) say that our company will have a bumper year of profits.

You should be able to read a sentence, omit the information in parentheses, and still make sense of that sentence.

# Semi-colons

A semi-colon can be used to join two closely related sentences.

> Jack took the photograph and Jill developed it.

> Jack took the photograph; Jill developed it.

> They had trained very hard; however, the victory was out of their reach.

Some students have difficulty using the semi-colon and the comma with transitional adverbs, such as *however, moreover, therefore.* If you keep in mind that these adverbs are not conjunctions, like *but, when,* and *although,* you will remember that they cannot join two sentences. A semi-colon, therefore, is sometimes used to join the sentences instead. In addition, to properly punctuate these sentences, remember that the transitional adverb is separated from the rest of the sentence with commas.

> The meeting became chaotic; therefore, the chair adjourned the proceedings.

> The Canadian flag, however, has only existed since 1965.

Semi-colons are also used to separate items in a list where you also use commas.

> At the pot-luck dinner, Jan and Dean brought fruit salad; Sally, lasagna; Leslie and Joe, brownies; and Mary, wine.

# Colons

The colon signals a detailed illustration of a main idea.

> There can be only two interpretations: the poet is being ironic or he is earnest.

A colon is often used before lists, but not after the verb *to be*, when the list forms part of a sentence.

> For class, you should bring the following items: your notebook or paper, a pen, a pencil, your textbooks, and a dictionary.

> *In the carol, there are: five gold rings, four calling birds, three French hens and a partridge in a pear tree.

In addition, a salutation in a business letter is usually followed by a colon, as in *Dear Sir:* Colons are also used between the main title and subtitle: this book is called *Groundwork: Writing Skills to Build On.*

# Space

Space can also be considered an element of punctuation. For instance, an indentation of five spaces shows the beginning of a paragraph. If block style paragraphs are used (as in business letters), blank lines indicate paragraph boundaries. When a line does not extend to the right margin, the space indicates the end of a paragraph.

Some students incorrectly space around punctuation marks. They might leave a space between a word and the comma or period, even putting the punctuation mark at the beginning of a line. Note that most punctuation marks, like commas, periods, colons, and semi-colons, take a space after but not before. M-dashes have no spaces. Open quotes take a space before, but not after.

Some of the confusion related to space may be caused by the widespread use of computers. We think of the space as nothing, but the computer views it as an element that is inserted into a document. In handwriting, spaces are not as fixed in size. Traditionally, typists were taught to put in two spaces after periods, but the use of proportional fonts in word-processing software means that one space after periods is now preferable.

White space can also determine the readability of a document. When you are writing a business letter, a résumé, or a brochure, make sure you leave enough space on the page so that the text does not look cramped. In school assignments, leave enough space to give instructors room to write corrections and comments. When text is printed in narrow columns, as in newspapers and magazines, short paragraphs are used to make it easier to read.

Some students like to use full justification in their word-processed document. This means that the computer lines up the text so there is a straight right-hand margin as well as a straight left-hand margin. Books and newspapers are printed this way. However, this leaves uneven spaces between words and can create distracting rivers of white space running through a paragraph. For your essays, it is usually preferable to use left justification only.

# Capitalization

The basic rules of capitalization are quite simple: Capitalize the first word of a sentence, the main words in book and article titles, and proper nouns, including names of people, languages, religions, countries and other geographical names, government departments, course titles, and organizations. While these simple rules explain most capitalization practices in English, there are some problem areas.

Many people forget to capitalize country names when the names are used as adjectives: English class, Spanish dancing.

As for the name of school subjects, capitalize when it is a formal title but not if it is the general subject name.

> I need to take another science course, so I'm thinking of Introduction to Biology 101.

Sometimes capitalization depends on personal preference or approved style. Consult a style guide or dictionary if you are unsure.

---

**E X E R C I S E   16.2**

---

Put capital letters where necessary in the following sentences:

1. i am writing an essay on capital punishment for my english course.

2. johannes and maria steuer are the winners of the getaway to the bahamas contest.

3. they have some old textbooks for sale—mostly history, science, and french.

4. i'm hoping to go to the united states during the christmas vacation.

5. for her birthday, i'm giving her a cd by the tragically hip.

# Formatting

In the days of typewriters, students did not have many options for formatting. For example, underlining was used instead of italics. Now that most students do assignments on computers, they are exploring the different formatting options available to them. They can use different fonts, boldface, and even graphics.

On the whole, however, you should avoid fancy typefaces. Instructors are interested in a clear, easy-to-read printout, with lots of room for their comments and marking. For most standard typefaces, a 12-point size produces letters clear enough to read. Generally, a fancy cover page is also unnecessary and will not give you extra marks for your assignment.

## Italics and boldface

Italics are used for foreign words and for titles of books, newspapers, magazines, and movies. Titles of works that appear in longer works, such as short stories and poems, should be given in quotation marks, in normal print.

> The article "Making the Grade" was first printed in *Newsweek* magazine.

You can see more examples of this in Chapter 8. Some instructors may insist on the old typewriter style of underlining instead of italics.

When you talk about a word itself, you use italics to show that you are not using the word in the regular way: The word *italics* comes from the name *Italy*; Italian hand meant sloping writing.

Italics are also used for emphasis, but writers should use them judiciously, and beginning writers should avoid them. Boldface, like italics, can be used to stress a word. It should be used sparingly.

### EXERCISE 16.3

Put the proper punctuation and capitalization in the following paragraph:

all too often the consumer is tricked into believing that designer jeans give better fit and wear than the generic brand x such may not be the case the pair of calvin kleins, gwgs or levis that the consumer finds beside the pair of brand x in a department or clothing store may have been cut styled and sewn by the same person moreover the sizing and 14-ounce-cotton weight are all uniform even universal whenever the name brands come out with a new style or look brand x is sure to follow within a short while and with a lower price tag so why pay more for a designer patch that only gives the manufacturer free advertising

## SUMMARY

## *Assignment format*

Your instructor may give you specific instructions on the format of course assignments. Some teachers are very strict about essay format; others are not. All, however, want to see work that is easy to read and mark. Here are some general rules you can follow:

- Use a word processor for your assignment and take advantage of the spelling and grammar checker.

- Double-space your work. There should be a full blank line between each line of print. Use the "2" setting for line spacing in your word processor.

- Use a basic font, in an easily read size, usually 12 point.

- Make sure your printout is easy to read, with dark enough print.

- Indent your paragraphs with five spaces or with a tab set to five spaces.

- Leave at least one inch of margin on all four sides of the page.

- Use left justification and a ragged right margin.

- Use only one side of the paper.

- Make sure all your sentences are clearly delineated, with a capital letter at the beginning and a period at the end.

- Make sure spacing around punctuation marks is correct.

- Paginate assignments with page numbers bottom centre or bottom right.

- Hand in your assignments with a cover page which gives your name, your student number, the course code with section number, the date, the instructor's name, and the title of the assignment. (See example in Figure 16.1.)

- Do not use folders. Staple the sheets of paper in the left hand corner.

## FIGURE 16.1   Sample of a Cover Page

Note that the format you are required to use in your school might be slightly different.

<br>

The Importance of Music Studies

Assignment # 2

by

Antoine LeRoy

# 23986547

Date: October 6, 2001

For: Prof. G. Engkent

Course: ENG 149 TK

# PART 3

# Readings

# Reading Selections

It is difficult to complete any writing course without including some readings. Students cannot improve writing skills in a vacuum. Reading selections can serve as models and give you ideas and topics for your own writing. Most importantly, developing reading skills goes hand in hand with developing writing skills. Good writers tend to be avid readers.

The reading selections here are not meant to serve primarily as models for academic writing; the sample paragraphs and essays in the text are the models. While there are some excerpts from academic texts, most of these selections are from newspapers and magazines, so they are written in a conversational style. Sometimes the writers break the rules of formal English that you are taught in this text; for example, some writers use sentence fragments. Don't let this usage trouble you too much. As we discussed in Chapter 13, we ask you to develop a more formal style of writing that is suitable for academic, business, or technical writing. To do this, you must be able to recognize informal styles of writing.

The readings have several purposes:

- to improve your reading skills
- to give you reading practice
- to increase your vocabulary
- to allow you to learn about sentence structure
- to give you ideas and topics for discussion and writing
- to increase your general knowledge
- to make you more aware of other views of the world
- to challenge you to look at an issue in a different way
- to encourage you to read more outside class

# Reading fiction

We have included two short stories among the reading selections. While fiction is usually relegated to literature courses, it is sometimes included in general composition courses because it is as important to students studying maths and sciences as to those in the humanities. Fiction can teach you about human behaviour. It can take you to places you have never been—even places that do not exist. Historical fiction can teach you about how people lived in the past. Following the plot of a novel can help you develop your thinking skills. Reading novels and short stories will expose you to vocabulary you won't see in textbooks.

You don't have to read classic literature to get these benefits. You should be reading novels that are easy enough for you to enjoy without working too hard. As your readings skills improve, you can challenge yourself with more difficult books.

Some students do not realize that reading fiction is important. It is not just for relaxation and entertainment. While few post-secondary students have the leisure time to read novels, they should try to fit in as much as they can, especially during breaks from school.

# About the selections

Some of these reading selections appeared first in newspapers. Newspapers articles are made up of very short paragraphs so that the text is more readable in the narrow columns. Thus, they do not have the developed paragraphs taught in this text. Moreover, newspapers use headlines instead of titles. A title may tell you the topic or theme, whereas a headline can be a short summary of the article. We have retitled some of these pieces, sometimes giving them a rather prosaic title that makes it easy for teachers and students to refer to the article. For example, "Work is all hell for footsoldiers in corporate trenches" has become "Corporate footsoldiers."

The newspaper pieces are often "op-ed" articles. Op-ed is short for "opinion and editorial." While news stories concentrate on facts, op-ed pieces interpret the facts and state a point of view. When you read the newspaper, you should seek out the editorials and opinion articles, especially those with opposing viewpoints. They are good examples of argumentation.

We have tried to get a range of readings on topics of general interest that can stimulate further discussion and writing. Many of the readings deal with business and consumer issues because we have found these topics work well with our students. We encourage instructors to supplement the reading selections with current newspaper and magazine articles and website readings.

# Using the reading selections

Each reading is accompanied by an introduction, vocabulary study, comprehension and discussion questions, and topics for assignments. The readings are introduced by a few words about the author, some information about the article or story, and some contextual information. The Vocabulary sections are designed to help you increase your vocabulary. We do not have notes on words that are fairly straightforward, so you should use your dictionary to help you with unfamiliar words. You might use the ideas presented here to do your own vocabulary study. For instance, a couple of the reading selections are accompanied by vocabulary charts. If you find these charts useful, you can make your own for other readings. Each reading selection is accompanied by Comprehension and Discussion sections as well as suggestions for Assignments. These, of course, can be tailored by your instructor. For example, instead of discussing a question in class, you may be asked to write a paragraph on the topic.

# How to read effectively

When you read an article, you may have to read it several times. The first time through, concentrate on the main ideas and don't stop to look up words you don't know. Checking unfamiliar words in the dictionary can make reading laborious. Try to use context clues to help you understand a word you don't recognize, then resort to your dictionary if you are really stuck.

One ESL student we knew tackled each reading text as a puzzle. He used his bilingual dictionary to translate words he did not know. He labelled words as to their parts of speech. He parsed sentences, breaking them down into component bits. In other words, he analyzed texts, but he did not really read them. He was a poor reader, concentrating too much on the bits of language without seeing the whole content.

The primary function of a piece of writing is to communicate; you read successfully when you understand the reader's message. You may not understand every single word the author uses, but you should be able to see the main point and how the author supports that point.

# Reading comprehension tests

As part of your English course, you may be called upon to take reading tests. Usually, tests have a variety of questions: You may be asked to give the main idea of the article, to explain the author's ideas, or to paraphrase a sentence from the article. The Comprehension and Discussion sections following the reading selections contain typical reading comprehension questions.

One of the most important strictures included in reading tests is that you must answer in your own words and not copy phrases and sentences from the article. Your instructor can tell nothing about your reading comprehension skills if you repeat what is in the article word for word. Students with little knowledge of English could get lucky and copy the right piece of text as an answer, without understanding what they read at all.

It does help to use part of the question to help frame your answer. For example, if a question asks "Why does the policeman refuse the assignment?" you could begin your answer with "He does it because…"

Accepted practice is to refer to authors by their last names, after you have identified them first with their full name. If you use the first name, you are implying that you know the author personally. Only use *he* or *she* to refer to an author if you know which pronoun to use. The author's first name might indicate whether you should use "he" or "she," but this is not foolproof. Be careful not to call all authors "he" by default.

# How to improve your reading skills

Just like writing, reading skills improve gradually. Whether or not you understand a piece of text depends on your familiarity with the vocabulary, your ability to decode the sentence structure, your understanding of the concepts and context, and your ability to see the relationship between the ideas in the text. The writer's responsibility is to make the text clear to the reader, but the writer has a specific audience and purpose in mind, and sometimes the reader is just not part of that assumed audience. For example, you can buy a book about psychology written for a general reading audience or one that is written as a textbook for advanced students. The latter will be much more difficult to understand.

You can build up your reading skills by starting with relatively easy texts and gradually moving to more difficult texts. When elementary-school students choose books to read at their level, librarians may advise them to read a page and count how many words they do not understand on that page. If it's more than five, the book is too difficult.

Another factor that determines comprehension is familiarity with the subject. The more you know about a certain topic, the more you will understand what is written on that topic. If you study sociology in school, you can read more difficult texts than general readers can. Therefore, it is important to keep reading to build your knowledge in certain subject areas.

One thing you have to accept is that you will not understand every word you read. Even highly educated people come across words, expressions, or ideas that they do not understand. Most of the time they just keep reading and try to get what they can out of the passage. Sometimes they consult reference books to look up unfamiliar words.

You also must be aware that even published materials may be badly written or have mistakes in them. If you don't understand what you read, it might be the writer's fault. The Plain English movement acknowledges that many documents are written in unnecessarily complicated language, especially examples of business and legal writing.

# Finding other reading materials

This book can only offer a few reading selections. Your instructor may supplement these with current newspaper articles or texts from the Internet. It is also important that you keep reading on your own as much as possible. Some students find they can barely keep up with their textbook reading, and they don't want to read anything at all during school breaks. Unfortunately, this kind of thinking does not help them develop the language skills they need.

One good strategy is to broaden the range of materials you read. You can gradually increase the complexity and difficulty; for example, if you like science fiction, you may start with Star Trek books or other genre novels, and then work towards more literary science fiction by authors such as William Gibson. If you read only non-fiction, expand to fiction books by reading ones dealing with the subjects you are interested in.

Use your public library. Ask the librarian for recommendations. When you've read all the books by your favourite author, look up lists of writers who write similar types of novels.

There is a wide range of material available. If you find regular novels difficult, try the simplified novels in the "Literacy" section of the library or youth (young adult) novels. If English is your second language, children's books can supply some of the background cultural knowledge you need. For example, you should know fairy tales such as Cinderella, Snow White, and Sleeping Beauty, as references to such tales are common in the media and even in psychology.

Facing a whole newspaper each day can be daunting. Follow a couple of stories that you are interested in, and be sure to read columns, opinion pieces, editorials, and letters to the editor that follow up on the stories.

Above all, keep reading.

# Why My Mother Can't Speak English

All writers use their own experiences in their stories and articles. Fiction that is closely based on the author's life is called autobiographical. The following short story is autobiographical fiction; it is based on the author's life, but it is not meant to be an accurate account of what actually happened.

Stories are told either in the third person using *he, she,* or *they* to refer to the main character, or in the first person using *I.* When you read a story in the first person, you have to distinguish the narrator (the "I" person) from the author. In this story, the author and the narrator are similar, but in some stories they may be quite different. For example, the book *Memoirs of a Geisha* is told in first person, but its author, Arthur Golden, is not a geisha, Japanese, or even female. In Anne Michaels' novel *Fugitive Pieces*, both narrators are male. The narrator of "Why My Mother Can't Speak English" is unnamed in this story.

Notice that in dialogue a new paragraph is started for every change in speaker.

## *Why My Mother Can't Speak English*

### *by Garry Engkent*

1   My mother is 70 years old. Widowed for five years now, she lives alone in her own house except for the occasions when I come home to tidy her household affairs. She has been in *gum san* for the past 30 years. She clings to the old-country ways so much so that today she astonishes me with this announcement:

2   "I want to get my citizenship," she says as she slaps down the *Dai Pao,* "before they come and take away my house."

3   "Nobody's going to do that. This is Canada."

4   "So everyone says," she retorts, "but did you read what the *Dai Pao* said? Ah, you can't read Chinese. The government is cutting back on old age pensions. Anybody who hasn't got citizenship will lose everything. Or worse."

5   "The *Dai Pao* can't even typeset accurately," I tell her. Sometimes I worry about the information Mother receives from that bi-weekly community newspaper. "Don't worry—the Ministry of Immigration won't send you back to China."

6    "Little you know," she snaps back. "I am old, helpless, and without citizenship. Reasons enough. Now get me citizenship. Hurry!"

7    "Mother, getting citizenship papers is not like going to the bank to cash in your pension cheque. First, you have to—"

8    "Excuses, my son, excuses. When your father was alive—"

9    "Oh, Mother, not again! You throw that at me every—"

10    "—made excuses, too." Her jaw tightens. "If you can't do this little thing for your own mother, well, I will just have to go and beg your cousin to..."

11    Every time I try to explain about the ways of the *fan gwei* she thinks I do not want to help her.

12    "I'll do it, okay? Just give me some time."

13    "That's easy for you," Mother snorts. "You're not 70 years old. You're not going to lose your pension. You're not going to lose your house. Now, how much *lai-shi* will this take?"

14    After all these years in *gum san* she cannot understand that you don't give government officials *lai-shi*, the traditional Chinese money-gift given to persons who do things for you.

15    "That won't be necessary," I tell her. "And you needn't go to my cousin."

16    Mother picks up the *Dai Pao* again and says: "Why should I beg at the door of a village cousin when I have a son who is a university graduate?"

17    I wish my father were alive. Then he would be doing this. But he is not here, and as a dutiful son, I am responsible for the welfare of my widowed mother. So I take her to the Citizenship Court.

18    There are several people from the Chinese community waiting there. Mother knows a few of the Chinese women and she chats with them. My cousin is there, too.

19    "I thought your mother already got her citizenship," he says to me. "Didn't your father—"

20    "No, he didn't."

21    He shakes his head sadly. "Still, better now than never. That's why I'm getting these people through."

22    "So they've been reading the *Dai Pao*."

23    He gives me a quizzical look, so I explain to him, and he laughs.

24    "You are the new generation," he says. "You didn't live long enough in *hon san*, the sweet land, to understand the fears of the old. You can't expect the elderly to renounce all attachments to China for the ways of the *fan gwei*, white devils. How old is she, 70 now? Much harder."

25    "She woke me up this morning at six and Citizenship Court doesn't open until ten."

26    The doors of the Court finally open, and Mother motions me to hurry. We wait in line for a while.

27    The clerk distributes applications and tells me the requirements. Mother wants to know what the clerk is saying so half the time I translate for her.

28    The clerk suggests that we see one of the liaison officers.

29    "Your mother has been living in Canada for the past 30 years and she still can't speak English?"

30    "It happens," I tell the liaison officer.

31    "I find it hard to believe that—not one word?"

32    "Well, she understands some restaurant English," I tell her.

33    "You know, French fries, pork chops, soup, and so on. And she can say a few words."

34    "But will she be able to understand the judge's questions? The interview with the judge, as you know, is a very important part of the citizenship procedure. Can she read the booklet? What does she know about Canada?"

35    "So you don't think my mother has a chance?"

36    "The requirements are that the candidate must be able to speak either French or English, the two official languages of Canada. The candidate must be able to pass an oral interview with the citizenship judge, and then he or she must be able to recite the oath of allegiance—"

37    "My mother needs to speak English," I conclude for her.

38    "Look, I don't mean to be rude, but why didn't your mother learn English when she first came over?"

39    I have not been translating this conversation, and Mother, annoyed and agitated, asks me what is going on. I tell her there is a slight problem.

40    "What problem?" mother opens her purse, and I see her taking a small red envelope—*lai-shi*—I quickly cover her hand.

41    "What is going on?" the liaison officer demands.

42    "Nothing," I say hurriedly. "Just a cultural misunderstand-ing, I assure you."

43    My mother rattles off some indignant words and I snap back in Chinese: "Put that away! The woman won't understand, and we'll be in a lot of trouble."

44    The officer looks confused and I realize an explanation is needed.

45    "My mother was about to give you a money-gift as a token of appreciation for what you are doing for us. I was afraid you might misconstrue it as a bribe. We have no intention of doing that."

46    "I'm relieved to hear that."

47    We conclude the interview, and I take Mother home. Still clutching the application, Mother scowls at me.

48    "I didn't get my citizenship papers. Now I will lose my old age pension. The government will ship me back to China. My old bones will lie there while your father's will be here. What will happen to me?"

49    How can I teach her to speak the language when she is too old to learn, too old to want to learn? She resists anything that is *fan gwei*. She does everything the Chinese way. Mother spends much time staring blankly at the four walls of her house. She does not cry. She sighs and shakes her head. Sometimes she goes about the house touching her favourite things.

50    "This is all your dead father's fault," she says quietly. She turns to the photograph of my father on the mantle. Daily, she burns incense, pours fresh cups of fragrant tea, and spreads dishes of his favourite fruits in front of the framed picture as is the custom. In memory of his passing, she treks two miles to the cemetery to place flowers by his headstone, to burn cere-monial paper money, and to talk to him. Regularly, rain or shine, or even snow, she does these things. Such love, such devotion, now such vehemence. Mother curses my father, her husband, in his grave.

51    When my mother and I emigrated from China, she was 40 years old, and I, five. My father was already a well-established restaurant owner. He put me in school and Mother in the restaurant kitchen, washing dishes and cooking strange foods like hot dogs, hamburgers, and French fries. She worked seven days a week from six in the morning until

eleven at night. This lasted for 25 years, almost to the day of my father's death.

52    The years were hard on her. The black-and-white photographs show a robust woman; now I see a withered, frail, white-haired old woman, angry, frustrated with the years, and scared of losing what little material wealth she has to show for the toil in *gum san*, the golden mountain.

53    "I begged him," Mother says. "But he would either ignore my pleas or say: 'What do you need to know English for? You're better off here in the kitchen. Here you can talk to the others in our own tongue. English is far too complicated for you. How old are you now? Too old to learn a new language. Let the young speak *fan gwei*. All you need is to understand the orders from the waitresses. Anyway, if you need to know something, the men will translate for you. I am here; I can do your talking for you.'"

54    As a conscientious boss of the young male immigrants, my father would force them out of the kitchen and into the dining room. "The kitchen is not place for you to learn English. All you do is speak Chinese in here. To survive in *gum san*, you have to speak English, and the only way you can do that is to wait on tables and force yourselves to speak English with the customers. How can you get your families over here if you can't talk to the Immigration officers in English?"

55    A few of the husbands who had the good fortune to bring their wives over to Canada hired a retired school teacher to teach a bit of English to their wives. Father discouraged Mother from going to those once-a-week sessions.

56    "That old woman will get rich, doing nothing. What have these women learned? *Fan gwei* ways—make-up, lipstick, smelly perfumes, fancy clothes—like whores. Once she gets through with them, they won't be Chinese women any more—and they certainly won't be white, either."

57    Some of the husbands heeded the words of the boss, for he was older than they, and had been in the white devils' land longer. These wives stayed at home and tended the children, or they worked in the restaurant kitchen, washing dishes and cooking *fan gwei* foods, and talking in Chinese about the land and the life they were forced to leave behind.

58    "He was afraid that I would leave him. I depended on him

for everything. I could not go anywhere by myself. He drove me to work and he drove me home. He only taught me to print my name so that I could sign anything he wanted me to, bank cheques, legal documents…"

59   Perhaps I am not Chinese enough any more to understand why my mother would want to take in the sorrow, the pain, and the anguish and then to recount them every so often.

60   Once I was presumptuous enough to ask her why she would want to remember in such detail. She said the memories didn't hurt any more. I did not tell her that her reminiscences cut me to the quick. Her only solace now is to be listened to.

61   My father wanted more sons, but she was too old to give him more. One son was not enough security he needed for old age. "You smell of stale perfume," she would say to him after he had driven the waitresses home. Or, to me, she would say: "A second mother will not treat you so well, you know," and, "Would you like another mother at home?" Even at that tender age, I knew that in China a husband could take a second wife. I told her that I didn't need another mother, and she would nod her head.

62   When my father died five years ago, she cried and cried. "Don't leave me in this world. Let me die with you."

63   Grief-stricken, she would not eat for days. She was so weak from hunger that I feared she wouldn't be able to attend the funeral. At his grave side, she chanted over and over a dirge, commending his spirit to the next world and begging the goddess of mercy to be kind to him. By custom, she set his picture on the mantel and burned incense in front of it daily. And we would go to the cemetery often. There she would arrange fresh flowers and talk to him in the gentlest way.

64   Often she would warn me: "The world of the golden mountain is so strange, *fan gwei* improprieties, and customs. The white devils will have you abandon your own aged mother to some old age home to rot away and die unmourned. If you are here long enough, they will turn your head until you don't know who you are, what you are—Chinese."

65   My mother would convert the months and the days into the Chinese lunar calendar. She would tell me about the seasons and the harvests and festivals in China. We did not celebrate any *fan gwei* holidays.

66      My mother sits here at the table, fingering the booklet from the Citizenship Court. For thirty-some years, my mother did not learn the English language, not because she was not smart enough, not because she was too old to learn, and not because my father forbade her, but because she feared that learning English would change her Chinese soul. She only learned enough English to survive in the restaurant kitchen.

67      Now, Mother wants *gum san* citizenship.

68      "Is there no hope that I will be given it?" she asks.

69      "There is always a chance," I tell her. "I'll hand in the application."

70      "I should have given that person the *lai-shi*," Mother says obstinately.

71      "Maybe I should teach you some English," I retort. "You have about six months before the oral interview."

72      "I am 70 years old," she says. "*Lai-shi* is definitely much easier."

73      My brief glimpse into Mother's heart is over, and it has taken so long to come about. I do not know whether I understand my aged mother any better now. Despite my mother's constant instruction, there is too much *fan gwei* in me.

74      The booklet from the Citizenship Court lies, unmoved, on the table, gathering dust for weeks. She has not mentioned citizenship again with the urgency of that particular time. Once in a while, she would say: "They have forgotten me. I told you they don't want old Chinese women as citizens."

75      Finally, her interview date is set. I try to teach her some ready made phrases, but she forgets them.

76      "You should not sigh so much. It is bad for your health," Mother observes.

77      On the day of her examination, I accompany her into the judge's chamber. I am more nervous than my mother.

78      Staring at the judge, my mother remarks: "*Noi yren.*" The judge shows interest in what my mother says, and I translate it: "She says you're a woman."

79      The judge smiles "Yes. Is that strange?"

80      "If she is going to examine me," Mother tells me, "I might as well start packing for China. Sell my house. Dig up your father's bones, I'll take them back with me."

81    Without knowing what my mother said, the judge reassures her. "This is just a formality. Really. We know that you obviously want to be part of our Canadian society. Why else would you have gone through all this trouble? We want to welcome you as a new citizen, no matter what race, nationality, religion or age. And we want you to be proud—as a new Canadian."

82    Six weeks have passed since the interview with the judge. Mother receives a registered letter telling her to come in three weeks time to take part in the oath of allegiance ceremony.

83    With patient help from the same judge, my mother recites the oath and becomes a Canadian citizen after 30 years in *gum san*.

84    "How does it feel to be Canadian?" I ask.

85    "In China, this is the eighth month, the season of harvest." Then she adds: "The *Dai Pao* says that old age pension cheques will be increased by nine dollars next month."

86    As we walk home on this bright autumn morning, my mother clutches her piece of paper. Citizenship. She says she will go up to the cemetery and talk to my father this afternoon. She has something to tell him.

## Vocabulary

The author uses Chinese words and phrases to add flavour to the story. Knowing that these will be unfamiliar to most of his readers, the author makes the meaning clear by translating and by giving clear context clues. In prose, translations or explanations often appear in appositive phrases, usually set off by commas, such as in this example:

> "You are the new generation," he says. "You didn't live
> long enough in hon san, the sweet land, to understand
> the fears of the old. You can't expect the elderly to
> renounce all attachments to China for the ways of the
> fan gwei, white devils."

The author translates *hon san* as "the sweet land" and *fan gwei* as "white devils." From the context we know that *hon san* refers to China and *fan gwei* refers to non-Chinese people.

Note how the author builds the context clues and gradually reveals the meaning of *Dai Pao* in paragraphs 2 to 5. At first, we notice the term is capitalized, so we know it is a proper noun, the name of something. The mother slaps it down, so we know it is something she can hold. The references to reading it and typesetting make it clear that the *Dai Pao* is a publication. Then the author gives the meaning: "that bi-weekly community newspaper."

Examine the other clues the author gives to the Chinese expressions: *lai-shi, gum san, noi yren*. Try to figure out the meaning. Even if the words or phrases are not English transliterations of the original, you can still figure them out in context. For example, when the mother says, "*Lai-shi* is definitely much easier," you know from the earlier scene at the Citizenship office that she means a bribe.

In the same way, use context clues to help you try to figure out the English words you do not understand. If you are stuck on a word, use your dictionary.

## Comprehension

1. Why did the narrator's mother not learn English?

2. What other factors contributed to the mother not knowing English?

3. Explain in your own words the author's reference to "her Chinese soul."

4. How did the father feel about the mother learning English? How is this a double standard (different rules for different people)?

5. Why is citizenship important for the mother?

6. What is ironic about the last dialogue in the story?

7. Explain the sentence: "Despite my mother's constant instruction, there is too much *fan gwei* in me."

## Discussion

1. What do you think are the factors important in determining whether or not someone will acquire a second language easily?

2. We use the term "generation gap" to explain the differences in perspective that two generations may have, and thus the conflict between parents and grown children. In this story there is also a culture gap, because the narrator is Canadian while his mother is Chinese. Discuss your experiences with culture gap or generation gap.

3. What kind of difficulties do second generation immigrants face? Second generation refers to immigrants' children, those who are born or raised in the new country.

## Assignments

1. Describe the process of becoming a Canadian citizen.

2. Explain how immigrants adapt to their new country.

3. Should Canada's immigration laws encourage new immigrants?

4. Examine Canada's immigration laws. Do you think they are fair?

# House Guests

Raheel Raza is originally from Pakistan, and she now lives in Toronto. This article originally appeared as "Those lazy, crazy, summer visitors."

This article is written in conversational style. It includes many expressions that you would not use in an academic essay, such as "love to bits" and "Yeah right!"

## House Guests

### by Raheel Raza

1    I'm glad summer's over—not only so the kids can return to school. They were the least of my problem—I hardly saw them. I spent my summer waiting on guests from back home.

2    Apart from physical and emotional exhaustion, I swear I can drive to the airport blindfolded, I've seen Niagara Falls at least a dozen times in two months, every salesperson in the Eaton Centre knows me and I've run out of cheap places to feed guests.

3    I'm not being mean. I pride myself on South Asian hospitality, but give me a break! When we moved to Canada, relatives groaned, "Oh, you're going so far away to that cold land, we'll never be able to visit you." Yeah right! So who told them about summer in Canada?

4    While griping to friends, I realized I'm not the only one who suffers the onslaught of inconsiderate guests. Many of us (South Asian by birth) are inundated with packs of ill-informed relatives (and *their* distant relatives) who descend on us every summer with short notice, expecting to be picked up and dropped off, driven around, fed three home-cooked meals a day, entertained, wined, dined and given gifts as they depart with two extra suitcases. Not to mention the phone bill that indicates they called everyone coast-to-coast in North America.

5    I believe you can take the South Asian out of South Asian but you can't take Asian customs out of the person. I'm referring to myself and the fact that I don't have the gumption to tell my guests to ride the TTC, feed them one meal a day, give them sandwiches for lunch, point them in the direction of the shops and insist they take the bus tour instead of waiting for me to take them sightseeing after work every day. Every time I

think of cutting corners, my mother's spirit haunts me and preaches the virtues of being a good host.

6      A friend, drained from lugging a dozen family members to Wonderland for the whole day, commented "we must be stupid to emotionally, financially and physically exhaust ourselves for our guests; we ignore our kids, go to work bleary-eyed, take vacations to accommodate their needs and don't even get a thank-you note in return because it's not done in our culture." Her aunt had handed her a hundred rupee note (approx. $2.50) while leaving!

7      It wouldn't be so frustrating if they came with an open mind (an open wallet would also help). Some of them arrive here with preconceived notions about Canada and constantly compare their lifestyle to ours, so we have the added onus of defending our choice of living here.

8      Take my sister (whom I live to bits, in case someone sends her a copy of this piece). Having seen too much *Geraldo* and *Baywatch*, the two most popular TV programs in Pakistan, she came to Toronto recently, expecting the worst. When she saw families with kids, her comment was, "I thought Canadians were not the family type!" Other things she thought: homes get cleaned by themselves, everyone drinks and smokes, incest and abuse are common, women walk around in bikinis and there are only white Christians in Canada.

9      It didn't take long to set her straight. My sister dresses traditionally and covers her head. While traveling, an airline attendant asked me if she understood English. Sis, a graduate who majored in English literature, said "how ignorant, all this is gleaned from the media." One night, she decided to take a walk outside and triggered our burglar alarm. When multi-coloured neighbours rushed to our assistance, Sis saw the light. She confessed she understands what stereotyping means and that it can work both ways. While she's not moving to Canada, she's gone back a bit enlightened, carrying a few instructions for the next batch of visitors, who may arrive any day.

10      While I recharge my batteries and gear up for the onslaught, I've thought of a few precautions I might take next year:

• Get an unlisted phone number and change my name to Smith or Jones;

- Tell relatives I've moved to Yellowknife—they won't even look for me;
- Tell them the Falls are closed for cleaning;
- Best of all, lock up the house and go there for the summer.

## Vocabulary

*Baywatch*: a one-hour American drama about lifeguards, known for attractive actors running around the beach in skimpy bathing suits

cut corners (idiom): to do something in an easy or less expensive way, usually by eliminating something

Eaton Centre: a large shopping centre in downtown Toronto

*Geraldo*: an American talk show that deals with sensational personal stories, often with confrontation

mean: Note that this is the adjective, not the verb. What are some synonyms?

open mind: The adjective form is *open-minded*; related words are *close-minded*, *narrow-minded*, and *broad-minded*.

see the light (idiom): Compare this expression to the verb *enlighten*. The idea of light means understanding.

stereotype: an image people have of a certain kind of person. For example, the stereotype of a computer programmer is a young man with few social skills, dressed conservatively, wearing glasses.

TTC: Toronto Transit Commission, the name of the public transit system in Toronto

Wonderland: a large amusement park near Toronto

## Comprehension

1. What are the author's two main complaints about her guests?

2. What does the author do for her house guests? How would she like to cut back? Why doesn't she?

3. What do you think the author's friend thinks about the hundred-rupee note her aunt gave her?

4. What does the author mean when she says, "you can take the South Asian out of South Asia but you can't take Asian customs out of the person"?

5. What lesson did the sister learn about stereotyping?

## Discussion

1. Discuss the idea of stereotyping. What are some common stereotypes? What is the danger of stereotyping?

2. Answer the following questions about the behaviour of guests and hosts. If your answer is "that depends," explain what circumstances should be considered.

   a) Should house guests bring a gift to the hosts? Should they give a gift at the end of their stay?

   b) Should hosts give guests a going-away gift?

   c) What kind of gifts are appropriate?

   d) Should guests help with the housework?

   e) Should hosts take time off work to take guests to tourist sites?

   f) Should guests expect three home-cooked meals every day?

   g) If hosts take guests to a tourist attraction, should the hosts pay for admission, meals, and souvenirs?

3. When do guests wear out their welcome?

## Assignments

1. Write a paragraph explaining what kind of behaviour you expect from a host, or from an overnight guest.

2. Compare/contrast ways guests are treated in two different cultures.

3. Choose a custom from another country, and explain why immigrants have difficulty keeping that custom in Canada.

4. It often happens that we rarely visit our own region's tourist attractions unless we are accompanying visitors from out of town. Choose a tourist attraction and write a paragraph describing it, convincing local residents to visit.

5. Take one of the actions of hosts and guests from the discussion section and write a paragraph explaining it.

6. Write a developed paragraph restating Raza's complaint in academic English.

# Making the Grade

Kurt Wiesenfeld is a physics professor at the Georgia Institute of Technology.

Notice how Wiesenfeld starts his article with a narrative—a story telling what happened to him. From this introduction he goes to the heart of his argument. Consider the audience for this article. If Wiesenfeld were simply addressing students, how would the article be different?

## *Making the Grade*

*Many students wheedle for a degree as if it were a freebie T shirt*

### *by Kurt Wiesenfeld*

1    It was a rookie error. After 10 years I should have known better, but I went to my office the day after final grades were posted. There was a tentative knock on the door. "Professor Wiesenfeld? I took your Physics 2121 class? I flunked it? I wonder if there's anything I can do to improve my grade?" I thought: "Why are you asking me? Isn't it too late to worry about it? Do you dislike making declarative statements?"

2    After the student gave his tale of woe and left, the phone rang. "I got a D in your class. Is there any way you can change it to 'Incomplete'?" Then the e-mail assault began: "I'm shy about coming in to talk to you, but I'm not shy about asking for a better grade. Anyway, it's worth a try." The next day I had three phone messages from students asking me to call them. I didn't.

3    Time was, when you received a grade, that was it. You might groan and moan, but you accepted it as the outcome of your efforts or lack thereof (and, yes, sometimes a tough grader). In the last few years, however, some students have developed a disgruntled-consumer approach. If they don't like their grade, they go to the "return" counter to trade it in for something better.

4    What alarms me is their indifference toward grades as an indication of personal effort and performance. Many, when pressed about why they think they deserve a better grade, admit they don't deserve one but would like one anyway. Having been raised on gold stars for effort and smiley faces for self-esteem,

they've learned that they can get by without hard work and real talent if they can talk the professor into giving them a break. This attitude is beyond cynicism. There's a weird innocence to the assumption that one expects (even deserves) a better grade simply by begging for it. With that outlook, I guess I shouldn't be as flabbergasted as I was that 12 students asked me to change their grades after final grades were posted.

5      That's 10 percent of my class who let three months of midterms, quizzes and lab reports slide until long past remedy. My graduate student calls it hyperrational thinking: if effort and intelligence don't matter, why should deadlines? What matters is getting a better grade through an unearned bonus, the academic equivalent of a freebie T shirt or toaster give-away. Rewards are disconnected from the quality of one's work. An act and its consequences are unrelated, random events.

6      Their arguments for wheedling better grades often ignore academic performance. Perhaps they feel it's not relevant. "If my grade isn't raised to a D, I'll lose my scholarship." "If you don't give me a C, I'll flunk out." One sincerely overwrought student pleaded, "If I don't pass, my life is over." This is tough stuff to deal with. Apparently, I'm responsible for someone's losing a scholarship, flunking out or deciding whether life has meaning. Perhaps these students see me as a commodities broker with something they want—a grade. Though intrinsically worthless, grades, if properly manipulated, can be traded for what has value: a degree, which means a job, which means money. The one thing college actually offers—a chance to learn—is considered irrelevant, even less than worthless, because of the long hours and hard work required.

7      In a society saturated with surface values, love of knowledge for its own sake does sound eccentric. The benefits of fame and wealth are more obvious. So is it right to blame students for reflecting the superficial values saturating our society?

8      Yes, of course it's right. These guys had better take themselves seriously now, because our country will be forced to take them seriously later, when the stakes are much higher. They must recognize that their attitude is not only self-destructive, but socially destructive. The erosion of quality control—giving appropriate grades for actual accomplish-

ments—is a major concern in my department. One colleague noted that a physics major could obtain a degree without ever answering a written exam question completely. How? By pulling in enough partial credit and extra credit. And by getting breaks on grades.

9    But what happens once she or he graduates and gets a job? That's when the misfortunes of eroding academic standards multiply. We lament that schoolchildren get "kicked upstairs" until they graduate from high school despite being illiterate and mathematically inept, but we seem unconcerned with college graduates whose less blatant deficiencies are far more harmful if their accreditation exceeds their qualifications.

10   Most of my students are science and engineering majors. If they're good at getting partial credit but not at getting the answer right, then the new bridge breaks or the new drug doesn't work. One finds examples here in Atlanta. Last year a light tower in the Olympic Stadium collapsed, killing a worker. It collapsed because an engineer miscalculated how much weight it could hold. A new 12-story dormitory could develop dangerous cracks due to a foundation that's uneven by more than six inches. The error resulted from incorrect data being fed into a computer. I drive past that dorm daily on my way to work, wondering if a foundation crushed under kilotons of weight is repairable or if this structure will have to be demolished. Two 10,000-pound steel beams at the new natatorium collapsed in March, crashing into the student athletic complex. (Should we give partial credit since no one was hurt?) Those are real-world consequences of errors and lack of expertise.

11   But the lesson is lost on the grade-grousing 10 percent. Say that you won't (not can't, but won't) change the grade they deserve to what they want, and they're frequently bewildered or angry. They don't think it's fair that they're judged according to their performance, not their desires or "potential." They don't think it's fair that they should jeopardize their scholarships or be in danger of flunking out simply because they could not or did not do their work. But it's more than fair: it's necessary to help preserve a minimum standard of

quality that our society needs to maintain safety and integrity. I don't know if the 13th-hour students will learn that lesson, but I've learned mine. From now on, after final grades are posted, I'll lie low until the next quarter starts.

## Vocabulary

Use your dictionaries to fill in the following chart. Some spaces have been filled in to give you examples. Some spaces you will have to leave blank. Usage tags show how or where a word is used. For example, some words are British or American English. Some are slang, colloquial, or derogatory.

| WORD | PART OF SPEECH AND USAGE TAGS | MEANING | SYNONYMS OR ANTONYMS | WORDS WITH THE SAME ROOT |
|---|---|---|---|---|
| blatant | | | obvious | |
| cynicism | | | | cynic (n.), cynical (adj.) |
| disgruntled | adj. | | | |
| flabbergasted | | | | |
| flunk | v. slang | | | |
| freebie | | | | |
| indifference | | | | |
| jeopardize | | | | jeopardy (n.) |
| outlook | | | | |
| overwrought | | | | |
| plead | | | | |
| relevant | | | | irrelevant (opp.) relevance (n.) |
| rookie | | | | |
| saturated | | | | |

| WORD | PART OF SPEECH AND USAGE TAGS | MEANING | SYNONYMS OR ANTONYMS | WORDS WITH THE SAME ROOT |
|---|---|---|---|---|
| tentative | | | | |
| wheedle | | | | |
| woe | | | | |

## Comprehension and Discussion

1. Why did Professor Wiesenfeld write this article? What is his argument?

2. What does the title "Making the Grade" mean?

3. Explain the reference to "declarative statements" in the first paragraph. (Hint: it's a grammatical term.)

4. Explain the sentence: "What alarms me is their indifference toward grades as an indication of personal effort and performance."

5. Does Wiesenfeld feel guilty about giving the students low grades? Why or why not?

6. What does Wiesenfeld say that he learns from his experience?

7. Do you think Wiesenfeld is being fair? How would you feel if you were one of his students?

8. The author implies that our society is too focused on buying and selling. How else does over-commercialization affect our society?

## Assignments

1. It doesn't really matter what you learn in college—as long as you have your diploma, you have a ticket to a good job. Agree or disagree with this statement.

2. Explain why some students may think they can buy, rather than earn, a degree.

3. Wiesenfeld says that it is important to society that educational standards are maintained. In an essay, explain why it is important specifically to students, to the institution, or to employers.

# Teenagers and Part-time Jobs

This selection is by Ken Dryden, a famous hockey player, who also became a lawyer and a writer. He was goalie for the Montreal Canadiens in the 1970s, helping the team win several Stanley Cups. After his NHL career, he practised law. He wrote books about hockey, including the well respected *The Game.* In 1997 he became president of the Toronto Maple Leafs.

Dryden spent the 1993-94 school year in a Mississauga, Ontario high school, Thomas L. Kennedy Secondary School. He sat in on classes and interviewed students and teachers. His book *In School: Or Kids, Our Teachers, Our Classrooms* reports his experience. Here is an excerpt.

## *Teenagers and Part-time Jobs*

### *by Ken Dryden*

1    The part-time job may be the single biggest change in the life of teenagers since the time their teachers were young. Except for paper routes and babysitting, almost none of them had outside jobs. When public education became universal about a century ago, most kids had chores to do around the house, the farm, or in the family business. But only a handful went to school for more than a few years, so the collision of increased homework in higher grades and family responsibilities rarely happened. This century, families moved from farms to cities, household appliances cut time needed for chores, education became more important to futures, so more kids stayed in school longer. For decades, there was no conflict between studies and paid work. Any money earned outside the home was handed over to the parents for the family's shared benefit. A kid had no money of his own, and there was little for him to buy. The teenager as consumer had yet to be invented.

2    By the late 1940s, after years of depression and war, the North American economy was burgeoning. There was money to make, and money to spend. Families that had been put on hold were rapidly taking shape. More people got married, more kids were born, "baby boomers" as they would be called.

More houses were built, suburbs grew, more cars were sold. A larger family bounty meant larger allowances for kids, finally money of their own to spend. Teenagers became a separate group with its own identity. It was money that did it. Blue jeans and white T-shirts gave teenagers a look; rock and roll music, a sound; jalopies, the residue of those millions of new cars, gave them independence. An allowance was no longer enough: the part-time job at the local supermarket or gas station was necessary to afford all the stuff manufacturers provided for teenagers to buy. But there weren't enough supermarkets or gas stations. The real revolution came with fast food restaurants, and the explosion of the service sector.

3      Hamburgers at 59 cents or 49 cents: with pressure on prices, there was also pressure on wages. People were exchanged for machines and process, higher-priced people exchanged for lower. And who were they? In the growing economy of the sixties and seventies, the only adults available were the long-term unemployed or new immigrants who spoke little English—both second choices for many employers. Why not hire instead the bright-eyed teenaged sons and daughters of neighbours and friends, with their "go get 'em" energy? That made sense to employers; it made sense to kids and their parents. A part-time job would give kids a dose of responsibility, an appreciation of what they have, make them learn that in this life they have to work for what they get. That's how it had been for families earlier in the century, thought their parents, memories of their own parents' era frozen and idealized in their adult minds. Those families had worked together and stayed together. Even if work today took family members into different places, it still represented an important shared experience.

4      A part-time job gave kids the chance to experience the discipline of work. Kids can ignore parents and finesse teachers, but this was a boss, unimpeded by affection or stature, who had no obligation to put up with them. These kids had to produce or they would be fired. It was a chance to work beside older people, to learn from them and about them; to learn some practical skills they could take with them into some future workplace. Far better than the fun and games of clubs and

sports whose lessons, so indirect, seemed nearly invisible. A job was the direct route to maturity. It was also another way to keep kids busy, off increasingly mean streets. For those who might drop out, it was a few hours a week in a workplace that held no bad memories, earning money for some of the freedom and independence they craved, perhaps helping to keep them in school longer.

5      But if part-time jobs have achieved some of their goals, their unintended effect has been more significant. Some work disciplines are learned on the job, some skills too, though many fewer than parents would like to think. For kids, most work time is spent not in the company of older workers, but with kids like themselves. It is from the money that kids have taken their greatest lessons. Money that doesn't go into a family pot. I worked for it, it's mine, kids today say. Though in the last fifteen years family incomes have struggled to keep up with inflation, "designer" tastes and expectations have taken hold among teens in part because of this additional pocket of income. A kid wants new Doc Martens and Birkenstocks. His parents refuse to buy them. They're too expensive, they say; but crumbling under his relentless pressure, they agree to a bargain. We'll give you the money it costs for the entirely adequate no-name clothes and running shoes we always bought you, and you can buy what you want, using your own money to pay the difference. So the kid works and buys the coveted item, and feels the sense of achievement and success that comes from having bought it himself. But he hasn't really bought it himself. And now he has designer tastes, designer standards of success and achievement to take into the future, where soon he'll have to pay the entire price for these tastes, as well as for his own shelter, his own food, and so on and so on. More than anything, part-time jobs have created a false standard of living and a false sense of independence among teens. They have helped to generate the destructive impatience kids feel when, out of school, unable to find immediately the job they want at the salary they want, they complain, "There are no jobs out there," and feel the weight of personal failure and disappointment.

## Vocabulary

baby boomers: people born between 1946 and 1965, a period when a population explosion occurred. Because of the large size of this group, they dominate society.

Birkenstocks: a brand name for sandals, popular in the 1990s

Doc Martens: a brand name for boots, popular in the 1980s and 1990s

"go get 'em" energy: ('em is short for them) enthusiasm and aggressiveness in business. A person with this quality might be called a "go-getter."

## Comprehension and Discussion

1. Explain the changes in society that Dryden mentions.

2. Why do employers in the service sector prefer to hire teenagers?

3. Why do parents want their children to work part-time?

4. Explain what Dryden means when he says, "part-time jobs have created a false standard of living and a false sense of independence among teens."

5. Make a list of advantages and disadvantages of part-time jobs for students.

6. Another reason that high school students work is to earn money for post-secondary studies. How much could a high school student earn working part-time in a school year and full-time in the summer? Compare these amounts to tuition fees.

## Assignments

1. Describe a work experience you had and explain what it taught you.

2. Some children are not expected to work part-time or to do housework. Discuss the advantages or disadvantages of a life in which a child's only responsibility is schoolwork.

3. Many businesses, such as the movie industry, rely on teenaged clientele. Choose an industry and explain how it attracts teenaged consumers.

# The Baby Boom

Demographics is the study of population distribution. The location and concentration of population can give a lot of information for government and business. For example, an aging population needs more investment in health care, while a young population needs more in education.

This reading is an excerpt from *Boom, Bust and Echo 2000*, the second edition of a book that appeared on the best-seller charts for months. The word *boom* refers to an explosion—in this case a population explosion. In this book, the authors explain the phenomenon of the baby boom and its aftermath. The sudden influx of millions of babies creates problems and opportunities as they grow from childhood, through adolescence and middle age, to the age of senior citizens. At each stage of the boom, governments and businesses must adapt to the needs of the many.

Note that the book is by David K. Foot *with* Daniel Stoffman. What do you think this type of author credit means? Dr. Foot is a professor at the University of Toronto, while Mr. Stoffman is a journalist. Does this information give you an idea of how this collaboration might have worked?

This reading selection is an example of a more academic text than other selections in this chapter. It is a definition, explaining what the baby-boom generation is. The definition includes comparison and cause/effect. This passage is composed of developed paragraphs with topic sentences.

Since this is an excerpt from a book, there are references to what has been mentioned in the previous pages. For example, the authors had already explained the Depression generation. To help you put this information in context, here are some of the other cohorts (groups of people) of the 20th century described in the book:

The Depression Babies (1930–1939): They had a hard time during their youth, through the depression and World War II, but once they joined the workforce they had an easy time getting work. They are part of a small group, but they are the parents of the baby boom. They made a lot of money from real estate and the stock market. Their large families boosted the economy.

The Baby Bust (1967–1979): This is a small cohort, so the members have had little competition. Although they have to compete for jobs with late boomers, they can get entry-level jobs more easily, and they have the computer skills employers want.

The Baby-Boom Echo (1980–1995): These are the children of the boomers. They make a mini-boom: a boom because there were a lot of boomers having children, but small since boomers had fewer children than their parents.

## *The Baby Boom*

### *by David E. Foot with Daniel Stoffman*

1    Even people with no knowledge of demographics have heard of the group born from 1947 to 1966. These are the boomers. Some members of this particular cohort seem to think they are pretty special. To hear them talk, you'd think they were the most innovative and creative bunch of people Canada had ever seen, infusing all of society with new ways of thinking and new ways of doing things. This is nonsense. In fact, when they were 20, boomers weren't much different from the 20-year-olds who had preceded them. And now that many of them are in their 40s and early 50s, they are behaving just as middle-aged people have always behaved.

2    The only thing special about the boomers is that there are so many of them. It seems hard to imagine now, but at the height of the boom, Canadian women were averaging four offspring each. Canada produced more than 400,000 new Canadians in each year of the boom, peaking at 479,000 in 1959. But examining Canadian births alone isn't sufficient to define the baby boom. The largest single-year age group in Canada is those born in 1961, even though 3,600 fewer people were born here in that year than in 1959. That's because the 1961 group includes immigrants born in that year somewhere else. The boom, both those born in Canada and those born elsewhere, totalled 9.9 million people in 1998, or 32.4% of the Canadian population.

3    Canada's was the loudest boom in the industrialized world. In fact, only three other Western countries—the United States, Australia, and New Zealand—had large booms. Part of the reason was that these four countries were immigrant receivers, and immigrants tend to be in their 20s, the prime childbearing years. The U.S. boom started earlier, in 1946, and it also ended earlier, in 1964. At its peak in 1957, the U.S. boom hit 3.7 children per

family, nearly half a baby fewer than Canadian women were producing at the peak of the Canadian boom. The Americans started their boom earlier because more of their war effort was in the Pacific, and the Pacific war wound down sooner. The U.S. troops were brought home in 1945 and kids started appearing in 1946. Canadian troops came home later, so Canadian births did not leap upwards until 1947. As for the Australians, they never got much higher than three babies per woman, but they compensated by continuing their boom ten years longer than Canada did. That happened because Australians were slower to adopt the birth-control pill and because Australian women were slower than their North American counterparts to enter the workforce in large numbers.

4    Because the Canadian boom was so big, Canadian boomers are a slightly more important factor in Canadian life than American boomers are in American life. Almost one-third of Canadians today are boomers, and for that reason alone, when they get interested in a particular product or idea, we all have to sit up and take notice. It's not that the product or idea is so great, it's just that everyone seems to be talking about it. The result is that phenomena such as the return to "family values" are often mistakenly identified as new social trends rather than the predictable demographic events they really are. (There is nothing new or remarkable about 35-year-olds raising families being interested in family values.)

5    Why did the boom happen? A likely explanation is that during those 20 years, Canadians knew they could afford large families. The postwar economy was robust, the future seemed full of promise, and young couples wanted to share that bright future with a big family. A second reason was the high immigration levels that prevailed during the 1950s; immigrants tend to be people of childbearing age, and they made an important contribution to the boom. The combination of two ingredients—lots of people in their high fertility years and high incomes—is a surefire recipe for filling up maternity wards. But you need both: immigration levels were raised in the early years of the 1990s but the fertility rate didn't respond because incomes were falling, and Canadians, immigrants and non-immigrants alike, didn't think they could afford extra mouths to feed.

6    Why did the boom end? Towards the end of the 1960s, an increasing number of women were pursuing higher education or entering the workforce. As a result, they were postponing childbirth and deciding to have fewer children. The introduction of the birth-control pill made this easier than ever to achieve. The more rapid acceptance of the pill in the United States may explain why the American boom ended before Canada's.

7    Like the seniors, the boomers break down into separate subgroups. The front-end boomer, in his early 50s, with a bulging waistline and equally bulging Registered Retirement Savings Plan, doesn't share much in the way of cultural attitudes or life experiences with the Generation-Xer, in his mid-30s, whose career hasn't yet got off the ground and who has trouble scraping up rent money every month. But as boomers, they have one very important thing in common: they are part of a huge cohort. For the front-end boomers, this was an advantage they could exploit. For the back-end boomers of Generation X, it is the cause of most of their problems.

8    It's important to grasp this point because the mass media have thoroughly confused it. Newspaper articles, media pundits, and even Statistics Canada often confuse Generation X with the baby-bust generation that followed it. Even as the millennium looms, the media are still calling Gen-Xers "twentysomethings" although all of them have celebrated their 30th birthdays. Some writers are so confused they seem to think Generation X is the children of the boomers. But it isn't. Most boomers weren't yet old enough to have children when Generation X came along. To clarify matters, we'll look at the characteristics of each subgroup of boomers in turn.

9    The front-end boomers have done pretty well for themselves. There are a lot of them, so they had to compete for jobs when they entered the workforce over the 1960s. But the entry of vast numbers of younger boomers into the marketplace through the 1970s and 1980s created wonderful opportunities for the front-enders already entrenched in business and government. New products, new services, new government programs, new universities—it was a period of seemingly endless expansion. The front-end boomers got there first, so they are

the ones in good jobs now in both the public and private sectors. They understand the needs of the boom because they are the leading edge of it.

10  Those born towards the end of the 1950s also understand the boom but, unlike the front-enders, they have been less well positioned to profit from that knowledge. Most members of this boomer subgroup have got a house and are in a career, but that career seems to be going nowhere because the rungs ahead of them are clogged with older boomers who are still 15 to 20 years from retirement.

11  Things are tough for the late-1950s group, but not nearly as bad as for the back end of the boom that arrived just after them. These are the 3.2 million people born from 1961 to 1966. They are the same age as the characters in Douglas Coupland's novel *Generation X*, which gave the early-1960s group its name. Many of them were still living at home with their parents at their 30th birthday because, faced with the horrendous obstacles in the labour market, they had a terrible time getting their careers on track. That is why, while front-end boomers were earning 30% more than their fathers by age 30, back-enders were making 10% less than their fathers at the same age.

12  Gen-Xers' life experience has led them to distrust any sort of large institution, whether in the public or private sector. It didn't take them long to learn that, in an overcrowded world, they had no choice but to "look out for number one." On their first day in kindergarten, the Gen-Xers discovered there weren't enough seats for them. In elementary school, many of them were squeezed into portables. They have been part of a crowd ever since. Whether it was trying to enrol in a ballet class, get into a summer camp, or find a part-time job, waiting lists have been a way of life for Generation X.

13  The millions of boomers who preceded them drove up rents, drove up house prices, drove up interest rates, and claimed all the best jobs and opportunities. As if that weren't enough, the Gen-Xers entered the labour market in the late 1970s and early 1980s, just when a brutal recession gripped the Canadian economy. In the best of circumstances, there would have been few jobs; in the recession there were virtually none. And when economic recovery finally began to create new demand for labour,

the Gen-Xers were told they were too old for entry-level jobs and too short of experience for more senior ones. They kept hearing the same story right through the 1990s.

14        One of the worst things the Gen-Xers have to cope with is their parents—the Depression generation. These are the 60-year-olds sitting at the top of the corporate ladder or recently retired from very successful careers and unable to fathom why their 35-year-old offspring still hasn't got a permanent job. Tension is tremendous in these families. Often the father is certain that his own success is based solely on his own merit while he sees his son's failure as a result of lack of drive and ambition.

## Vocabulary

cohort: originally a group of warriors; used in sociology to refer to a defined group of people

GenX: a term frequently used in the media; but it is often misused to describe people born after the baby boom rather than people born at the end of the baby boom

Notice that in English we say "He is twenty years old" but "He is a twenty-year-old." When *years* is used in an adjective phrase before the noun, the singular *year* is used. Here are some other examples of this structure:

>   I wouldn't touch it with a <u>ten-foot</u> pole. (The pole is <u>ten feet</u> long.)

>   He went on a <u>three-day</u> fast. (He fasted for <u>three days</u>.)

## Comprehension and Discussion

1. What did you know about the baby boom before you read this article? Have you often read references to boomers?

2. Which other countries were affected by the boom and why? How where those booms different than the one in Canada?

3. Explain why those born in 1961 are the largest group even though fewer babies were born in Canada in 1961 than in 1959.

4. When was Generation X born? How did it get its name?

5. Explain the three subgroups of boomers that the authors define.

6. Explain this statement: "Often the father is certain that his own success is based solely on his own merit while he sees his son's failure as a result of lack of drive and ambition." Would the authors agree with this view? Explain.

7. What role do you think governments should play in encouraging or discouraging large families?

## Assignments

1. The time when you were born can affect your life a great deal, not only within the society but within your family. You may have been born during a time of economic prosperity or a time of hardship. Perhaps you were the youngest child in the family with a large age gap between you and your siblings. Write an essay describing what the timing of your birth has meant in your life.

2. Find out about population policies in different countries. China instituted a one-child policy to reduce its population. Quebec offered financial incentives to try to encourage larger families because its birth rate was low. Write an essay explaining the situation in one area.

3. Choose one decade of the late 20th century and explain how boomers left their mark on it. For instance, the youth culture of the 1960s (with its saying "don't trust anyone over thirty") was a product of the baby boom.

# Sales Pitches

Masud Alam is a writer who lives in Toronto. He worked as a door-to-door salesman for three days. This article originally appeared as "Learn to live with those sales pitches."

Notice how Alam uses sentence fragments (incomplete sentences) to give the article an informal, conversational tone.

## Sale Pitches

### by Masud Alam

1    Buying and selling. The two fill the gap between the first candy purchase at the school cafeteria and the final investment in a funeral plan.

2    And yet, many of us find it so hard to come to terms with the concept of selling.

3    "I can't stand salespeople," you'll hear your friends complain. "Don't trust him, he is an insurance salesman," and the classic threat, "If you are calling to sell something, I am putting the phone down."

4    So palpable is the fear and mistrust of sellers and agents that no legislation, no consumer protection committee and no business ethics watchdog are going to satisfy the skeptic.

5    Many writers have denounced sales hounds, suggesting innovative ways to "defeat" solicitations. It's a shame: even those writers had to first sell their ideas to an editor.

6    Don't get me wrong. I, too, am uncomfortable at being solicited. It brings out the worst in me—I impulsively tell lies to put a quick end to the conversation.

7    I sometimes behave impolitely, and, as a result, later feel embarrassed.

8    But my impulsive wariness of salespeople hasn't stopped me from buying things. I switched my long-distance carrier only a couple weeks after signing it, on the basis of information I received from the competition through a telemarketer. That information was incorrect. So I switched a second time, again over the phone, and am quite happy with the rates and services. I am neither bitter with one company nor ecstatic with the other. Just accept it as part of my education as a buyer in the '90s.

9   Selling may be the oldest occupation in human history. And the most enduring, too. The success of modern capitalist economies is built on the principles of right to choose and unhindered access to consumer markets.

10   Buying and selling patterns have undergone a considerable change but the bottom line remains the same: For a manufacturer or service provider to stay in business and keep paying its employees, it must find buyers.

11   And if the potential buyer—which is every one of us—shuts his door on a salesman, the latter is going to come through the phone, through television, in the mailbox, in the newspaper, through home computers...

12   In Canada, an overwhelming number of new jobs—permanent, temporary and contract—are being created in the sales and marketing fields. Last year, retail sales topped the list as the most common job for Canadians, with more than half a million men and women reported to be employed in this sector.

13   And this does not include countless telesales persons and outdoor canvassers who do not fall under any of the 700 or so occupations listed with Statistics Canada, and therefore remain unaccounted for.

14   So there. Half a million people—among them our friends, relations, neighbours—trying to sell us things which we may or may not want.

15   The more unwelcome of them—telemarketers and door-to-door canvassers—are ironically, just as likely to be solicited in their off-duty hours as the rest of us.

16   The person at your door or on the phone is simply doing his or her job, for the same reason you do yours. And if you are irritated by this person's intrusion into your private life, chances are he or she is quite aware of it and therefore wouldn't have ventured to test your patience if he or she had a choice.

17   They are simply little teeth on a giant flywheel which is powered by that awesome and utterly unstoppable engine called "free enterprise."

18   We are all beneficiaries of this system and that's worth remembering when a tooth on that flywheel shows up at your doorstep.

## Vocabulary

can't stand (idiom): be unable to tolerate something

come to terms with so: accept, agree

hound: a kind of dog (as in *foxhound, bloodhound, greyhound*), used to describe people who pursue something (as in a *newshound*, a *publicity hound*); also a verb—to harass or pursue someone relentlessly.

so there: an expression used when someone makes a point in an argument or accomplishes something

watchdog: a person or organization that monitors business practices

## Comprehension and Discussion

1. What is the author's main point?

2. What are the author's personal feelings towards salespeople?

3. Explain the author's reference to a flywheel in the last two paragraphs.

4. Paraphrase (write in your own words) the first paragraph of the article.

5. What are the benefits of the free enterprise system? What are the disadvantages?

6. How do you deal with door-to-door salespeople or telemarketers?

7. How do people try to sell things on the Internet? Discuss these techniques from the point of view of the seller and the potential buyer.

8. In 1999, an artist displayed an unusual piece of art—a phone and a list of names of people who had been rude to him when he worked as a telemarketer. He invited gallery visitors to call these people and be rude to them. What do you think of this? Is this art?

## Assignments

1. Describe an encounter you had as a seller or a buyer and explain what you learned from this.

2. Write a process essay describing buying or selling. For example, describe the steps a buyer should go through to purchase a house, car, or computer. Or describe the techniques used by a telemarketer.

3. Define a good salesperson.

4. Should there be any restrictions on selling practices? Why, or why not?

5. Choose a benefit (or disadvantage) of the free-enterprise system, and explain it in a paragraph.

6. Take another job or profession that is not well respected in society and write an essay defending it.

# TV Advertising and Children

This is an excerpt from a book, *Television and Your Child*, by Carmen Luke. It is written in a more academic style than the newspaper pieces in this part of the book. Notice the developed paragraphs. The author cites other research works with the use of endnotes.

The opening words "just as" link this section to what has already been discussed in the book. This excerpt is from a chapter called "Television and Socialization," which explains what television teaches, and describes consumer, political, and gender socialization. (Socialization is the act of preparing someone to live in a society.)

## *Consumer Socialization*

### *by Carmen Luke*

1    Just as the appeal of children's programs provides an easy transition to adult shows, so the enticement of children's commercials prepares young viewers to accept advertisements aimed at adults. Ads geared for children typically emphasize fun and increased popularity among peers and portray peer interaction. These elements tend to increase viewers' attention to the commercial. A *Dukes of Hazzard* bike guarantees a proud and lucky 5-year-old-boy not only the friendship (and envy) of other boys on the block, but also an admiring smile from the girl next door. Children quickly learn the association with increased physical attractiveness, profit or fame. They have no trouble understanding that the use of Right Guard deodorant or Crest toothpaste equates with the chime of wedding bells, or that using STP will compel attractive women to throw themselves wantonly on the hood of the sleek late model car which the driver has treated to the additive. In all, through both programming and commercials, children begin learning what is to count as success, beauty, and happiness.

2    Learning to buy requires learning the skills to make informed decisions about products, to comparison shop, to read labels and count money. TV does not teach these skills. Instead, as many parents complain, ads manipulate the child viewer with promises of fun and popularity resulting from ownership of a particular toy, game or snack. This illusory appeal

encourages children to pressure their parents into buying extra crunchy peanut butter, the electronic humanoid, or that oh-so-cuddly doll which will make that little princess feel like a real mom. We all have seen the results of consumer training via TV commercials. When parents cannot fulfill their children's product demand, family conflict breaks out, especially in the supermarket or department store.

3      Another form of the commercial manipulation of children entails the use of complex verbal messages that are not understood by children, but that make it quite clear to parents that "batteries are not included", or that the purchase of Barbie "does not include the gymnasium". The cognitive ability of five- and six-year-olds allows them to focus only on a single dimension of an ad (for example, "big", "fast", "colourful", instead of on the accompanying verbal or textual message. Production features grab children's attention while complex verbal messages ("balanced and nutritious breakfast", "partial assembly required") go unnoticed.[8] Yet when a disclaimer such as "partial assembly required" is rephrased to "it must be put together before you can play with it", children immediately understand the message.[9]

4      Witness a parent and child in the toy department. They have just bought a Barbie aerobics outfit. Jennie loves it but starts whining about needing the gym as well. Dad explains to Jennie that this time Barbie is getting only the outfit without the gym: she may get the gym some other time. Jennie throws a tantrum and refuses to accept the outfit without the gym, believing the gym should go with the aerobics leotard just like it did on TV. How can Jennie play exercise with Barbie wearing the leotard unless she has the gym? Product dependency is the principle at work here. The child has an image of the whole ensemble and, while parents worry about their credit limit, the child won't be satisfied until that image becomes reality.

5      Fun and popularity are not inherent in any product, as most of us know. Young children, with their more limited social experience, do not always have this understanding, nor do a surprising number of educated adults. Neither nursery school nor TV will teach children the difference between fabricated wants and authentic needs. Neither will teach them to discern

the relationship between a product and the effects of owning that product, or give them the skills to evaluate a product's usefulness relative to its cost. Youngsters can, too easily, become hooked on the televised version of reality, too easily turn into ad addicts singing along with every commercial jingle for a game, toy or cereal, or become toystore tyrants unable to accept a simple "no" from parents in response to product requests. But it is up to parents to intervene in TV's consumer socialization of children.

8. Palmer, E.L. & McDowell, C.N. (1981). Children's understanding of nutritional information presented in breakfast cereal commercials. *Journal of Broadcasting*, 25(3), 295-301.

9. Liebert, D., Sprafkin, J., Liebert R., & Rubinstein, E. (1977). The effects of TV commercial disclaimers on the product expectations of children. *Journal of Communication*, 27(1).

## Vocabulary

*Dukes of Hazzard*: a comedy-adventure television show popular in the early 1980s. It was set in the southern United States and featured many car chases.

STP: brand name for a motor oil additive

throw a tantrum: (also called a "temper tantrum") make an angry outburst, in childlike behaviour

## Comprehension and Discussion

1. Explain "illusory appeal."

2. Describe the "family conflict" that might be seen in a supermarket or department store.

3. Explain "product dependency."

4. How do commercials intentionally deceive the consumer, especially a child viewer?

5. How much wiser are you as a consumer now that you have read this article?

6. As an adult, have you fallen into the trap of buying something you have seen on commercials and later regretted it? Elaborate.

## Assignments

1. Analyze a TV commercial—one aimed at children or adults—and discuss how effective it is in its sales pitch.

2. How does what Luke is describing relate to teenagers and their desire for brand-name clothes? Have these teenagers learned how to buy, according to Luke's definition: "Learning to buy requires learning the skills to make informed decisions about products, to comparison shop, to read labels and count money."? Write an essay on consumerism among teenagers.

3. Write an essay on the benefits of ads or of our consumerism-oriented society.

# When Bigger is Not Necessarily Better

Charles Gordon writes a column called "Another View" for *Maclean's* magazine. This piece originally appeared on October 20, 1997, just after the World Series in baseball. The Florida Marlins won the Series, and many critics say they bought the win, as they had many expensive stars on their team that year. After they had accomplished their goal, they got rid of most of those players to cut their payroll; therefore, in 1998, they did poorly.

Gordon is describing a trend towards bigger organizations. He gives examples of "big box" stores. These are large stores usually grouped together in suburban areas, but not in malls. He also makes a reference to the government blocking American bookstores. This is a controversial trade issue. Canada wants to protect its cultural industries in order to preserve a Canadian voice in books, movies, television, and radio. However, the American view is that this not culture so much as part of the entertainment industry, and therefore open for business.

## *When Bigger is Not Necessarily Better*

### *by Charles Gordon*

1    The bedazzled consumer gapes: thousands of books are spread out before him; there are comfy chairs upon which to sit down; more flavours of coffee than he ever dreamed possible. Just down the street, there is another store: more books, more comfy chairs, and this time, wine and beer. And next, who knows? Bookstores with coffee and beer and wine and—what?—acupuncture, perhaps, or bullfighting. Anything can happen in our modern economy. Anything, that is, except the survival of anything small.

2    The signs are all around us that big money makes bigger money and that little money disappears. The signs are also all around us that no particular conspiracy is involved. The fault is mostly our own.

3    Look at the sports pages. In the baseball playoffs, the teams with the biggest payrolls were there—Florida, Atlanta, Baltimore, the New York Yankees. The baseball teams (such as the Montreal Expos) that elected not to compete in signing expensive free agents are, as they say in the sports world, on the

golf course. Because of their unwillingness or inability to pay $10-million salaries, those teams face extinction, their players heading off to larger and considerably greener pastures.

4 "Small market teams," they are called, although it is difficult to consider places such as Montreal and Pittsburgh small. We have already seen some of those smaller market teams disappear from the National Hockey League, the teams in Quebec City and Winnipeg moving to cities where bigger arenas, richer owners and fatter television contracts are available. Indications are that the process has not ended there. We will see more teams go away, some of them Canadian, because they cannot match the outrageous bids for star players that hit the headlines every day from places like Philadelphia and New York. "The teams that spend the money end up winning," is how the general manager of the Philadelphia Flyers, Bob Clarke, put it the other day.

5 Players make ridiculous salaries, cities with rich hockey traditions cannot afford to have teams, which move to such hockey meccas as North Carolina and Arizona. The process is destined to alienate fans, and some evidence of that is being seen at the box office. But the process of alienation is not complete. The fans still turn out, still turn on the televisions, still buy the team sweaters and wristbands. Whatever is needed to bring the players and owners to their senses has not yet materialized. If nothing changes, hockey will become bigger, less affordable and more remote.

6 It would be wonderful to be able to restore the innocent and happy relationship between the home team and its fans. Many of us grew up on it; in its uncomplicated way, it was one of the joys of childhood. But the young sports fan now, it is safe to say, is worldly wise, fully conversant with the ways of owners and agents, endorsements and corporate boxes. The age of pure hero worship is over, which may please the kind of people who don't like Santa Claus much, but is sad for the rest of us.

7 Hockey is not alone in becoming bigger and more remote. The neighbourhood sporting goods store goes under when a superstore opens up. Independent booksellers fight the threat posed by the giant Chapters stores, and now the giant Indigo stores (and maybe after—as soon as the Liberal government

loses its nerve—the giant Barnes & Noble stores from the United States). The neighbourhood computer store (that ancient institution) suffers at the hands of the "big-box" outfit on the outskirts of town. In each case, the lure is the same: more variety, discounted prices. The lure of the neighbour-hood operation—familiarity, service, knowledgeable staff, and the neighbourhood itself—doesn't seem to have the necessary drawing power.

8    Bigness itself may be a factor. Watch theatregoers flock to the mega-musicals—*Phantom of the Opera, Showboat, Miss Saigon*—despite their mega-prices. And watch smaller-scale theatre, where the real creativity is (not to mention the real Canadians), struggle to break even.

9    In all walks of life, bigness sells. And bigness gets bigger. Anyone who has followed the trend over the years knows at least two things about it. First, it represents the natural incli-nation of the free enterprise system. Second, it is not being foisted upon an unwilling consumer. The consumer is a willing accomplice.

10    While protecting the small businessman is an article of faith among political parties, particularly at election time, today's politician is thoroughly imbued with the myth of the market. The market is wise; if the market makes it happen, it is good. If the market takes the team away or kills the little store, too bad, but, hey, that's the market.

11    So don't count on politicians to help. Which leaves our-selves. As consumers, we have become as enslaved as govern-ment and business to the myth of the bottom line. At the level of the individual, it means that if it is cheaper, buy it. Never mind that it is cheap because it is being dumped across the border by a multinational or discounted by a large domestic company to drive the local guy out of business. It is on sale and off we go. Eventually and inevitably, our destinations are bigger and far from the neighbourhood. But we don't seem to mind.

12    It may be that this is what we want: a world of superstores and superteams (we are also getting superschools and super-hospitals, you will notice). If that's what we want, fine. It's what we're getting. If what we want is something else, we have to know that the power to change it is ours and ours alone.

## Vocabulary

goes under: goes bankrupt, closes (used for businesses)

Use dictionaries and thesauruses to fill in the following chart. Some spaces have been filled in to give you examples. Some spaces you will have to leave blank. Usage tags show how or where a word is used. For example, some words are British or American English. Some are slang, colloquial, or derogatory.

| WORD | PART OF SPEECH AND USAGE TAGS | MEANING | SYNONYMS OR ANTONYMS | WORDS WITH THE SAME ROOT |
|---|---|---|---|---|
| accomplice | | | | |
| alienation | | | estrangement | alienate (v) |
| bottom line | | | | |
| bring to one's senses | idiom | | | |
| comfy | adj. informal | | | |
| conspiracy | | | | conspire (v) conspiratorial (adj) |
| conversant | | | | |
| drawing power | | | | |
| elect | | | | |
| endorsement | | | | |
| extinction | | | | |
| greener pastures | | | | |
| hero worship | | | | |
| imbue | verb (+ with) | | | |
| lure | | | | |
| materialize | | | | |

| WORD | PART OF SPEECH AND USAGE TAGS | MEANING | SYNONYMS OR ANTONYMS | WORDS WITH THE SAME ROOT |
|---|---|---|---|---|
| mecca | | | | |
| mega- | | | | |
| myth | | | | |

## Comprehension

1. What is the main idea of this article?
2. Explain Gordon's criticism of professional sports.
3. What does Gordon mean when he calls the consumer "a willing accomplice"?
4. What does Gordon like about smaller enterprises?
5. Explain Gordon's criticism of politicians.

## Discussion

1. What is important to you when you shop?
2. Discuss examples of the "bigger is better" principle in your area. For example, smaller cities are often amalgamated to become one large city, and multi-national corporations swallow up smaller companies. What are the gains and what are the losses?
3. Does the world of professional sports have too much emphasis on the business aspects rather than the sports activity?
4. How does the market for high-priced players hurt the game for the fans?

## Assignments

1. Write a paragraph describing your favourite place to shop, explaining why it is so good.
2. Write an essay comparing two different kinds of stores or places to shop, such as a mall and a downtown area, or a small store and a "big box" store.
3. Bigger is better. Agree or disagree with this statement. Limit your essay to a particular area (such as health care, education, corporations).

# In Praise of Gouging

Karen Selick is a lawyer and writer in Belleville, Ontario, one of the regions hit by the ice storm of January 1998. The storm affected Kingston, Ottawa, Montreal, and the regions around these cities. Freezing rain coated trees and power lines. Some people were without electrical power for as long as six weeks. Some left their homes to stay in shelters while others stayed home. Much in demand were supplies and equipment like candles, firewood, electrical generators, and water.

This article is about the basic economic principle of "supply and demand." When items are in short supply and many people demand them, the price goes up.

## *In Praise of Gouging*

### *by Karen Selick*

1    Central Canada's ice storm has brought with it the inevitable: complaints of price "gouging" by merchants. Candles, formerly $1 a box, were marked up as high as $4, reports say. Prices skyrocketed for batteries, firewood, propane, gasoline, bottled water and a host of other items. "No one should be permitted to profit from the misery of others," people rage.

2    The truth is, these sudden, exorbitant price increases serve a useful purpose. Instead of vilifying the so-called gougers for their greed, we should accept them as necessary players in the price system—the system that keeps the economy of a distressed region operating as smoothly and impartially as possible under the circumstances.

3    Take candles. Ordinarily, most people have little use for them. During a power failure, suddenly everyone needs them. Storekeepers have only enough in stock to satisfy their normal low demand. Faced with a surge in demand, they can continue selling them at their normal price, or raise the price. At the normal price, they will quickly sell out and there will be none left for the latecomers, no matter how desperate.

4    Suppose instead that merchants quadruple the price of candles. Among the shocked shopper will be some who already have a supply of candles or some other alternative, such as kerosene lamps, and were merely intending to stock up for

good measure. They may well use what they have first and defer buying until the price returns to normal. Others will say, "At that ridiculous price, I'll take one, not three." The result? More candles will be left for latecomers to buy. Those who didn't already have a supply and needed them quite desperately will find some, even though the price may be steep.

5    As well, all shoppers will be alerted to the shortage of candles—something they might not have realized if they had been able to buy them at the normal price. Spontaneous candle conservation will occur once they realize how difficult to replace they are. The severity of the shortage will be alleviated.

6    Price increases also induce a rapid increase in supply. Storekeepers suddenly able to make a huge profit will do their utmost to get in a new supply of candles. Suppliers outside the stricken region will rush to the area with stocks of candles. This will further assist in alleviating the severity of the shortage. As truckloads of candles flow into the area, competition among vendors will soon reduce the price to its former level.

7    Price increases are simply one method of rationing scarce goods among competing users. It's not perfect, but the alternatives are even worse. Suppose the government simply froze candle prices at $1 a box. Knowing that they would immediately sell out at that price, storekeepers could choose which customers they wished to favour. That would present an opportunity to curry favour with local bigwigs. A system that allocates goods by "pull" is surely no fairer than one that allocates goods by price. In normal times, we call this corruption.

8    Or suppose ration coupons had been issued, so that everyone was entitled to buy an equal but restricted number of candles at $1 a box. This system would allocate candles to people who don't need them (those with an emergency supply or alternatives) and deny an adequate supply to people who need them most urgently (those with none). A black market in ration coupons would soon develop. Those who need more candles than their coupons allow would end up paying inflated prices for them anyhow—because they would first have to buy black-market ration coupons, then the candles. The only difference is that the windfall profit would go to those who sell their unneeded ration coupons, rather than to storekeepers.

9     There is nothing to commend such an outcome as more fair than simply allowing candle prices to rise. And there is a major disadvantage to this rationing scheme: It eliminates the incentive for vendors and outsiders to rush in with increased supplies.

## Vocabulary

curry favour: to try to win favour and attention

pull: power and influence

windfall: unexpected luck, as in apples blown from a tree to the ground

Use dictionaries and thesauruses to fill in the following chart. Some spaces have been filled in to give you examples. Some spaces you will have to leave blank. Usage tags show how or where a word is used. For example, some words are British or American English. Some are slang, colloquial, or derogatory.

| WORD | PART OF SPEECH AND USAGE TAGS | MEANING | SYNONYMS OR ANTONYMS | WORDS WITH THE SAME ROOT |
|---|---|---|---|---|
| alleviate | | | | |
| allocate | | | | allocation (n.) |
| conservation | | saving | | |
| corruption | | | | |
| defer | | | | |
| exorbitant | | | excessive | |
| impartially | | | | |
| incentive | | | | |
| ration | verb | | | |
| scarce | | | | |
| severity | | | | |

| WORD | PART OF SPEECH AND USAGE TAGS | MEANING | SYNONYMS OR ANTONYMS | WORDS WITH THE SAME ROOT |
|---|---|---|---|---|
| spontaneous | | | | |
| surge | noun | | | |
| vilify | | | | vilification (n) vile (adj) |

## Comprehension and Discussion

1. What is Karen Selick's main argument? How does she support it? Write a point-form outline detailing her argument.

2. Why is the word *gouging* in quotation marks in the article?

3. Explain the statement "A system that allocates goods by 'pull' is surely no fairer than one that allocates goods by price."

4. What counter arguments can you think of to refute Selick's statements?

5. Which paragraphs are developed paragraphs starting with a clear topic sentence?

## Assignments

1. Discuss an experience you had with any of the situations the author mentioned—for example, a disaster like an ice storm, a power blackout, the black market, steep price increase— and what you learned from it.

2. Supply and demand explains prices and wages to some extent. Write an essay discussing other factors which determine prices or wages. For example, the amount of training required for a job can determine the salary range.

3. The ice storm gave us some incredible pictures and stories. Check out two books by Mark Abley: *The Ice Storm: An historic record in photographs of January 1998* and *Stories from the Ice Storm.*Write a description of one of the pictures, or write a summary of one of the stories.

# Corporate Footsoldiers

Joanne Milner is a writer who also has her own business. This opinion piece originally appeared as "Work is all hell for footsoldiers in corporate trenches." In this article she talks about the demands of one of her previous jobs.

Milner calls the employees footsoldiers, making an analogy, or comparison. Soldiers do as their commanding officers tell them, have little to say about their work, and suffer the most in the front line of battle. Milner does not actually write about the similarity between workers and soldiers, but by calling the workers footsoldiers she underscores the similarity between them.

An unequal distribution of work is a problem in our society. While some people put in long hours, others are unemployed or can only find part-time or contract work. Downsizing has meant that companies are trying to get by on a smaller staff, and employees fearful of losing their jobs do not complain about the overwork. It is important to remember that overwork is not the same thing as overtime. We use the term *overtime* to refer to the paid work of hourly wage earners who can earn time and a half for extra hours. Salaried workers do not get overtime pay but often put in extra hours.

## Corporate Footsoldiers

### by Joanne Milner

1    I was recently in a job that required me to put in 60-hour work weeks. I was in the office at the crack of dawn. I worked right through the day. Lunch was a five-minute break. I'm skinny and I lost 10 pounds on the job—and this was a paper shuffling office job, not a high-energy aerobic position. I'd finish work when it was dark outside, taking my work home on the public transit, editing documents on the bus.

2    When I got home, I was stressed. I'd complain to my husband for five minutes, open a can of dinner, eat it, work some more, then go to bed, worrying that I still didn't get it all done.

And the next morning, it started all over again.

3    Weekends were no exception, well, except for taking maybe 15 minutes for lunch. On Friday afternoon my boss would tell me I had to work that night and on the weekend. We would

have a Monday deadline he had just found out about. Put any weekend plans aside, my life aside. Work comes first.

4    The casualties of doing corporate battle are high. One friend works 80-hour weeks. He's 30 years old. He suffers from regular migraines accompanied by vomiting that sends him on regular trips to the emergency department. Sometimes he can't feel his legs.

5    My husband, a psychiatrist, says when people can't deal with mental stress, it can get converted into physical symptoms.

6    Food is lousy in the trenches. Soldiers go into battle armed with junk food, fast food or no food. Not to mention tanking up on caffeine: coffee, cola, chocolate, while other soldiers just get tanked to blow off steam. Poor nutrition and no exercise make for weak soldiers. Yet corporate Canada ignores the battle fatigue.

7    Many of these soldiers are angry, stressed, depressed and filled with resentment that they don't have a life. For one friend, Marvin the Martian ("You make me very angry, very angry indeed") has become the mascot for those in the corporate trenches.

8    There is no leave from this war. Many soldiers are guilt-ridden at taking a break for the weekend, evening, or just for lunch. There is no escape from the corporate army. We voluntarily joined the war, they have our pledges—our mortgage payments, our car loans.

9    Back on the home front, life is not good. You may as well scratch out friends' home phone numbers in your directory. They don't live there any more. Double ink their work numbers—that's where you'll find them.

10   Their homes fall into disrepair as chores wait in line behind spouses, family and friends of the overworked, all are also victims of this corporate carnage. It's as if the overworked have ceased to exist. We make plans with them, then they always drop the bomb—we can't join you, we have to work. We cease to see them at get-togethers and family functions. And if we do see them, it is as if their spirits have left their bodies, their minds are elsewhere. They are the working wounded, shell-shocked and over stressed.

11   Most of these ridiculous hours result from poor management. A lot of managers are so disorganized, they waste our

time, give us redundant projects and don't set priorities. They don't think of us as human beings. These so-called managers are turning motivated people into overworked, resentful entities. Corporate Canada harbors the illusion that people who are unhappy, depressed and stressed make great employees. What it doesn't understand is that by not looking out for those on the front lines, it's not looking out for the bottom lines.

## Vocabulary

Marvin the Martian: a character in Bugs Bunny cartoons. You may not know his name, but you probably would recognize his image. If you are not familiar with him, look him up on the Internet.

In groups, use context clues and dictionaries to find meanings for the following words and expressions:

| | |
|---|---|
| bottom line | home front |
| carnage | in the trenches |
| corporate Canada | mascot |
| crack of dawn | paper shuffling |
| double ink | scratch out |
| front lines | shell-shocked |
| harbour an illusion | tanked |
| high-energy aerobic position | tanking up |

## Comprehension

1. What is the main idea of this article?

2. Explain the comparison Milner is making when she talks about workers.

3. Why do the workers put up with such conditions?

4. What different areas of life suffer because of overwork?

5. Explain the sentence: "The casualties of doing corporate battle are high."

6. What message does Milner give to corporate Canada?

7. When is Milner talking about real soldiers in this article?

# Discussion

1. How can the bottom line be hurt by overworked workers?

2. Sleep deprivation is another problem caused by our long work hours. Industrial accidents have been linked to mistakes by tired workers. In hospitals, interns and residents routinely work around the clock and are expected to make critical decisions on few hours sleep. Yet, society continues to expect people to work long hours. Why? Do you think this will change? What could help solve this problem?

3. Decades ago, futurists predicted that we would have more leisure hours as technology did our work for us. Yet many of us are working long hours. Why were the futurists wrong?

# Assignments

1. Describe the ideal balance between work for pay, time for personal business (housework, shopping), and leisure.

2. Write an essay arguing that we should (or should not) have a shorter work week.

3. While some people work incredibly long hours, many others are either unemployed or underemployed (working part-time or at jobs that don't meet their skill level). What could be done to solve this problem in our society?

4. Technology is supposed to make our work easier. Why have technological advancements not led to greater amounts of leisure time?

5. Define a workaholic.

# Rest Day

This article first appeared as "Let's hear it (softly) for Rest Day." It was written by a husband and wife who live in Hull, Quebec. Like many Canadians, they are feeling the stress of coping with work and family responsibilities.

It has often been suggested that Canadians have a holiday in February, and it has been brought before the House of Commons as a bill. However, a national holiday has not yet been declared. February 15 has been designated as Heritage Day; if it were made a statutory or legal holiday, it would be celebrated on the third Monday in February.

## *Rest Day*

### *by Josie Marino and Jean-Francois Rioux*

1    Canadians often complain about the lack of a long weekend between New Year's Day and Easter. It is paradoxical that the longest period of the year without a break is also the most difficult one in terms of climate. In any case, Canada has fewer public holidays than the U.S. and most countries in Europe.

2    Therefore, it is high time that Canada created a new holiday for the dead of winter, beyond half-baked innovations such as Flag Day and Heritage Day that have not caught on.

3    We suggest that the last Monday of February be declared "Rest Day," a day dedicated to sleep, relaxation, even laziness. On Rest Day, Canadians would be required to sleep in late, spend an inordinate part of their day in their pajamas, and have a late breakfast or brunch.

4    In the afternoon, many might enjoy a nap, and perhaps an early bedtime that evening. Rest Day Eve sleepovers would become *de rigueur*, at least for children old enough not to wake up their parents in the morning. Grownups could be invited to attend such activities, though many would elect to organize more formal brunches.

5    Before Rest Day, people could exchange gifts of pajamas, nightgowns, bathrobes, sheets, covers, pillows, cushions, stuffed animals, etc. Cards for the holiday would express the sender's wishes for rest, relaxation, tranquillity for the recipi-

ent. The commercialization factor—the essential ingredient of any major holiday—would therefore be guaranteed.

6    The colours of Rest Day would be white, light blue and pink. A hibernating bear, wearing a nightgown and toque, might be chosen as its emblem. Stores would schedule their biggest white sales of the year for the period immediately preceding Rest Day. Manufacturers would issue their new lines of sleeping clothes or bedroom stuff for the occasion. However, Rest Day Monday would be a real holiday with all stores shut tight.

7    Another advantage of Rest Day is that it would cross religious, ethnic, linguistic, regional and class boundaries in honouring something common to all Canadians: the need to rest.

8    It would be a time to celebrate the virtues of sleeping, napping, relaxing, daydreaming, and basically doing nothing. Rest Day would be a public health event. Physicians and psychologists would be invited by TV and other media to talk about the benefits of sleep and the use of relaxation techniques. They would warn Canadians about typical stress-related diseases such as hypertension, burn-out, sleeplessness, and workaholism. Children would be socialized into accepting that rest and even a tad of languor can improve life, in its psychological, moral and physical dimensions.

9    Rest Day would be especially welcomed by the B-types, the relaxed and the laid-back, those who would enjoy seeing the dynamo A-types, the doers, taking a back seat for at least this one day. Teenagers could sleep all day without fear of being harassed by their parents. Finally, a holiday spent with Mom and Dad that even they might find cool.

10   Our politicians should establish Rest Day as the midwinter break that Canadians need. We don't need religious, civil or historical justification for taking a day off in February. Rather, the holiday should be honest and direct about its aim: keep Canadians in bed longer that morning.

## Vocabulary

In order to explain hypertension and stress, doctors have classified people as A and B types. An A-type personality is ambitious and driven, whereas a B-type is more relaxed.

*de rigeur:* one of the many French expressions used in English. It is more emphatic than its synonyms "required" or "necessary."

Use your dictionary to find the meanings of these French expressions used in English: *au contraire, au courant, déjà vu, flambé, gauche, résumé, RSVP.*

white sale: a sale of linens (sheets, towels, etc.)

In groups and with the aid of dictionaries, discuss the meaning of the following idioms and expressions:

| | |
|---|---|
| a tad | it is high time |
| catch on | laid-back |
| dead of winter | sleep in |
| half-baked | take a back seat |

## Comprehension and Discussion

1. Why is February a good time to have a national holiday?

2. In point form, write down the arguments that Marino and Rioux use to support their argument.

3. How would Rest Day be celebrated, according to the authors? What do you think of these celebrations? Suggest other ways to celebrate Rest Day.

4. Explain why rest is so important.

5. What is a workaholic?

6. Do you consider yourself a Type-A or Type-B personality?

7. Explain: "Another advantage of Rest Day is that it would cross religious, ethnic, linguistic, regional and class boundaries in honouring something common to all Canadians: the need to rest."

8. Discuss holidays from other cultures. Which ones would make good national holidays for Canadians?

## Assignments

1. Design a greeting card for Rest Day.

2. Make up your own holiday. In an essay explain why this holiday is necessary and how it would be celebrated.

3. What is your favourite holiday? Why?

4. Do Canadians have too few holidays? You can compare Canada with another country.

5. How should Canada Day be celebrated?

6. Make a list of Canadian holidays. Find out which are statutory holidays and which make a long weekend.

# How Isolation has Bred Our Uncivil Society

John Barber has a regular column called "Semi-detached" in *The Globe and Mail.*

Many people have observed that our lifestyle is hectic and that people are less polite than they used to be. Aggressive behaviour in automobiles has become so common that it now rates its own term—road rage. People aggressively cut off other drivers or make rude gestures. Extreme cases include violence such as beatings and shootings.

## How Isolation Has Bred Our Uncivil Society

### by John Barber

1   You're walking along the sidewalk. It's crowded and slow. Then some jerk who can't wait cuts right in front of you. You slam your heel to the ground in a desperate attempt to stop, veer hard to the left and just about slam into a lamppost.

2   The next thing you know, you're running to catch up with the guy. You get right into his face and scream so hard you shower him in spit, saying things so harsh the dogs are whimpering a block away.

3   You've never done anything like that, you say? So let's change one detail. You're not walking along the sidewalk, you're driving your car.

4   Suddenly it all clicks together. You've done it. You're guilty, whether you're just another big-boned boor or whether you're as refined and delicate as a porcelain figurine. Everyone's a monster with a steering wheel in their hands.

5   We've heard lots of vague sociological reasons advanced to explain the alarming decline of civility in modern life. We hear about the high levels of stress entailed in our "hectic lifestyles," we hear about the added pressures experienced by dual-income families, about time poverty and economic security.

6   It's hard to understand how any of that can explain change, however, because none of it is really new. The day isn't any shorter than it ever was, and there is no long-run increase in the proportion of dual-income families—the alleged golden age when Mom stayed at home was a historical anomaly that lasted less than 20 years. Work hours shorten with every generation, and life

for the vast majority of us is easier than it has ever been.

7    On the other hand, our ancestors never spent half their waking hours driving around in cars.

8    Does that explain why there is so little restraint displayed in public life today, why so much of our expletive-drenched discourse degenerates so quickly into foaming rage, why even the moralists who crave a return to "civil society" rely on merciless humiliation to bring it back?

9    Of course not. That simplistic explanation neglects the fact that our ancestors didn't spend the other half of their waking hours lying in front of the tube. Mix cars and television together, sprinkle with a few other artifacts of modern technology, and a complete picture of modern barbarism magically appears.

10    Consider why people who bump into each other on the sidewalk say "sorry," whereas people who almost bump into each other in cars scream bloody murder. In the latter case, people are barely part of the equation. They are encapsulated within separate worlds; they share no common ground. The disagreement occurs between machines. As a result, rudeness has no consequence.

11    Television has the same isolating effect. The discussions, disputes and ceremonies that once brought people together in actual physical space now occur in millions of individual, darkened rooms. If you talk back to a television set, you might as well scream. It screams back.

12    That doesn't happen when you actually meet neighbours and strangers in public. Civility only becomes real in such unregulated, unmediated, personal encounters. It may be expressed in the form of mere niceties, but it signifies something much deeper: Every "excuse me" acknowledges a bottomless reservoir of mutual obligation. But the habit of getting along dies out when people are always alone.

13    So you drive to the mall, but your diminished social skills are no more exercised there than they are at home. The corporate landlord and his security force ensure that the challenges that make civility necessary in the first place—mainly encounters with people unlike yourself, who say and do things you may not appreciate—never occur. They are zoned out.

14    You drive home, fuming as usual at all the idiots on the road, turn into a lifeless street lined with garages, press a button on the dash and disappear back into the cave. You emerge an hour later with your encapsulated children and drive them to a highly regulated activity where authority figures endlessly elaborate "the rules."

15    When it's all set out for them so neatly, they never have to learn for themselves. They might do so if they were ever let out to play freely by themselves, but that's far too dangerous. Across the continent there are neighbourhoods filled with children who are never seen, except in fleeting glimpses through tinted glass.

16    The street is deserted. You go for months without ever passing through your own front door. Your living room, a formal space originally conceived as the place where a private family greeted the public world, might as well have a velvet rope strung across its entrance. And in the family room, way in the back, you click on Jerry Springer and wonder how life ever got so coarse.

## Vocabulary

living room and family room: The term "living room" denotes a general-usage sitting room in most houses. However, if a house has a family room as well as a living room, the living room is the company sitting room, often at the front of the house, while the family room is the room where the family does many everyday activities, like watching television.

Jerry Springer: a TV talk show known for rude behaviour, confrontation, and violence

velvet rope: as in a museum where rooms are roped off to prevent people from entering

## Comprehension and Discussion

1. What is the main point of this article?

2. Barber's use of *you* is deliberate and effective. (He is not using it to give the article an informal tone.) What effect does the use of *you* have?

3. In the fifth paragraph, Barber repeats the phrase "we hear." What does this usage signify?

4. What are the usual explanations for the lack of civility in society today?

5. Does Barber agree with these usual explanations? Why or why not?

6. What does Barber mean when he says that "expletive-drenched discourse degenerates so quickly into foaming rage"? Put this phrase into simpler English.

7. How does Barber criticize the way children are raised today?

8. Explain Barber's criticism of television.

9. What does Barber mean by the "discussions, disputes and ceremonies that once brought people together in actual physical space"? Give examples.

## Assignments

1. How do Internet chat lines affect social skills?

2. Write an essay illustrating the lack of civility in our society today. Do not use the same examples Barber uses.

3. Explain how parents teach children social skills.

4. In an essay, discuss road rage. You can describe it, explain the causes, or suggest solutions.

5. A relatively new phenomenon is air rage. Research the topic and write an essay explaining the causes.

6. Write an essay agreeing or disagreeing with one of the points Barber makes:

   a) We are a less social, more isolated society now.

   b) Technology isolates us.

   c) We are a less civil society.

   d) Children do not get a chance to learn how to get along with others.

   e) Television leads to less social interaction.

   f) Drivers are less polite because of the influence of the car itself.

# Personal Privacy

This reading selection is an example of academic writing. It was taken from a sociology textbook. It is written for a more general audience than some academic texts because it is an introductory textbook. A more specialized sociology text might contain more jargon and discuss more complex topics. Note how the authors handle the citations.

The process of assembling consumer profiles is one aspect of data mining. Data mining is the analysis of data to find relationships that can be exploited for marketing purposes. For example, data miners might study buying patterns to see if people who buy sports videos buy more beer. With this kind of information, advertisers can target their marketing more effectively.

Technology is developing quickly, and laws and policies are unable to keep up with the advances. You can use the Internet to find out what current regulations exist and what kind of controls are being proposed to safeguard people's privacy.

## Are Large Organizations a Threat to Personal Privacy?

*by John J. Macionis and Linda M. Gerber*

1    As he finishes dressing, Joe calls an 800 number to check the pollen count. As he listens to a recorded message, a Caller ID computer identifies Joe, records the call, and pulls up Joe's profile from a public records database. The profile, which now includes the fact that Joe suffers from allergies, is sold to a drug company, which sends Joe a free sample of a new allergy medication.

2    At a local department store, Nina uses her American Express card to buy an expensive new watch and some sleepwear. The store's computer adds Nina's name to its database of "buyers of expensive jewellery" and "buyers of sexy lingerie." The store trades its database with other companies. Within a month, Nina's mail includes four jewellery catalogues and a sex-videotape offer (Bernstein, 1997).

3    Are these cases of organizations providing consumers with interesting products, or violations of people's privacy? The

answer, of course, is both: the same systems that help organizations operate predictably and efficiently also empower them to invade our lives and manipulate us. So, as bureaucracy has expanded in Canada, privacy has declined.

4     The problem reflects the enormous power of large organizations, their tendency to treat people impersonally, and their practice of collecting information. In recent decades, the danger to privacy has increased as organizations have acquired more and more computers and other new information technology that stores and shares information.

5     Consider some of the obvious ways in which organizations compile personal information. As they issue driver's licences, for example, provincial departments generate files that they can dispatch to police or other officials at the touch of a button. Similarly, Revenue Canada, Health and Welfare, and government programs that benefit veterans, students, the poor, and the unemployed all collect extensive information.

6     Businesses in the private sector now do much the same thing although, as the examples above suggest, people may not be aware that their choices and activities end up in someone's database. Most people find the use of credit cards a great convenience (people in North America now hold more than one billion of them, averaging more than five per adult), but few people stop to think that credit card purchases automatically generate electronic records that can end up almost anywhere.

7     We also experience the erosion of privacy in the surveillance cameras that monitor more and more public places, along main streets, in the shopping malls, and even across campuses. And then there is the escalating amount of junk mail. Mailing lists for this material grow exponentially as one company sells names and addresses to others. Bought a new car recently? If so, you probably have found yourself on the mailing lists of companies that market all kinds of automotive products. Have you ever rented an X-rated video? Many video stores keep records of the movie preferences of customers and pass them along to other businesses whose advertising soon arrives in the mailbox.

8     Of particular concern to Canadians is the information stored in connection with our Social Insurance Numbers (SINs), which

in some organizations have become employee identification numbers as well. The amount of personal information associated with one's SIN, the multiple uses of the number, and the possibility of merging massive files makes SINs a particularly sensitive issue. Access by one government department or agency, such as Revenue Canada or the RCMP, to SIN-related data or Statistics Canada files would also be a worrisome invasion of privacy. It is possible, as well, for unauthorized users—from anywhere in the world, in fact—to gain access to and link the various files containing personal information about us.

9    Concern about the erosion of privacy runs high. In response, privacy legislation has been enacted in Canada by provinces and the federal government. The federal *Privacy Act* (1978; amended in 1982) permits citizens to examine and correct information contained about them in government files. Canadians also have access to information (e.g., consultants' reports) that contributes to the making of government decisions and policy. But the fact is that so many organizations now have information about us that current laws simply can't address the scope of the problem.

Sources:

Bernstein, Nina. "On the Frontier of Cyberspace, Data is Money and is a Threat." *New York Times* (June 12, 1997): A1, B14-15.

Miller, Michael. "Lawmakers Begin to Heed Calls to Protect Privacy." *Wall Street Journal* (April 11, 1991): A16.

Rubin, Ken. "Privacy." In *The Canadian Encyclopedia.* 2d ed. Vol. 3. Edmonton: Hurtig Publishers, 1988: 1761.

Smith, Robert Ellis. *Privacy: How to Protect What's Left of It.* Garden City, N.Y.: Anchor/Doubleday, 1979.

## Vocabulary

Caller ID: an electronic method of visually identifying the name and phone number of the caller.

X-rated video: sexually explicit movies on videotapes, often called adult movies or films; "X-rated" usually denotes something not for children to see.

Social Insurance Numbers (SINs): a number issued by the Canadian government to keep track of income and federal benefits, but which is widely misused as an identification number

Revenue Canada: a ministry of the federal government which oversees income taxes and other financial matters of the country.

RCMP: short for Royal Canadian Mounted Police, the federal police force with jurisdiction across Canada.

Statistics Canada: a ministry of the federal government which collects data from public and private sources and administers the census.

## Comprehension and Discussion

1. Explain: "the same systems that help organizations operate predictably and efficiently also empower them to invade our lives and manipulate us."

2. What do you think of the two examples the authors give at the beginning of the piece? Do you object to businesses handling data in this way?

3. Why is the linking of government files about individuals more worrisome than that of business files?

4. Explain the limitations of the Privacy Act as explained by the authors. What should the government law be?

5. What experience have you had with mailing lists? When a company asks if you want to be on a mailing list, do you agree? What kind of restrictions should be places on the use of such lists?

6. Are surveillance cameras an invasion of your privacy?

## Assignments

1. Find out more about the federal and provincial laws on consumer privacy and write an essay describing one such law and its strengths and weaknesses.

2. Describe what an individual can do to safeguard his privacy.

3. Explain what privacy means to you.

# Another View of the True North

Amanda Touche was raised in Canada but now lives in Dallas, Texas.

The relationship between Canada and the United States is a complicated one. People from other parts of the world tend to lump Canadians and Americans together, seeing very little difference. Americans are woefully ignorant of Canada whereas Canadians are better informed about the States because of the influence of the American media. Some American businesses, such as the film industry, see Canada as an extension of the domestic market rather than a foreign market. Some Canadian politicians would like to see our country being more like the U.S., with lower taxes and greater freedoms; others fight this goal, defending our social programs and our deference to authority. While some Canadians admire Americans, others have the resentfulness typical of being the underdog—a feeling of powerlessness that sometimes erupts in anti-American sentiments.

## *Another View of the True North*

### *by Amanda Touche*

1    My last image of Canada was of my mother standing on top of a small hill that rose from one of the pastures of our farm near Calgary. Both her arms were stretched to the sky, and she waved her hands back and forth like flags. The road rolled away from her and took me with it. I wept all the way to the Montana border.

2    That was 17 years ago. I was leaving Canada with my American bridegroom to live in the U.S. My tears then were more for the home I was leaving than for my country. After all, I was only 25 and in love with the idea of American living. For much of my adolescence I had been influenced by *Seventeen* magazine. To own a pair of U.S.-purchased white painter's pants was for me the height of coolness.

3    The longer I was away, the more I grew to love Canada. I noted our reputation as a kind and compassionate country. A nation of peacekeeping. A land of goodness. A clean country. In contrast to the Americans, we were nice people, not given to self-promotion and excess.

4    I missed concrete things about Canada—CBC, *The Globe and Mail, Maclean's,* the lilt of Canadian voices. I began to define myself strongly as a Canadian. I subscribed to *Maclean's.* I hung out with Canadians. I squealed with delight whenever I spotted a Canadian licence plate. On my yearly visits to Calgary, I loaded my suitcase with Rich Tea cookies, Coffee Crisps and Red Rose tea.

5    This behaviour shaped my three children. They ate the Rich Tea cookies and Coffee Crisps. Once they watched in amusement as I followed a car with Alberta plates to a parking lot.

6    "Where are you from?" I called out, drawing alongside.

7    "Edmonton."

8    "Oh great, I'm from Calgary."

9    And then we two strangers stared at each other with nothing more to say.

10    My car-chasing subsided, but my children's sense of belonging to two countries remained strong. They loved their visits to Calgary and the farm. I took them to Canada as often as I could, and they returned with a sense of belonging. By Grade 2, my elder daughter announced in class she was Canadian-American.

11    Last summer, the three of them wanted to go to camp together. A friend from high school suggested a camp outside Calgary, nestled in the Canadian Rockies. On blind faith I signed them up for a two-week experience. My friend was sending her children there, and the idea was intoxicating for a rootless Canadian.

12    The children went willingly; at 15, 13 and 11, they were excited about a mountain adventure. In the week preceding camp, my son slept in his new sleeping bag in our air-conditioned house while the temperature outside reached 102° F. We talked about homesickness, but they felt it would be eased in a country that was a second home.

13    We received only one letter during the two weeks. This came from our middle child, Anne. It was a long letter written on the second day of camp and it started with her homesickness and ended with a single sentence: "They don't like Americans up here."

14     The rest of this tale is sad. I picked them up and my 11-year-old son cried all the way to Calgary. It was as if he was in shock. He had been taunted for being American. His junior counsellor had burned an American dollar one night in front of all the boys in the tepee. Sam had argued that such a burning was illegal. The counsellor had laughed. Sam had also tried to use my citizenship as a shield, claiming "My mother is from Calgary." "Yeah, but you're not," came the retort. Not all his tepee mates were hostile, but there were enough to keep Sam off balance.

15     The girls had happier times, but they were strong in their conviction that Canadians are anti-American. Anne played a continual bantering game of "The U.S. sucks/No it does not" with several of her tepee mates. Sarah was confident that "Americans are just not liked."

16     I felt stunned and stung. What had happened to tolerant Canada? One American friend suggested the attitude was tied to the slide of the Canadian dollar last summer. But does a tepee full of 11-year-old boys understand the economy? Someone is teaching intolerance.

17     The camp responded quickly to a fax I sent regarding our experience, releasing the junior counsellor from his duties. When the camp registration arrived this week, I asked the children about returning. I thought time might have muted their feelings. Anne's answer sums up the general consensus. "Why would I go somewhere I am not liked?"

    How do I answer her?

## Vocabulary

painter's pants: wide pants, usually white, with big pockets and loops to hold tools

tepee (also spelt teepee and tipi): a tent shaped like a cone, used by Aboriginal peoples on the prairies

suck (v.) (slang, somewhat vulgar expression): to be very bad, disgusting, offensive, disappointing (a strong negative comment about something)

# Comprehension

1. Why did Amanda Touche move to the United States?

2. How did she feel about leaving?

3. How did her feelings about Canada change once she moved?

4. Explain what happened to the Touche children at camp.

5. What happened to the counsellor afterwards?

6. Why does Touche claim that "Someone is teaching intolerance"?

# Discussion

1. Have you ever suffered from homesickness? Describe your experience and what you missed from home.

2. How are Canadians and Americans different?

3. Why do you think some Canadians have anti-American feelings? What kind of anti-American feelings can be found in other countries?

# Assignments

1. Write a letter to Anne Touche, the author's daughter, answering the question she poses at the end of the article.

2. Write a letter to the camp complaining about the behaviour of the counsellor, as Touche would have written it. Write a response from the camp to the letter Touche faxed.

3. Describe an incident of prejudice you have experienced.

4. Describe some stereotypes of Canadians or of Americans.

# Letters to the Editor

Newspapers and magazines generally have a "Letters to the Editor" section where they print responses to articles. These letters may agree with, disagree with, or add information to an article. You can see different points of view when you read the letters.

Here are four letters to the editor that appeared in *The Globe and Mail* in response to Amanda Touche's essay.

1    It was sad to read about the summer camp experience of Amanda Touche's children. I am an American whose childhood and adolescence were highlighted by many summers at a Canadian summer camp with experiences directly opposite of what the author describes. My immigration to Canada in 1981 was largely influenced by friendships that originated during those summers and endure today.

2    As part of a group of children from the New York City area, we were welcomed by our fellow campers and counsellors from Canada. The differences in our cultures served to provide a learning experience for all of us. I recall friendly rivalries that surfaced in events such as Canadian v. American softball games, but nothing like what Ms. Touche describes. My own children now attend a summer camp in Ontario where Americans and other nationalities are represented and they have not experienced those negative attitudes.

3    I would hope that what happened to the Touche children was an isolated incident and not indicative of Canadians' attitudes today. I believe that the positive aspects of Canada that Ms. Touche notes are still the norm. Her children might try a different camp.

— Mel Kellner, Thornhill, Ontario

4    I can't blame Amanda Touche's children for not wanting to return to the Canadian camp where they felt they were disliked because they were American. I find it very sad, but completely understandable, and although I can't change it, maybe I can help them understand it.

5    Ms. Touche has to do something that most Americans don't do: She has to educate her children about more than just

America. Expand their horizons so they will understand how the rest of the world sees them because of the country they belong to. Make sure they're aware of how that country treats its closest neighbour and best ally. How it economically bullies and demands concessions it would never dream of conceding to its other closest neighbour, Mexico, where the free-trade shoe is on the other foot. Explain to them how the rest of the world feels when the United States demands centre stage in the Theatre of global negotiations and then refuses to pay its fair share to maintain that very theatre, the UN.

6    And finally, in answer to her daughter's question, "Why would I go somewhere I am not liked?"—if being liked as an American is her criterion for travel, it's very sad, but she isn't going to be going anywhere except America.

— Susan Lawson, Burlington, Ontario

7    Hear, Hear! How wonderful to hear someone openly discussing this hypocritical Canadian conceit over our "arrogant" American cousins.

8    During the two years I lived in California, I cannot count the number of times my friends and acquaintances, upon hearing that I was a Canadian, related stories to me of their mistreatment in Canada, Europe and the rest of the world by my fellow Canadians. I was ashamed, humbled and saddened. The nationalist insults hurled at these people belong properly in accounts of pre-First World War Europe, and certainly not in 1990s Canada.

9    I submit that anyone looking for examples of arrogant, jingoistic nationalism need not look south of the 49th parallel.

— Gavin Peters, Toronto

10    The children of transplanted-Canadian-now-Texan Amanda Touche were exposed to some mild anti-American antics at the hands of Canadian campgoers in Alberta. "What had happened to tolerant Canada?" asks Amanda. I can answer her: not much. The trials of her children sound remarkably similar to my own experiences in 1972, when I arrived in suburban Toronto as an awkward 11-year-old with a very noticeable Indiana twang. Kids will be kids, and it doesn't sound to me

like Canadian teens are any more or less tolerant than they were 26 years ago.

11      Amanda's daughter asks, "Why would I go somewhere I am not liked?" The answer is this: to give them a reason to like you.

12      And remember, if Amanda's children are lucky enough to be dual citizens, a good college education still costs a lot less up here than down there. So wait a while and then consider staying for a few years. You'll find the reception warmer at 20 than at 13.

—Derek Riehm, Vancouver

## Vocabulary

49th parallel: Canada-U.S. border

"Hear! Hear!": an expression of agreement and may be heard after someone gives a speech.

jingoistic: aggressively nationalistic

Indiana twang: Indiana accent—Americans from the mid-west are sometimes described as having a "twang" (a nasal sound) in their speech

v., vs.: abbreviations for *versus*, a word which shows opposing sides in a sport or legal battle

## Comprehension and Discussion

1. Which letters support the original article?

2. What is the main point of each letter writer?

3. How does Susan Lawson criticize Americans? Do you think this criticism is valid?

## Assignments

1. Write your own letter to the editor in response to Amanda Touche's article.

2. Take one of the points one of the letter writers makes and write a paragraph giving your own explanation or argument on it.

# Soap and Water

This reading selection is a short story. What looks like a simple story has many layers. Fiction can tell us much about human behaviour and society. For example, in "Soap and Water," we see what the main characters care about most by what they say and by how they act. Moreover, we tend to categorize people by their profession, by what they wear, and by social expectations. However, Frei plays with the stereotypes, and finds humour and compassion in an unwanted, awkward situation.

## *Soap and Water*

### *by Urs Frei*

1    The other day a man walked into the store, carrying a cat. I don't know which I noticed first, the cat, or how the man was crying. The cat was his, I guess. Its legs were mangled and blood was dripping through his fingers. He was crying so hard he didn't notice that this wasn't a vet hospital anymore.

2    "I need you to put my cat to sleep," he said.

3    There he stood, dripping onto the carpet. We had three customers in the store. Of course they were staring.

4    "The vet moved out last month, sir," I said. I came around the counter to show my concern. But also to move him out of there. You have to understand, we'd only been open a month. "We sell computers."

5    The man was silent. The cat was crying low, strange cries.

6    "Where's the vet?" he said.

7    "Where'd that vet go?" I said. Robert, one of my sales reps, was staring back at me. It was a pointless question, actually, because I knew the vet hadn't moved anywhere near. I was pretty sure there was no vet within a mile. "Have a look in the phone book," I told him.

8    The man was sobbing again. I couldn't decide if the best thing to do would be to ask him to step outside, or if this would antagonize the customers. I had a closer look at him. He had earrings in both ears. His hair was shaved on the sides of his head. He was wearing a leather jacket, and it was hard to say for sure, but he seemed to be handsome, the kind of man who

would talk about his successes with women. What was he doing crying about a cat?

9   The stock boy had heard the cat and come in from the stock room. He wasn't supposed to be in the store.

10   Robert said, "There's a vet over on K- road."

11   K- road was the other side of town.

12   "Should I call them?" he said. "They have a pet ambulance, it says here."

13   "Call the pet ambulance," I said. "Get that pet ambulance over here."

14   The stock boy wasn't a boy at all. He was a Mexican man, about forty years old, named Ricardo, who spoke almost no English. He was wearing dirty blue-jeans and a blue work shirt. Also, he wasn't legal. He was taking off his shirt. I thought, Lord in heaven—Lord in heaven. There was that cat, dripping on my new carpet, and there was the stock boy, taking off his shirt.

15   He walked up to the man, spreading the shirt on his palms, and took the cat, and wrapped it in the shirt. The man said nothing. Ricardo turned his back so that no one could see, but everyone heard the snap as he broke the cat's neck. The cat went silent. One of the customers, a lady, made a horrified sound. Then Ricardo, with his head bowed, handed the cat back, along with his shirt.

16   I was glad I'd got that in about the pet ambulance. You have to understand that this was before I learned that blood comes out easily with just soap and water. It was that lady customer who told me.

## Vocabulary

legal: (shortened form) a legal immigrant, someone with proper immigration papers

put an animal to sleep: (euphemism) to kill an animal, usually because it is old, sick, or dangerous

sales reps: (shortened form) sales representatives

vet: (shortened form) veterinarian, a doctor who takes care of animals

## Comprehension and Discussion

1. How would you describe the store owner?

2. Would this story be the same if the store sold something else, such as health food? Why?

3. Compare the store owner and the stock boy.

4. What is the store owner concerned about?

5. What is the narrator apologizing for in the last paragraph?

6. What is the stereotype of someone who works with computers?

7. What would you do in this situation? Who do you identify with more, the store owner, the cat owner, or the stock boy?

8. What is the significance of the soap and water?

## Assignments

1. Modern city dwellers have lost many of the survival skills their grandparents had. For example, how many of us could kill a chicken and prepare it as a meal? In a paragraph or an essay, explain why losing these skills is unfortunate, or why it is not.

2. What kind of rules should govern euthanasia (mercy killing), for animals or for people? In a paragraph, explain one rule; or, in an essay, explain a number of rules.

# Answers

## Exercise 2.1

The nouns are underlined. (Capitalized nouns are proper nouns.)
The pronouns are in italics with their antecedents in parentheses.

The Trojan War started with the gift of an angry goddess. Eris, goddess of strife, was not invited to a wedding on Mount Olympus, so *she* (Eris) tossed a golden apple, inscribed "To the fairest," into the middle of the party. Three goddesses vied for the apple: Hera, Zeus's wife, and two of Zeus's daughters, Aphrodite, the goddess of love, and Athena, goddess of wisdom. The gods and goddesses called on Zeus to make a judgement, but *he* (Zeus) did not want to decide among *his* (Zeus's) wife and daughters. *He* (Zeus) called for an impartial judge. The judge chosen was Paris, the son of Priam, the king of Troy. Paris was living as a herdsman because *he* (Paris) had been sent away from the city when a prophecy said that *he* (Paris) would cause *its* (Troy's) destruction. The goddesses tried to bribe Paris. Athena offered *him* (Paris) the gift of wisdom, Hera offered power, and Aphrodite offered the most beautiful woman in the world. Paris picked Aphrodite. The most beautiful woman was Helen, the wife of Menelaus of Sparta. When Paris stole Helen and took *her* (Helen) to Troy, Menelaus went to *his* (Menelaus) brother Agamemnon, a mighty Greek ruler, who assembled an army of Greek heroes. *They* (heroes) sailed to Troy and surrounded the city in a siege that lasted ten years. Eventually, the Greeks won the war and took Helen back home.

## Exercise 2.2

Verbs are underlined. Verbals are in italics with type (gerund, participle, infinitive) in parentheses.

The verb "*to coin,*" (infinitive) *used* (participle) *to describe* (infinitive) the action of *introducing* (gerund) a new word into the language, has a double meaning when the names of coins enter the language. When the loon was chosen as the image on Canada's dollar coin, it made an indelible mark on the vocabulary of Canadian English. The new coin was dubbed the "loonie," and now the word <u>is</u> synonymous for the Canadian dollar as *shown* (participle) in newspaper headlines *proclaiming* (participle) "Loonie's value <u>drops</u>." It <u>is</u> fitting, perhaps, that the word "loon" <u>refers</u> not only to the waterfowl with the haunting cry but also to a crazy person, a "lunatic," someone *touched* (participle) by the moon (from the Latin *luna*). With the loonie *accepted* (participle) into Canadian pockets and the language, a new bi-metallic two-dollar coin <u>was introduced</u>. The image on one side of the coin <u>was</u> a polar bear, another representative of Canadian wildlife. Several names <u>were suggested</u>. Some <u>were built</u> on the precedence of the loonie: "Doubloon" <u>brought forth</u> images of pirate gold, and "twonie" or "toonie" <u>suggested</u> a doubling of the loonie. Other names <u>played</u> on the image of the polar bear. "Bearback" and "bearbutt" <u>were</u> irreverent suggestions for a coin with the image of the Queen on the other side. However, simplicity <u>won out</u> in common usage, and the coin <u>is</u> now <u>accepted</u> as the "toonie." Coin designers <u>must consider</u> language as well as image when they <u>choose</u> symbols.

## Exercise 2.3

Adjectives:

1. most, flexible, part-time, fair, reasonable

2. much, work-related

4. some, repetitious, demanding, unwilling

5. high, dead-end, younger, innovative, senior, active, extra

Adverbs:

2. generally

3. really

4. unfortunately, hard

5. aggressively

## Exercise 2.4

1. Every year <u>in</u> (preposition) high school, the <u>class</u> (noun) studies a <u>different</u> (adjective) <u>play</u> (noun) by <u>Shakespeare</u> (proper noun).

2. My parents <u>play</u> (verb) Scrabble every evening, and then <u>they</u> (pronoun) go for a <u>walk</u> (noun).

3. I <u>walk</u> (verb) <u>quickly</u> (adverb) <u>and</u> (conjunction) my sister <u>always</u> (adverb) has trouble keeping up <u>with</u> (preposition) <u>me</u> (pronoun).

4. After the <u>reorganization</u> (noun), a <u>calmer</u> (adjective) <u>atmosphere</u> (noun) <u>prevailed</u> (verb).

5. <u>When</u> (subordinate conjunction) I go <u>to</u> (preposition) the <u>movies</u> (noun), I <u>like</u> (verb) to see a film with lots of <u>special</u> (adjective) <u>effects</u> (noun) that take <u>advantage</u> (noun) of <u>the</u> (definite article) big <u>screen</u> (noun).

## Exercise 2.5

1. <u>Once upon a time</u>, there was a man, <u>dressed in a red suit</u>, who wanted <u>to please children</u>.

2. <u>Living in the North Pole</u> <u>for most of the year</u>, he was sheltered <u>from the everyday hustle and bustle</u> <u>of crowds and other distractions</u>.

3. <u>For eleven months</u>, <u>he and his merry elves</u> made toys <u>of every sort</u> and stored them <u>for one special day</u>.

4. <u>During this time</u>, some<u> of his helpers</u> kept a list <u>of children</u> who were naughty or nice.

5. <u>With the help</u> <u>of eight tiny reindeer</u>, he rode <u>through the sky</u> <u>to every household</u>.

6. Children, <u>believing that this jolly old man would be wanting something good to eat after all this work</u>, often placed cookies and milk <u>near the fireplace</u>, <u>just for him</u>.

## Exercise 2.6

1. Complex sentence
   Relative clauses: (that) he could about home-based businesses
   Subordinate clause: before he set up his office
   Main clause: James learned all

2. Complex sentence
   Subordinate clause: while he still had a full-time job
   Main clause: he started his consulting business

3. Complex sentence
Subordinate clause: once he was sure he could be successful
Main clause: he quit his job

4. Simple sentence

5. Complex sentence
Subordinate clause: when he could talk shop by the water cooler and share a confidence or two
Main clause: James yearned for the good old days

6. Compound sentence
Clauses: he enjoyed the challenge of his new work
he never regretted his decision

7. Simple sentence

8. Complex sentence
Subordinate clause: although he had prepared for the millennium bug
Main clause: he could not imagine the magnitude of his troubles

9. Compound sentence
Clauses: some hacker broke into his files
[some hacker] stole all his data

10. Simple sentence

## Exercise 2.7

1. S: attendant; V: couldn't give

2. S: his brother; V: distributed

3. S: advertisement; V: was

4. S: power-walking; V: can be

5. S: the manager and her assistant; V: were looking for

6. S: I; V: came home and found

7. S: you; V: can say

8. S: employees; V: were

9. S: that our government is undemocratic; V: can be debated

10. S: store; V: is closing

## Exercise 2.8

There is no one right answer in this exercise, but here are some possible answers.

1. After considering Kingston, Montreal, and Toronto, Queen Victoria chose Ottawa, a small lumber town, as the capital of Canada because it was farther from the American border.

2. A chain of candy shops is named after Laura Secord, a heroine of the War of 1812. After she overheard American officers planning a surprise attack, she walked 30 km. through swamps and forests to warn the British troops.

3. Louis Riel was a Metis leader in Manitoba who wanted his people to have some choice in their place in Canada. After he led the Red River Rebellion, he was hanged for treason on November 16, 1885.

4. D'Arcy McGee was one of the few Canadian politicians to be assassinated. He was shot on Sparks Street, just two blocks south of Parliament Hill, in 1868, supposedly by a Fenian, an Irish revolutionary.

5. John A. Macdonald, the first prime minister of Canada, wanted British Columbia to join the new Canadian confederation, so he proposed a national railway to link that Western province with the ones in the East. Based on this commitment, British Columbia joined in 1870.

## Exercise 3.1

__4__   The solution to this problem was packet-switching—data would be broken up into packets and transferred over a network of computers.

__3__   The Americans wanted a way to keep communication going in the event of an attack of Soviet nuclear missiles.

__7__   Scientists soon found this network convenient for sharing research findings and discussing problems with other scientists.

__11__   These providers became large companies as more people came online and the Internet became more commercial.

__5__ If one system was down, the packet would be rerouted another way. Then the electronic packets were reassembled at the final destination.

__10__ When they left the school community, they wanted to maintain their Internet access, so they turned to Internet service providers.

__2__ It started as an American military project.

__6__ Military computers were not the only ones on this early network; scientific institutions, including universities, were also connected.

__12__ The development of the World Wide Web and web browsers made the Internet easy to use and led to its current popularity.

__8__ Gradually, more of the university community came online.

__1__ The Internet, a network of computers sharing information, has been growing steadily.

__9__ Students became accustomed to the speed and ease of e-mail communication.

The Internet, a network of computers sharing information, has been growing steadily. It started as an American military project. The Americans wanted a way to keep communication going in the event of an attack of Soviet nuclear missiles. The solution to this problem was packet-switching—data would be broken up into packets and transferred over a network of computers. If one system was down, the packet would be rerouted another way. Then the electronic packets were reassembled at the final destination. Military computers were not the only ones on this early network; scientific institutions, including universities, were also connected. Scientists soon found this network convenient for sharing research findings and discussing problems with other scientists. Gradually, more of the university community came online. Students became accustomed to the speed and ease of e-mail communication. When they left the school community, they wanted to maintain their Internet access, so they turned to Internet service providers. These providers became large companies as more people came online and the Internet became more commercial. The development of the Word Wide Web and web browsers made the Internet easy to use and led to its current popularity.

## Exercise 3.2

Other transition markers with the same meaning can be used.

1. The parade route gets lined with people quickly. Therefore, you should go early to find a good vantage point.

2. Parents with small children may want to leave early. However, they cannot because their children want to see the last float in the parade.

3. The clowns have several responsibilities. First, they distribute candy to the children in the crowd. Secondly, they entertain spectators with tricks during pauses in the parade action.

4. It is very difficult to march in step and play an instrument. Therefore, marching bands must practise more than other bands.

5. The parade marshall leads the entire parade. Thus, she sets the pace for the marching bands and floats.

6. Sometimes, unfortunate accidents happen. For instance, a horse bolted into the spectators last year, injuring two little boys.

7. The celebrities don't do much except ride on the floats, smile and wave at the crowds. Nevertheless, they get paid well and have lots of perks.

8. Normally the parade route remains the same. However, this year the organizers decide to shorten it by taking Elm Street instead of Maple Avenue.

9. I have two reasons why I avoid going to parades. First, I don't like crowds. Second, I get a better view from the television broadcast.

10. Parades are losing popularity in the 1990s. Moreover, they cost too much to produce.

## Activity 12.7

Words to read aloud for students to check in the dictionary to see how well they can figure out the spelling:

charisma

churlish

euchre

flagon

gamut

intangible

phonetics

rhyme

smidgen

yoke

## Exercise 12.1

1. widow

2. host

3. chauffeur

4. mayor

5. CEO (Chief Executive Officer)

6. landlady

7. thesaurus

8. immigrate

9. stroll

10. guests

## Exercise 13.1

1. He chickened out. c) He became scared and did not follow through.

2. Let's do lunch. g) Let us go for lunch sometime.

3. She just squeaked in. a) She was just barely able to get in.

4. It was one of those things. j) It was one of those unfortunate incidents.

5. He popped the question. e) He asked her to marry him.

6. Been there. Done that. i) I have already experienced what you are now experiencing.

7. She's a no show. f) She did not come.

8. She'll check it out. d) She'll investigate it.

9. He'll fix the grub. h) He will fix the meal.

10. He paid ten bucks. b) He paid ten dollars.

## Exercise 14.1

| NOUN | VERB | ADJECTIVE |
|------|------|-----------|
| admiration | admire | admirable |
| advice | advise | advisable |
| belief | believe | believable |
| competition | compete | competitive |
| development | develop | developmental |
| difference | differ | different |
| enjoyment | enjoy | enjoyable |
| function | function | functional |
| necessity | need, necessitate | necessary |
| proof | prove | provable |
| reason | reason | reasonable |
| success | succeed | successful |

## Exercise 14.2

1. I feel **comfortable** when I visit their home.

2. He is a **violent** man.

3. The **difference** between the two stories is the ending.

4. She was **successful** in her new career.

5. Is there a new **development** in the case?

6. He asked her to **define** the problem.

7. It's the **repetition** of the command that caused the problem.

8. She told me to take a deep **breath** and **relax**.

9. He is very **protective** of his family's privacy.

10. The child-care centre is a **necessity**, not a luxury.

## Exercise 14.3

1. The host's job is to greet guests, introduce them to others, and make everyone feel comfortable.

2. Instead of watching television, the children amused themselves by singing, playing games, and telling stories.

3. A voter must understand the election issues, listen to all the local candidates, and then cast his ballot on election day.

4. Eating nutritious foods, exercising, and sleeping at least eight hours a day will make you feel better.

5. She speaks with ease and confidence.

6. The government stopped the housing project because of the recession, lack of private sector investment, and changing policies.

7. Full-time students today suffer from these hardships: they have responsibilities to their family, they have no time to study, and the teachers are hard on them.

8. Fear of the unknown, media hype about the Y2K problem, and distrust in the political leaders are all valid reasons for millennium paranoia.

9. The causes of longevity in some people are they eat properly, live modestly and have forefathers who lived long lives.

10. Part of the building code states that during construction, the inspectors inspect the site regularly, work independently of the builders, and enforce all rules to ensure safety.

## Exercise 14.4

The shape of ____ Canadian houses follows both fashion and lifestyle changes. Attics and third storeys were popular in <u>the</u> first half of <u>the</u> 20th century. In <u>the</u> 1960s bungalows became popular. Today, buyers want <u>a</u> residence with several bathrooms, <u>a</u> large family room and <u>a</u> practical kitchen. Another change is the garage attached to <u>the</u> front of <u>the</u> house. It used to be separate and behind <u>the</u> main building. Verandas were popular when people actually sat there on _____ summer evenings and talked to passers-by. After many years of __ houses designed away from <u>the</u> street, <u>the</u> verandah is making <u>a</u> come-back. Patios and __ decks in <u>the</u> back extend recreation and entertaining space for <u>the</u> homeowner. Finished basements give children <u>a</u> playroom and teenagers <u>a</u> recreation room for __ parties. In <u>the</u> next century <u>Canadians</u> will see ___ smart houses wired to respond to their owners' commands.

## Exercise 14.5

Immigrants can improve their language skills in many ways. First, **they** can use the media by listening to the radio, watching TV, and reading the newspaper. If **they** read the newspaper every day, **they** can learn about important issues and improve their vocabulary. The library is a useful facility for immigrants because they can find information about the local area, as well as get books, magazines, videos, and audiotapes. **Immigrants** can also take continuing education courses. These courses do not have to be language classes. If **they** interact with English-speaking people, **they** will improve conversation skills. **They** need to take advantage of opportunities to practise English.

## Exercise 14.6

1. Yesterday we <u>walked</u> along the beach and <u>collected</u> sea shells.

2. While I was <u>cooking</u> supper, the phone <u>rang</u> three times.

3. Next week I <u>am going</u> to Prince George for a conference.

4. Mary-Anne <u>is</u> an epidemiologist. She <u>analyzes</u> health statistics. She <u>has worked</u> for the department for ten years.

5. I <u>forgot</u> my notebook, but I <u>think</u> Helena <u>has</u> a copy of those questions too.

6. They <u>started</u> the company in 1995. After five years they <u>wanted</u> to expand, but the expansion never <u>happened</u>. Today the company <u>is</u> not much bigger than when they <u>began</u>, but they <u>are making</u> a good income nevertheless.

7. He usually <u>takes</u> the seven o'clock train, but yesterday he <u>had</u> to accompany his sister, who <u>wanted</u> to leave earlier.

## Exercise 14.7

One of the worst disasters of the 20th century was the Halifax explosion. On December 6, 1917, at 8:45 a.m., the *IMO* collided with the French ship *Mont Blanc* in Halifax harbour. The Mont Blanc **was** a munitions ship carrying tons of explosives. The collision caused the explosives to ignite. About 20 minutes after the collision, the French ship **exploded** in a huge boom that **was** heard as far away as Prince Edward Island. More than two-and-a-half square kilometres of Halifax **was** levelled, and the force of the explosion was felt many miles away. A tidal wave was created and fires spread through the city. More than 1600 people died and 9000 **were** injured. It was a terrible time for the thousands left homeless because they **had** to endure a December blizzard with no proper shelter. The Halifax explosion was the largest non-nuclear man-made blast in the world. It was dramatized in Hugh MacLennan's novel *Barometer Rising.*

## Exercise 14.8

1. I should have **been** more careful.
2. The students were **applying** for summer jobs all week.
3. Angelica can **go** to university next year.
4. The players could **have** been traded easily.
5. I am **waiting** for an acceptance letter from the college.
6. Marshall might have **wanted** to go too.
7. Having **finished** the report, they were **cleaning** out the files.
8. I do **know** the answer.
9. They could not **understand** the problem.
10. Sylvie and Kyoko will be **taking** the children to the baseball game.

## Exercise 14.9

1. A tutor in the Writing Centre corrected the essay.
2. Our new development team put together the proposal.
3. The children performed the dance well.

4. They arrested the CEO for conspiracy.

5. The landlord did not listen to his tenants, and he soon evicted them from the housing complex.

6. The company trained her to keep the books for them.

7. They held the award ceremony in the gymnasium.

## Exercise 14.10

1. I <u>must meet</u> with the president to discuss that.

2. You <u>should</u> drink several glasses of water every day.

3. <u>May/Can</u> I borrow that book for a few days?

4. I <u>could</u> speak French fluently, but now I've forgotten so much of it.

5. If I had the time, I <u>would</u> join the parent council.

6. He <u>can</u> type 70 words a minute.

7. This project <u>may/might</u> take more time than we anticipated.

8. I really <u>must/should</u> go now.

9. <u>Would</u> you like to visit our Vancouver plant?

10. Anyone <u>can</u> improve writing skills with practice.

## Exercise 14.11

1. It seems <u>to make</u> no difference.

2. I expect <u>to finish</u> by noon.

3. I can't imagine <u>being</u> a firefighter.

4. Don't miss <u>seeing</u> that movie.

5. I hope <u>to see</u> you soon.

6. Laura refused <u>to take</u> on the extra assignment.

7. They're always talking about <u>learning to speak</u> Japanese.

8. He won't admit <u>writing</u> that memo.

9. I would like <u>to avoid</u> <u>calling</u> another meeting.

10. She's interested in <u>learning</u> to fly a helicopter.

## Exercise 14.12

1.  The win was a first for the premier, who became the leader of the party two years ago.

2.  The New Democratic Party (NDP) has always had strong union support. It opposes the domination of big business.

3.  Right wing refers to conservative values which embrace free enterprise; left wing believes in aid for the disadvantaged and in radical government intervention.

4.  The reason is that more women prefer entrenched social programs to tax rebates.

5.  Running on empty promises and disinformation, both candidates are bound to lose the election.

6.  The voters split the vote between the two established parties, so they inadvertently let the third choice party come from behind to form the next government.

7.  "Corporate welfare bums" was an expression first coined by David Lewis, leader of the national NDP, in the 1970s.

8.  The Bennet buggy was a horse towing a car without an engine, and the Diefendollar was a Canadian dollar worth 98 cents American.

9.  William Lyon MacKenzie King, the Liberal prime minister during WW II, secretly used a crystal ball and a talking dog to help him develop national policy.

10. Even though Sir John A. Macdonald was an alcoholic, he won two elections and weathered monumental scandals virtually unscathed.

## Exercise 14.13

1.  I don't agree <u>with</u> her plan because we can't depend <u>on</u> the schedule.

2.  He is always late <u>for</u> meetings.

3.  She is known <u>for</u> her use <u>of</u> vivid colours <u>in</u> her paintings.

4.  That university is located <u>in</u> a small town, so it dominates the economy.

5.  I am opposed <u>to</u> raising tuition fees.

6.  Are you acquainted <u>with</u> Dr. Patel?

7. Terry Fox will always be remembered <u>for</u> the courage he showed <u>against</u> cancer.

8. This textbook is suitable <u>for</u> a first-year class.

9. She is familiar <u>with</u> the new methodology we are using.

10. Harold is qualified <u>for</u> the managerial position.

## Exercise 14.14

1. I get <u>up</u> early in the morning and go jogging.

2. We can't put <u>off</u> this work any longer. We can't miss this deadline.

3. They need another income just to get <u>by</u>.

4. Her work always stands <u>out</u>. She's the best in the field.

5. All the papers burned <u>up</u> in the fire, and the computer files were not backed <u>up</u>.

6. Do you want to go <u>out</u> tonight?

7. They held a lottery for the residence rooms, and I lost <u>out</u>.

## Exercise 14.15

1. There are many ways for people to conserve resources and cut pollution in their everyday activities.

2. People can walk or bike to work to get exercise.

3. A woman's place is in the boardroom.

4. How many cups of coffee and tea can he carry in one hand?

5. Children's program are only on Saturday.

6. He lost both of his front teeth.

7. The deer run around free in the park, where the children often catch a glimpse of them.

8. There are three men and seven women working on the project.

9. That instructor gives the most homework of all the instructors.

10. Most of the athletes prefer to train in the morning.

## Exercise 14.16

1. The students in the band get time off from class to rehearse.

2. Sad movies and books make me cry.

3. Star Wars is my favourite movie.

4. The fact that he disrupted the meeting is irrelevant.

5. Deer are plentiful in this area, and skunks are a nuisance.

6. Many people want to live in a warmer climate.

7. Each of the students wants to take the make-up test.

8. The people who live in the surrounding area complain about the noise.

9. While many people applied for the job, it will be given to the person who has been with the company the longest.

10. If Jack really wants to go to Kitchener, I can take him next week.

## Chapter 15

### agree, develop, happen

Accidents usually happen when people are not paying attention.

The professor developed this theory last year.

I agree with this theory.

It happened when I opened the door.

### a lot

Many students have trouble with this course.

There is much to be thankful for.

### although, even though, though

Although he studied very hard, he couldn't understand the theory.

He applied for the engineering program although he didn't meet the requirements.

Even though he was late, he came into the meeting.

Even though she knew the answer, she didn't put up her hand.

## computer

Computers have changed the world.
The computer has changed the world.

I want to study computer science.

Computers are very useful for essay writing.
A computer is very useful for essay writing.

## easy, convenient, difficult, hard

I find it difficult to learn English.

Math is easy for him.

The meeting is convenient for him.

When they find something different, they have difficulty accepting it.

If I live on my own, it is difficult to finish all the housework.

## e.g., etc., i.e.

The program includes many arts courses, such as English, philosophy, and history.

The program includes many arts courses, such as English, philosophy, and history.

In the Ancient Civilizations course, we study Greece, China, Rome, and other civilizations.

## even

Even though he has the money, he will not go.

He couldn't do the work even if he spent hours on it.

Even when/though she was tired, she agreed to do the work

> interesting, boring, confusing, exciting
> (and other participles describing emotions)

I am interested in computer studies.

I am bored during the holidays.

I am confused about this grammar rule.

If they are bored, let's get out some games.

It's my first trip to Newfoundland. I am very excited.

## Exercise 15.1

1. It is **surprising** that he has never been out of the country.

2. That horror movie was the most **frightening** one I have ever seen.

3. I was very **confused** when I saw his filing system.

4. That advertisement is **misleading**.

5. The long winter season can be **depressing** for many Canadians.

6. I was **insulted** when he told me how much he thought my work was worth.

7. That part of the course was poorly **understood**.

8. She was **excited** when she heard the news.

9. The employees were **reassured** when the new owners offered to keep them on.

10. They are **interested** in taking another course.

> its, it's

It's a shame they can't go on the trip.

I can't understand its purpose.

It's beginning to look as if he did it on purpose.

The company lost its credibility when the scandal broke.

## many, most, almost

Most people like dancing.

Not only one but almost all the immigrants were homesick.

The worst difficulty the immigrants face is homesickness.

Many people drink coffee.

## suppose

I'm supposed to go to that meeting.

I suppose they will be late.

## used to

We have to get used to it.

I used to live downtown.

But I still cannot get used to living here.

## Countable and Uncountable Nouns

I have too much homework to do.

Where can we get the information?

You can get advice at the counselling centre.

I value honesty in an employee.

I must do much research to answer that question.

That company produces good software.

# Exercise 15.2

1. **You're** supposed to use this once a **week**.

2. It **does** not seem **right** that **women** are not **allowed** to join the club.

3. He will **accept** all the **advice except** for the part about not borrowing money from his brother-in-law.

4. **Where** are we going this evening? I want to know **which** jacket to **wear**.

5. I'm **too** full. I can't possibly eat any **dessert**.

6. She **complimented** me on my **choice**.

7. The **principal** of the high school said that they could not operate under those **principles**.

8. In your essay, you have to **cite** the Internet **sites** where you found that information.

9. **There** are many people asking **whether** the meeting will go on as scheduled.

## Exercise 16.1

1. In the 1960s, the Baby Boomers came into their own.

2. I got all A's and B's on my report card.

3. The children's room was a mess.

4. You shouldn't believe his story. He's always stretching the truth.

5. It's time we looked at the Smiths' place. It may be what we're looking for.

6. She always wants to outdo her sister.

7. The Sheridans decided to return to the farm.

8. The men's and ladies' restrooms are downstairs.

9. The students were looking for more posters for the library walls.

10. Susan's aunt is visiting from Prince George.

## Exercise 16.2

1. I am writing an essay on capital punishment for my English course.

2. Johannes and Maria Steuer are the winners of the Getaway to the Bahamas contest.

3. They have some old textbooks for sale—mostly history, science, and French.

4. I'm hoping to go to the United States during the Christmas vacation.

5. For her birthday, I'm giving her a CD by the Tragically Hip.

## Exercise 16.3

All too often the consumer is tricked into believing that designer jeans give better fit and wear than the generic brand X. Such may not be the case. The pair of Calvin Kleins, GWGs or Levi's that the consumer finds beside the pair of brand X in a department or clothing store may have been cut, styled and sewn by the same person. Moreover, the sizing and 14-ounce-cotton weight are all uniform, even universal. Whenever the name brands come out with a new style or look, brand X is sure to follow within a short while and with a lower price tag. So why pay more for a designer patch that only gives the manufacturer free advertising?

# Credits

**page 236**  "Why My Mother Can't Speak English," by Garry Engkent. Reprinted by permission of the author.

**page 246**  "House Guests," by Raheel Raza, originally appeared as "Those lazy, crazy, summer visitors" in *The Toronto Star*, September 14, 1998, p. A14. Reprinted by permission of the author.

**page 250**  "Making the grade," by Kurt Wiesenfeld. From *Newsweek*, June 17, 1996, p. 16. All rights reserved. Reprinted by permission.

**page 255**  "Teenagers and part-time jobs" is an excerpt (pages 119–122) from the 1995 book *In School: Our Kids, Our Teachers, Our Classrooms*, by Ken Dryden. Used by permission, McClelland & Stewart, Inc. The Canadian Publishers.

**page 259**  "The Baby Boom (1947-1966)" is an excerpt (pages 18–22), reprinted with permission from *Boom, Bust & Echo 2000: Profiting from the Demographic Shift in the New Millennium*, by David K. Foot with Daniel Stoffman (Toronto: Macfarlane Walter & Ross, 1998).

**page 266**  "Learn to live with those sales pitches," by Masud Alam, was in *The Toronto Star*, on June 15, 1998 on page A16. Reprinted by permission of the author.

**page 270**  "Consumer Socialization" is an excerpt (page 19–22) from *Television and your Child* by Carmen Luke, published by Kagan & Woo, 1988. Reprinted with permission.

**page 274**  "When bigger is not necessarily is better" by Charles Gordon, appeared in *Maclean's* on October 20, 1997, on page 11. Reprinted by permission of the author.

**page 279**  "In praise of gouging," by Karen Selick, appeared in *The Globe and Mail* on Jan. 24, 1998, p. D6. Reprinted by permission of the author.

**page 283**  "Corporate footsoldiers," by Joanne Milner, originally appeared as "Work is all hell for footsoldiers in corporate trenches" in *The Toronto Star*, July 31, 1997, p. A21. Reprinted by permission of the author.

**page 287**  "Rest Day," by Josie Marino and Jean-Francois Rioux, originally appeared as "Let's hear it (softly) for Rest Day" as a Facts and Argument essay in *The Globe and Mail*, Feb. 22, 1999, A22. Reprinted by permission of the authors.

**page 291**  "How isolation has bred our uncivil society," by John Barber appeared in his column Semi-detached in *The Globe and Mail*, Sat. Oct. 31, 1998, p. D7. Reprinted with permission from *The Globe and Mail*.

**page 295**  "Are large organizations a threat to personal privacy?" is an excerpt (p. 185) from *Sociology, Third Canadian Edition*, by John J. Macionis and Linda M. Gerber. Prentice Hall Canada. Reprinted with permission of Prentice Hall Canada Inc.

**page 299**  "Another view of the True North," by Amanda Touche originally appeared as a Facts and Arguments essay in *The Globe and Mail*, December 1, 1998, p. A22. Reprinted by permission of the author.

**page 303**  Follow-up Letters to the Editor reprinted by permission of the writers.

**page 306**  "Soap and Water," by Urs Frei, appeared in *The Fiddlehead*, Vol. 193, Autumn 97, pp. 9-10. Reprinted by permission of the author.